ABOUT THE AUTHORS

Simon Raven and Chris Raven were born in
England in 1974.
The *Linger Longer* is their second novel.

Also by the Raven brothers:

Living the Linger

www.samosirbooks.com

SIMON RAVEN   CHRIS RAVEN

The Linger Longer

samosir
BOOKS

SAMOSIR BOOKS

Published by Samosir Books, United Kingdom
www.samosirbooks.com
First published in Great Britain in 2006 by Samosir
Books

Printed in Thailand.

A CIP catalogue record for this book is available from the
British Library.

ISBN 0-9548842-1-3

Cover artwork by Clara Pages, Buenos Aires, Argentina

For George.

Contents

Map of the Trip:
Start: UK- Daventry
End: Vladivostok

---------- route

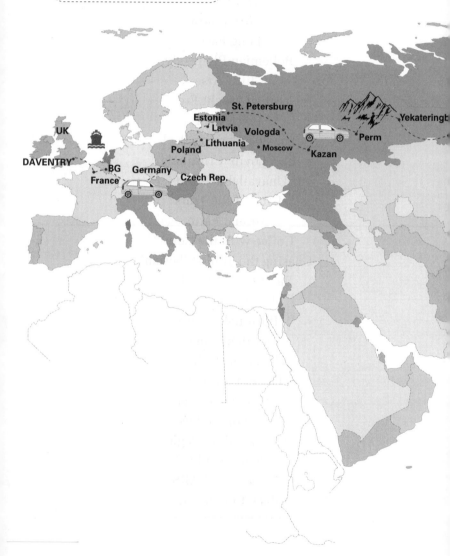

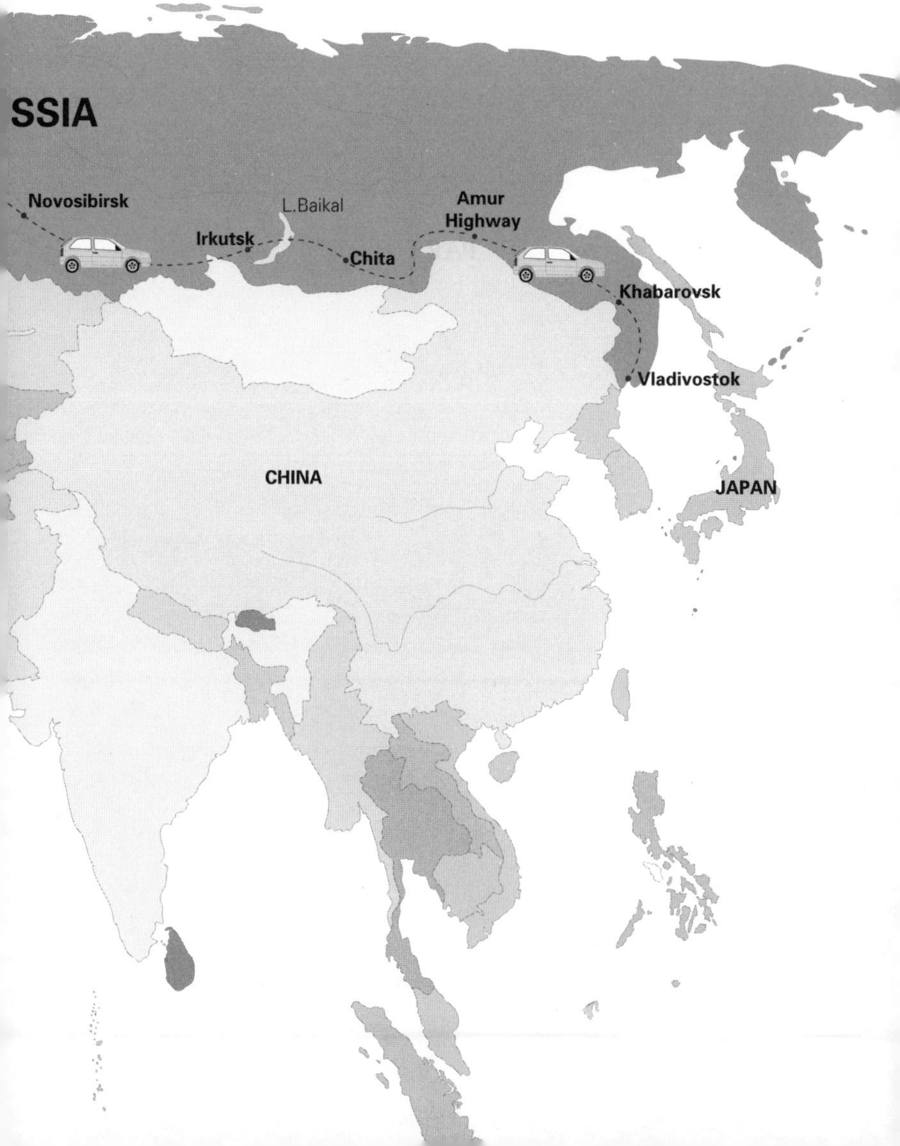

SSIA
Novosibirsk
L.Baikal
Irkutsk
Chita
Amur Highway
Khabarovsk
Vladivostok
CHINA
JAPAN

PART 1

The Cunnilingus King

'I could really eat a big bag of cheese curds,' Warren grins, wiping sweat from his burnt forehead. 'You know what I mean? A big bag of fucking cheese curds!'

Si scratches the back of his head. 'Yeah, sounds delicious.'

'I love them!' he laughs, rubbing his bloated stomach. 'I can't stop eating them.'

Warren reaches over and snatches my cigarettes out of my hand.

'Can I crash one?' he asks, placing a Marlboro between his lips. 'I've lost mine. I'll buy some more and give you...' he stops in mid sentence, '...actually, come to think of it, I probably won't.'

I turn to Si and shake my head in disgust. I've met a few freaks in my time, but this dude takes the biscuit. One minute we're watching The White Cliffs of Dover shimmering in the distance from the windy deck of this P&O ferry, and the next thing we know some total stranger, who introduces himself as Warren, plonks himself down beside us and spoils our beautiful view. I saw him earlier as we drove to the docks to catch the ferry to Calais. He was walking, or should I say waddling up the main road towards a busy roundabout. There was panic in his eyes and a look of concern in his fat red face. I remember smiling at his discomfort and thinking that any guy who has a tight 80's perm and wears a pair of paisley shorts ten sizes too small, should deserve to look worried.

'So where are you fuckers heading?' Warren sniffs, pulling hard on the cigarette.

'Vladivostok,' I reply.

'Vladifok-what?'

'Vladivostok.'

'Where the fuck's that?'

'It's in Eastern Siberia. It's about ten thousand miles … that way,' I smile, pointing in the direction of Calais.

'Fucking cool, man. Where you flying from?'

'We're not.'

'You're not?'

Si shakes his head. 'Nope. We're going to drive there in our Ford Sierra.'

Simon, my twin brother and travelling buddy extraordinaire, dreamt up the idea of driving across Russia whilst stacking boxes of frozen oven chips in a -30°C freezer. We'd bought the car for £300 from some dude with a twitch, and even though it had over 100,000 miles on the clock, attempting to drive the 1.8litre mean-machine halfway around the world seemed all too irresistible. Our family and friends thought we had finally lost the plot when we told them about our idea of driving to Vladivostok. They thought we were taking this new lifestyle of ours a little too far. OK, so maybe we were going a bit over the top. I mean, just because we had driven across the US six months before, it didn't really give us the right to worry everyone or give us the confidence to play fools and take on the world with this massive overland adventure. We hadn't even met anybody who had been to Russia before, let alone driven across it. Were we kidding ourselves? You could say it would be suicidal to even attempt such a journey, especially as we hadn't spent weeks researching the roads, or invested money on the correct equipment that would be required for such a huge expedition. Of course, we made sure we had oil, a few spare tyres, a GB sticker and an SAS Survival Guide, which Si bought from Oxfam for 50p, but apart from this, we took the attitude that we'd just see what happened along the way.

A few weeks before our departure, I jumped on the internet to find out what we were letting ourselves in for. I searched on Google to see if I could find any web sites by people who had driven to the Far East. It was quite worrying as I only found two. They were driving huge 4x4's and both had been heavily sponsored. On their web sites it showed pictures of them driving over dusty potholed roads and crossing deep rivers. It looked impossible, and neither of them had managed to complete the journey to Vladivostok without putting their vehicle on the train. What really put doubt in my mind, was the fact that there appeared to be a section of highway in Eastern Siberia that was still under construction. What chance did we have if the highway was still being bulldozed? How would we be able to make it across Siberia without a 4x4? I mentioned this to Si in passing, but he just shrugged his shoulders and told me not to worry. Deep down, I knew that if we were going to do it we might as well take the bull by the horns and go in blind.

'You're going to drive across Siberia?' Warren frowns. 'You're kidding me, right?'

'No,' Si replies.

'Why dude? Get the fucking plane. It's quicker!'

'Yeah, that would make a lot of sense, but it's not quite the plan we had in mind.'

'Well, fuck me hard with a dildo! Whatever floats your boat, guys. It sounds *far* too adventurous to me.' Warren leans forward. '...So, anyway, have either of you two had any pussy yet?'

I frown. 'Excuse me?'

'Pussy. You know, as in *sweet pussy!*' Warren sings,

adjusting his tight shorts from around his crotch. 'Are you getting any? Last night I made out with this chick from Dover. Fuck me she was hot. She had a face like Whoopi Goldberg and a body like Tina Turner. Damn, what a woman!'

Si looks completely horrified.

'Where did you meet this girl?' I ask.

'Some nightclub in town.'

'Which one?'

'OK, you got me, guys. It wasn't a nightclub at all. She worked in a massage parlor. You know how it is, I'm a fucking thirty-three year old Love God who needed some release. Normally, I've got girls coming at me from every direction. Back home they call me the Cunnilingus King!'

This guy has to be talking out of his fat ass. In the name of the Lord, what sane girl would let this grotesque specimen of a human being put his disease-ridden tongue anywhere near her clitoris? He must be over twenty stone, and if you squint your eyes for long enough he looks a bit like Jabba The Hut from *Star Wars*. This guy is ugly. He's so ugly I find it amazing he has so much confidence. If I looked like Warren, I'd be hiding in a dark hole somewhere suffering from a serious communication disability.

'*I'M THE CUNNILINGUS KING!*' he yells, pounding his chest. 'All the girls in Dover last night were obviously on their fucking periods. You know, I hate it when you spend an hour of your time chatting up a chick, telling her about yourself, complementing on how the kitty-cat looks, making her laugh, buying her drinks and all you get in return is jack shit! They walk away without even giving you a suck. That sucks! I like Dover, but it's full of frigid chicks and asylum seekers. The way I see it, it's all a numbers game. The more puppy dogs you chat up the more chance you have of getting some action. Last night was bullshit, so I paid for it. The bitch gets money to buy drugs and I-get-to-taste-the-pussy,' he sings, leaping back in his seat.

'MOTHER FUCKERS!'

A small group of French school kids sitting close by stop talking and look over.

'Hey, guys, listen to this,' Warren whispers, waving us closer. 'Have you two ever heard of klismaphilia?'

We both shake our heads and prepare ourselves for the answer.

'You don't know what klismaphilia is?' he repeats, looking concerned.

'No, but you're going to tell us, right?' Si replies.

'You bet ya!'

We move closer and wait with bated breath.

'OK, klismaphilia is the word for the sexual pleasure of flushing your asshole with water.'

There's a deadly silence. Warren sits on the edge of his seat in suspense, waiting for our reaction. But there isn't one.

'Flushing your asshole with water!' he cries, breaking the silence. 'Come on, it's pretty cool, man. I bet you didn't know that?'

'Uh ... no, we didn't,' Si grins.

'Fucking hell, guys, everybody knows what klismaphilia is! Look, here's some advice. The next hotel you stay in and there's brown scuff on the shower head – move rooms!'

Warren has to be the most disgusting person I have ever met ... well, apart from a kid in my class at school who used to eat shit and shag his cat, but apart from him this monster is pure filth. What is he trying to prove? Maybe nothing, maybe this is what he's normally like. He doesn't know us from Larry and he's talking to us like we've been best buddies for twenty years. OK, so the showerhead thing was good advice, but come on! This guy needs to return home and seek some professional help.

'To klismaphilia!' Warren cries.

The French kids sitting nearby look over again, and without a word they all get up out of their seats and move speedily back inside the ferry.

'So where in the US are you from?' Si asks in an attempt to change the subject.

'The US?' Warren spits.

'Yeah, which state?'

'You're a rude dude, man.'

'Why, what's the problem?' Si replies.

I turn to Si and try to indicate to him that it's time to leave.

'I'm fucking Canadian, man – Canadian! I live in Canada. Vancouver as a matter of fact.'

He reaches down between his hairy legs and picks up his rucksack. 'Look, I didn't stitch this Canadian flag onto my rucksack for the hell of it. I'm Canadian *not* American. My God, why can't people just shut the fuck up! Have you ever been to Canada?'

Si shakes his head. 'No, but I'd really like to go there someday.'

'I nearly killed an American guy in Hastings about a week ago,' Warren brags, his eyes darting suspiciously around the deck. 'He was pissing on my patch. I hate it when a guy pisses on my patch. Have you two ever pissed on someone else's patch?'

He looks at us coldly, waiting for an answer.

'No, I can't say that I have to be honest with you, Warren,' I reply.

'Good, because if I ever caught you making out with my girl, I'd…' he stops talking and uses the bottom of his T-shirt to wipe sweat off his face.'…Let's just say he was in a bad way by the time the medics arrived, red wine was pissing out of the back of his head. He was hurt real bad.'

I quickly interrupt. 'Warren, I hate to jump in like this, it sounds like an amazing story, but we've got to go and change some money before we get to Calais.'

Warren leans back in his seat and folds his arms. I avoid eye contact with him for a second. His face is so ugly. He looks concerned. It's as though he's trying to work out in his head the slowest and most painful way he can kill me. He wipes more sweat from his top lip before tilting his face in the sun. We both stand up and say goodbye before sprinting to the other side of the ferry. Calais is only a few miles away now. The sooner I'm in the Sierra and driving off this rust bucket the happier I will be.

Daventry

Before I can say "naturellement, quand la slitude me pese un peu, je me parle a moi-meme, ou a mes betes, en particulier a mon chien", Chris strikes up the Sierra's sixteen year-old engine and drives the car off the ferry onto French soil. It seems strange that not more than three hours ago we were stuck in a traffic jam on the M25, and now we're in a different country surrounded by weird road signs, weird number plates and weird people who speak a foreign language and eat frogs legs for their tea.

'Well, here goes,' Chris grins, pulling away from customs control.

'Yeah, n'ailez-pas! Ma-un-ami-a-une-chambre-avec-douche.'

'You what?'

'It means, "don't go! My friend has a room with a shower".'

'I thought you did German at school?'

'I did, but when in Rome, Chris, when in Rome. You never know when a little bit of French might come in handy, if you know what I mean?'

'Uh ... yeah, I know exactly what you mean,' Chris nods.

'So where are we heading first?' I ask, opening the road map out on my knee. 'I can't remember what we said. I think we decided to go north into Belgium, didn't we?'

'Yeah, from Calais to Belgium, Germany to Eastern Europe, through the Baltic States into Russia, and then head east over the Ural Mountains, across the entire length of Siberia until we hit Vladivostok and the Sea of Japan,' Chris replies, turning to me with a smug grin.

'Bliemy, is that it? You make it sound like we're about to go on a Sunday drive with Grandma.'

I peer down at the map and slide my finger across the globe from St. Petersburg to Vladivostok. The distance is immense. For a start, Siberia alone is *BIG*. It's *so* big you can scoop up the whole of the US and drop it into Siberia without even touching the sides. Add to this Alaska and all of the European countries, except Eastern Russia, and still there would be an incredible 300,000 square miles of territory left.

'If either of us want to chicken out, we should say so immediately,' Chris mutters, indicating onto the A16 to Dunkerque.

'I'm not chickening out. Are you chickening out?'

'Piss off! I didn't pay sixty pounds for a Russian business visa for the fun of it, you know.'

'What about the Russian Mafia and the KGB? Knowing our luck we'll be kidnapped by Chechen terrorists and held hostage in a dirty shed for fifty years.'

'Nah, we'll be all right, Si.'

'How the fuck do you know?'

'Well ... I don't, but it'll be OK. Trust me.'

'I suppose things do seem to have improved since Putin came on the scene.'

Chris frowns. 'Putin?'

'Uh-huh.'

'But that was years ago, wasn't it?'

'No.'

'Are you sure?'

'Of course I'm sure. He only came into power in 2000, since he left the KGB and worked his way into politics. I saw him recently standing outside Number Ten with Tony.'

'Oh ... you mean Vladimir Putin!' Chris smiles. 'The

Russian President.'

'Yes. Who did you think I was talking about?'

'I thought you meant the dude with the big beard from the eighteenth century.'

'What dude with the big beard from the eighteenth century?'

'You know ... the old Putin.'

'Chris, I don't know who you're talking about.'

'He saw a vision of the Virgin while working in the fields and started a cult.'

I narrow my eyes with irritation. 'You're talking shit!'

'No I'm not, you know who I mean. He charmed Catherine the Great with his beliefs that sinning through sex, then repenting could bring people closer to God. His orgies were legendary. Come on, Si, don't be a dipshit, you must have heard of him.'

'Wait a minute!'

'What?'

'His name wasn't Putin.'

'Wasn't it?'

'No. It was *Rasputin*, you fool!'

Chris clicks his fingers. 'That's the one, Grigory Rasputin ... the priest of sex. What a genius that man was.'

Six months ago, Chris and I travelled across the US in a brown van called Hank. Returning home after such an amazing journey had been an anti-climax. For the first few days we were treated like respected explorers - our presence to our family and friends had been a novelty, but sadly this quickly disappeared and before we knew it reality kicked in.

I hadn't lived at home for nearly eight years, not since I first flew the nest to go to college in London, and the idea of moving back to our mother's house in the small market town of Daventry was daunting to say the least. I was a 27 year-old man and dumping my rucksack on the floor of my old bedroom, which hadn't changed much since the day I'd left, could only feel like regression. What struck me the most about being back home was how people appeared to have little concept of what we had seen, or the effect our journey might have had on our lives. As far as they were concerned we'd been on a little holiday, got the travelling out of our system and we would now settle down again - slip back into working life and a career. Continue on as we had before.

Within a matter of weeks, we decided the only way to combat the travellers blues was to quickly find some short-term work - pay off our debts, store up some cash and buy ourselves some options. We didn't know where our next journey would take us, and smoking the last of our duty free cigarettes out of the kitchen door we'd spend most evenings trying to devise a cunning plan.

Daventry held a lot of memories from my childhood. I had gone to the local school until the age of sixteen - it was where I had kissed a girl for the first time, experienced my first fight. There were old class mates still living in Daventry that I hadn't spoken to since those days, and the idea of bumping into them in town made me feel unreasonably uncomfortable. I feared their questions. What have you been up to over the past ten years? What are you doing now? All I could think about was the negatives. How could I answer their questions without looking like a freak?

'Are you married?

'Uh … no, I'm single right now.'

'Where do you live?'

'I'm living with my mum at the moment.'

'With your mum? I heard you'd moved to London.'

'Yeah, I did for a while, but I decided to leave.'

'Why would you come back to Daventry? Someone told me you had a really good job.'

Mentioning my fears to Chris, he had tried to put my mind at rest.

'Don't worry about it, Si, school was years ago. Nobody gives a shit about what you're doing now. So you're living with your mummy, who cares!'

'But what if I bump into Kerry Middleton?'

Kerry Middleton? She was your girlfriend when you were fourteen, wasn't she?'

'Yeah.'

Chris sighs. 'That was fucking years ago. She's probably married with three kids by now. She doesn't give a fuck about you.'

'Three kids! Do you reckon?'

'Si, this is Daventry. People settle down a lot younger around here.'

'OK, what about a job, then? We're going to have to work in a warehouse with scumbags. What if we end up working with the Depford brothers? I don't think I could do it.'

'Si, you're living in the past, mate. All those lads are either in prison or they've moved away. Besides, you're forgetting something.'

'What?'

'They were young kids back then. They only seemed scary because you were a kid yourself. You're a twenty-seven year old man now. It's different.'

'Do you reckon?'

'Of course it is! All those lads got girls pregnant when they were eighteen. They don't want to fight anymore, they've got responsibilities.'

'But what will the people be like in the factories? What if they take the piss out of my hair?'

'Si, believe me, it'll be OK.'

Determined not to return to the mundane world of the office, I agreed to stay true to our plan and we quickly found temporary work in a gigantic freezer on an industrial estate close to our mother's house. From the Nevada desert and the Caribbean beaches of Mexico, to an ice cold distribution warehouse in the East Midlands. It certainly took a while for us both to get used to the change in temperature, but nothing was going to stop us from saving up some cash and doing another drive.

Our first night in the freezer had been an education. Emerging from the changing rooms wearing steel toe-capped boots, insulated dungarees and a large thick ski jacket that made you look twice your normal size, we were ordered to sit in the canteen and await instructions. To say I was nervous would be an understatement. I had never worked in a manual job before. Hunched over tables at 7 o'clock in the evening, the room fell silent as a large man in a high visibility vest entered the canteen and made his presence known.

'Right now, guys!' he bellowed. 'Great shift last night, we picked seventy four thousand in total with no accidents to report. The forecast for tonight is ninety thousand. We've got a few new lads starting on the agency, so we shouldn't have a problem. OK, let's get working. Big push, lads, *big push!*'

On that note, everyone stood up and headed for the freezer. A man with thick stubble nudged past me.

'Good luck,' he growled in my ear.

We had been warned by our employment agency that the work in the freezer was tough, but nothing was to prepare us for that first night. The place was like an enormous prison. The supervisors were our prison guards, walking around the factory spying on the workers and looking down from metal walkways. You couldn't stop for two seconds without one of them shouting at you. To the sound of loud thrash metal blasting from speakers around the warehouse, we lifted heavy boxes through the night. The only way to stay warm was to work, and the only way to stay sane was to think that with every hour that passed we were one step closer to being free again.

I wouldn't say working in the freezer had been any better, or worse, than my experience working in an office. In fact, after a few weeks I actually started to enjoy my new life as a factory worker. There was a real sense of achievement stacking boxes and loading lorries. We were distributing frozen food to the nation. We had a purpose, and finding many of my fellow workers to be very decent, intelligent men, there reached a point where I would actually look forward to a good nights graft. My fears of working in a factory had suddenly disappeared. For the years I worked in mundane office jobs, I had heard people consoling themselves with lines like, "At least we're not digging the roads". This statement no longer made any sense to me, and I quickly began to realise that the only negative aspect of work in any environment is that if you solely rely on a wage to support your existence – you're a slave to it.

Thirty Below

Without realising it we cross the invisible border into Belgium. It begins to get dark as Si directs me through Brussels, and determined to make some distance we thunder across the countryside with petrol pumping around the engine as fast as the adrenaline is pumping through our veins. Passing through Düsseldorf, I drive on the German autobahns late into the night. I feel wide-awake, which isn't surprising really as I'm still in nightshift mode.

When you work the nightshift you live like a vampire. It was new to us and in a weird, fucked up kind of way I soon began to enjoy my life living in the dark. Waking up as the sun was going down and returning home at the crack of dawn was *totally* crazy. There was a whole world at night that became our community, and I'd often find myself filling up a supermarket trolley at 3 o'clock in the morning.

Nobody worked in the freezer by choice, we had all ended up there through circumstance; a divorce, just got out of prison, left the army, business collapsed. Our reasons seemed less sane, we got bored of our cushy lives in London, we wanted to be flexible for a while and travel. In a strange way we had chosen to work in the freezer, but maybe it didn't seem all that bad to us as we knew it would only be for a short time. The fact that we were also with a temporary employment agency made our circumstances seem even more bizarre, particularly as we were literally the only English guys temping in the freezer. Well, that is except for Lefty, a young lad who seemed different to most people and who had become a great friend. Our fellow agency staff were from every country imaginable, predominantly Kurdish guys from northern Iraq, but also from other places around the world like Mozambique, Nigeria, Ghana, The Congo, Serbia, Romania, Afghanistan, Pakistan, Germany, Turkey, Portugal, France, Albania, and Syria – to name but a few. This made working in the freezer even more fascinating, and we'd spend much of the night jumping between chutes and chatting to people from all over the world. It felt like travelling, and it turned out to be as much an education as it was hard graft. One guy I got to know was called Abdul, a forty-year old man who was born in Afghanistan during the Taliban regime. He told me about the public floggings he'd received for not having a beard that was two fists in length. As a university student in Kabul, he had grown tired and fearful of the repression, and in a bid to start a new life he had fled across the border to Pakistan. He learnt Urdu and lived in Pakistan for a number of years, smuggling immigrants by camel across the border into Iran. He eventually moved to Iran himself and lived there during the entire bloody revolution and the Iraq-Iran war. After spending some time in Kazakhstan, where he learnt to speak Russian, he travelled across Europe and eventually made it to Great Britain as an asylum seeker. He had spent the past three years trying to scrape together a living as a tailor. The majority of the money Abdul earned in the freezer he sent back to his family in Tehran. He hadn't seen his family for over four years and had yet to meet his youngest son. We heard many stories like these during our time in the freezer. Like the guy from Mozambique whose best friend had been eaten by a Nile crocodile and the dude from the north-western frontier of Pakistan, who shot a dog with an AK47 and kept a rocket launcher in his bedroom. If this wasn't enough, the Iraq war kicked off in the last month we were working there. It was fascinating to be surrounded by the people whose country was being invaded, and to see their mixed reactions when the US army captured Saddam Hussein. From the impression we got, life was quite easy in Iraq when Saddam was in power, which seems strange when this monster murdered thousands of their people. Because of the oil in Iraq, food and cigarettes were free and it was only necessary for one member of a family of ten to go out to work and bring in cash to buy luxury goods such as satelite TV, or imported food or clothes. Most of the Kurds were from Mosel or Kirkuk and some were from Turkey. A few of them told me how they hid under lorries, and one guy claimed he had been involved with the Mafia and used to hijack cars in Baghdad. I could quite easily believe this, as he used to relieve his tension by head butting the metal cages at frequent intervals during the night.

In the beginning, working a twelve-hour nightshift was tough. You'd clock-in at the start of the shift feeling fit and healthy, but by the time you clocked-out you'd practically be in a wheel chair and sucking through a straw. I remember watching Si battling to stay warm from across the freezer. I could see a desperate man wrestling with his mind and fighting hard to keep up with the masses of boxes sliding down the chute. I felt angry with myself for pushing him into this hellhole. I wanted to tell him to leave and go back to London - to run as fast as he could out of this icebox and jump onto the next train bound for Euston. This wasn't the right job for him. It wasn't the right job for me, but I didn't have a choice – Si did! I felt responsible in some way for putting him through this torture. Before we left London to go on our first trip to the US, Si had a good career in the internet. He still had the option to go back to London for a while and earn money in a much easier way, but I knew he didn't want that. He was sticking to his guns. For the first time in his life he could see a light at the end of the tunnel, and over the following weeks as we became settled into the job, I began to notice that he actually seemed to be quite enjoying his labour.

It was around 2:30am whilst stacking boxes of frozen oven chips, when Si ran up to me with a big smile across his face and a plan that was to change everything.

'Put down that box and listen to this!' he yelled over the noise of a nearby hydraulic machine.

'Why, what's up?' I yelled back.

'I've got it!'

'Got what?'

'An idea!'

'Si, I'm working here. I've got to clear this chute before Bateman comes back.'

'Fuck, Bateman - *Vladivostok*!'

'You what?'

'How about we drive the Sierra to Vladivostok?' he beamed with excitement.

Throwing a box of oven chips into a cage, I patted my gloves together and tried to comprehend what Si was saying. 'You're joking, right?'

Si dropped his smile. 'No. I'm being deadly serious, you little shit ... think about it, what a journey! All the way from Daventry to Siberia ... overland.'

'It's not possible, is it?'

'I don't know, but I was thinking about an article I read in National Geographic. It was about the Trans-Siberian Railway that runs the entire length of Russia. Fuck getting the train ... let's drive!'

Suddenly, a voice cried out from across the freezer. '*RAVENS!*'

We turned to see Bateman, the evil nightshift manager, storming towards us.

'*RAVENS! WHAT YOU DOING?*'

Sticking out his chest, Bateman slid up beside us. He was a large man with dark heavy bags under his eyes, and had the manner of an army sergeant in some fucked up boot camp.

'What part of *work* don't you understand?' he growled. 'What part?'

I leaned against the chute, and smiled. 'We're just warming ourselves up.'

'Warming up your fucking mouths more like. Try doing some work, that'll warm you up.'

'We have been all night,' I replied. 'It just so happens that every time you walk past we're not working.'

'Look, guys, if you want to chat do it in your break – we've still got fifty thousand cases left to pick tonight. If I catch you both gossiping again like two housewives over the garden fence, you're out of here – understand. The Kurdish guys are bad enough, don't make me get rid of you two.'

'Leave them alone, Bateman, you bully!' a kid yelled as he ran past.

'Shut up, Lefty!'

Bateman pointed two fingers at his eyes and then at us. 'I'll be watching you.'

He stormed off and disappeared behind a chute rammed with boxes.

I turned to Si with a nod. 'Vladivostok. It's a crazy idea, but I love it!'

'Excellent, so in six weeks we go!'

'Yeah. In six weeks we commit suicide.'

After escaping the grasp of Köln, I force myself to pull over at a service station somewhere outside Nürnberg. Drawing to a sudden halt beside an orange VW Beetle, Si jerks forward and peers up over his fleece.

'Where are we?' he croaks.

'Uh … near Nürnberg,' I reply, tucking into a packet of salt and vinegar flavoured crisps.

'You what?'

'Nürnberg.'

'*NÜRNBERG?*' Si shouts, springing up in his seat. 'Nürnberg in Germany?'

'Yeah, why?'

'We can't be!'

'Why can't we be?'

'How can we be near Nürnberg? It's not possible!'

'We are – it's a fact.'

Si peers down at the map. 'Jesus Christ, you've driven fucking miles! What time is it?'

'I don't know the clock doesn't work. I think it's nearly morning.'

'Why didn't you wake me up?'

I shrug. 'Dunno. The past few hours have been a bit of a blur, to be honest with you.'

'What do you mean?'

'It's these German autobahns. I couldn't stop driving. I just wanted to drive and drive. It was like I was hypnotized … stuck on autopilot.'

'Fucking hell, Chris! The last time I looked out of the window we were just leaving Liège.'

'Liège? Nah, that was ages ago, wasn't it?'

'You should know, you've been driving.'

'All right, calm down.'

'NO, I won't calm down! It's a bloody good job you stopped when you did, otherwise we would have been in Vladivostok in about five days.'

I smirk. 'Yeah. I caught myself starting to drift off, so I thought I'd better pull over.'

'Drift off? You could have killed us both, you idiot! That's the last time I let you drive when I'm asleep. I've nearly missed the whole of Germany because of you.'

'You didn't miss much. There really wasn't anything to see ... well, apart from miles and miles of tarmac. Oh, I did have a race in a tunnel with some prick through the centre of Köln, though. That was quite interesting.'

* * *

After a quick freshen-up and a very strong coffee, I take over the driving and zoom down the autobahn towards Regensberg. Chris climbs into the back of the car and disappears beneath his sleeping bag. BMW's, Mercedes and monster size Audi's eat up the tarmac in the fast lane, and chasing their taillights we drive swiftly into the Bavarian countryside. Castles rise from the lush green forests that stretch out into the distance, and relieved to be away from the noise of industrial Germany we venture further towards the depths of Eastern Europe.

Glancing over my shoulder, I can see that Chris is sound asleep - most probably dreaming about being a gangster pimp in New York, or being stuck on a desert island with a hundred naked girls and fifty crates of beer. I'm not surprised that he's still dead to the world, especially after his mammoth eight-hour 'non-stop' autobahn experience, which I must admit I can totally understand now.

Avoiding the city of Regensberg, I happily turn off the autobahn and follow signs to a town called Passau on the Austrian border. It's early afternoon and spying a petrol station outside town, I decide to fill up the Sierra before we head north for the border with the Czech Republic. Not wishing to disturb Chris from his surreal dreams, I quietly remove the key from the ignition and unhook the hose. The petrol pump jumps into life and shoving the nozzle into the fuel tank, I press the lever and shoot the liquid into the car. Watching the numbers on the screen clock up at speed, the sound of the gushing fuel signals to my bladder that it needs to be emptied. Struggling to lock the petrol cap in place, I remove the key and hurry over to the garage to pay. A large Bavarian gentleman with a bushy-nicotine stained mustache stands at the till and talks loudly in a thick German accent to the guy behind the counter. They seem to be having a serious discussion, so I wait patiently to be served and try to distract myself from the fact that my bladder is ready to burst by thinking of other things … nice things … things that don't involve fast flowing water. Both guys can clearly see that I'm ready to pay, but they ignore me and continue with their debate. Feeling annoyed, I begin to tap my foot on the floor and hum a tune. The gentleman in front stops talking and turns to me. I beam a smile and peer over at the cashier. The large guy finally steps to one side and I slap my money on the counter. Running my purchase through the till, I take my change and leave without so much as a danke. I glance around in desperation for the toilet, and spot a small brick building around the back of the petrol station. I head swiftly in its direction. I enter the dark closet, flick on the light switch and slam the door shut behind me. The place is grim, with crusty shit plastered around the rim of the bowl and shit stained pieces of tissue paper spilling out of the bin. Trying to block these images from my mind, I feel relieved to see the toilet bowl and quickly tear open my flies just in the nick of time. Relaxing, I let out a deep sigh of relief as the pressure on my bladder is released. Shaking my fella dry, I pop him back in my pants and turn to the cracked mirror on the wall. I rinse my hands under the cold tap and dry them on the bottom of my T-shirt. Winking at my reflection I turn and reach for the door handle, but to my absolute horror there isn't one! Running my fingers frantically over the hole where the handle should be, I desperately begin to scan every inch of the doorframe.

'Oh, shit,' I whisper under my breath.

Panic hits me. Feeling my heart beating violently inside my chest, I look around the tiny room for an exit. Everywhere I look I see dirty black tiles, and I find myself holding onto the walls as the room begins to spin. Turning to the sink, I grab hold of the basin and lower my head.

'Fuck, stay calm!'

The room stops spinning and I try to gather my composure, but my pulse is sent racing out of control again as it suddenly occurs to me no one knows where I am. What if no one ever uses this toilet or Chris, the lazy fuck, sleeps for the next five hours. I'll be trapped in this cesspit, left to rot and die alone. Being trapped in a small space is one of my worst fears. You're helpless, confined between four walls, which at this moment in time seem to be closing in on me. The last time this happened was when Chris and I were seven years old. He thought it would be funny to lock me in the downstairs cupboard, and I've been terrified of being trapped in small spaces ever since. Looking up at my reflection in the mirror I can see the terror in my eyes. Turning away, I lean against the sink and look slowly around the room. There's a sky light in the roof and a small extraction fan on the wall to the outside, which sits motionless. It stares at me with its star shaped form and I try to find something else to focus on, but my eyes bounce around this shit hole and I'm forced to stare at the floor in an attempt to stop myself spinning again. Composing myself, I turn to the door.

'You're gonna have to do something, Simon,' I whisper to myself. 'What would Jack Bauer from the TV series *24* do in this situation? I know! He'd break down the door.'

Taking a step back, I brace myself against the wall.

'You can do it, buddy boy. One hard kick and the door will fly open.'

Releasing a high-pitched squeal, I leap into the air 'Matrix' style and karate kick the door. My right foot hits the lock, but instead of the door swinging open and handing me back my freedom, I find myself falling like a brick onto the concrete floor. Scrambling to my feet I contemplate karate kicking the door again, but I change my mind and resort to banging on it as hard as possible and screaming my tits off. Pausing to listen for a response, I lean back against the wall and look up at the ceiling. Returning my attention to the skylight in the roof, I stand on my tiptoes and reach up above my head. I can't quite reach the catch. Deciding to climb up onto the sink, I hoist a foot up onto the side and pull myself up. Balancing on the edge, I reach for the skylight and grab hold of the catch. Tugging at the metal handle, it appears to be wedged shut. Taking a moment to adjust my balance, I take a firm grip on the catch and prepare to wrench it open. Putting my full force into it I pull down with all of my strength, but hearing a crack below, I lose my grip and leap off the edge of the sink as it breaks off the wall and crashes to the floor. Stumbling forward, I slam into the far wall and skidding in the piss around the toilet bowl, I slip to my knees and plunge my right hand into the brown, foul smelling toilet water.

'*HELP!*' I scream.

Hearing the door swing open on its hinges, I look around and see Chris standing in the doorway with his hands in his pockets and a cigarette hanging from the corner of his mouth.

'Si, what you doing?'

'*IT'S NOT MY FAULT!*' I yell, vigorously scrubbing my hand with a brown stained towel. 'I've just put my hand down the frigging toilet!'

Chris peers over at the toilet bowl, and shivers. 'Why?'

'I didn't mean to do it, you twat. I was trying to get out!'

He nods reassuringly. 'I totally understand. Come on, let's

get the fuck out of here.'

Chris drags me out of the toilet and over to the Sierra.

'What took you so long?' I mutter, falling into the passenger seat.

'I didn't know where you were. I woke up and you weren't around.'

'I was stuck in the toilet, you numb-nuts. The lock was broken!'

'How was I supposed to know that? I'm not psychic!'

'We're twins – you should be!'

'Si, you know I don't believe in all of that GPS crap.'

'It's ESP, you idiot.'

'Whatever...'

'Jesus Christ, that was fucking horrible! Look at me I'm still shaking, I thought I was going to die in there.'

'Don't be so dramatic.'

'Piss off! I really lost it. I felt like a caged animal.'

'I can't believe you broke the sink?'

'I had to get out, I've never been so scared. My whole life flashed in front of my eyes, it was horrible. I'm telling you, Chris, just horrible!'

Driving north, Chris follows signs for the Czech border. Rain clouds fill the sky as we head deeper into the countryside, and approaching a barricade situated in the middle of nowhere, we draw to a halt in a torrential downpour. A stern looking border official wearing a long green raincoat, steps out of his guard box and peers through the passenger window. Water drips rapidly from the brim of his cap as he reaches out his hand and takes our passports. He then turns around and disappears back inside his guard box. Re-immerging a few minutes later, he hands back our wet documents and slowly nods as if to suggest everything is OK. With a friendly wave, we pass through the barrier and continue on into the Czech Republic and the forests of Sumava.

'Well, that was easy enough,' Chris grins, swerving around the large pools of water dotted along the roadside. 'So this is the Czech Republic, then?'

A bright bolt of lightening forks dramatically across the sky directly above us, followed closely by a loud crash of thunder.

'Fucking hell,' I mutter, watching the window wipers dance vigorously from side-to-side. 'I feel like I'm in the Michael Jackson 'Thriller' video.'

Shinning the torch down on the map, I follow the road with my finger. 'We need to find a turn off on the right for Cesky Krumlov.'

Chris dabs the brakes as we race past a woman sheltering beneath a small umbrella.

'Did you see that?' he cries glancing in the rearview mirror.

'Yeah, what the hell's she doing? Do you think we should offer her a lift?'

'Don't be stupid, Si. She's a hooker!'

'*Really!* What, out here in the middle of nowhere?'

Chris nods. 'Yep.'

'How do you know?'

'It was obvious, wasn't it?'

'Was it?'

'Of course! Couldn't you tell by the short skirt, or by the way she was stood with one hand on her hip and her arse slightly raised. Her tits were practically exposed to the Czech countryside. She's probably catching the rich Germans crossing the border.'

'She can't be!'

'Why not?'

'I haven't seen one single car since we left the border. Surely she must realise that tonight of all nights is a really bad night to be working. I mean, there's a full-on rainstorm going on here - a torrential downpour! She'll get struck by lightening holding that umbrella ... Hey! There's a sign for Cesky Krumlov, turn down that road.'

Another bright flash of lightening illuminates our faces, and is followed even more closely by a bone-shattering boom of thunder.

'Shit, that was too close for comfort!' Chris yells.

The rain begins to fall harder, and although the window wipers are on full speed they fail to clear the buckets of water pounding the screen.

'Si, this is dangerous, I can't see fuck all!'

'Pull over, then!'

'Where?'

'Anywhere!'

'I can't! A car might -'

The window screen suddenly turns white as hailstones engulf the car. Chris slams his foot on the brake pedal and the car skids to the left. I instinctively reach over and grab the steering wheel, and we both hang on for dear life as the Sierra spins 360 degrees in a perfect circle. While the sound of hailstones drown our screams, another bolt of lightening illuminates our frightened faces as the car mounts a small embankment and slides sideways into a hedge.

Continuing to scream at the top of our voices, Chris quickly flicks on the hazard lights.

'*WHAT THE FUCK HAPPENED?*'

'*NO IDEA!*' Chris shrieks, '*BUT I THINK I'VE JUST SHAT MY PANTS!*'

As quickly as it started, the hailstorm comes to an abrupt halt and peering through the now visible window screen, we gasp as we realise we're less than a few feet away from plunging into a deep dyke.

Still gripping the steering wheel Chris turns to me, and laughs. 'Welcome to the Czech Republic!'

Long Face

Following the road around the Krumlov chateau in the early evening, we find ourselves in the old part of the historic town of Cesky Krumlov. Si directs me through a labyrinth of narrow cobbled streets lined with beautiful old stone buildings, all restored to perfection. After our little nightmare drive through the torrential rainstorm, we decide to spend our first night in luxury ... well, I guess that's if you call a backpacker hostel, luxury. Crossing a small bridge we find an empty side street and park up beside the Vltava River.

'Right, then,' I mutter, grabbing the Russian phrasebook out of my rucksack. 'What words should I learn first?'

Si frowns. 'What you doing?'

'I'm going to learn Russian.'

'We've just arrived in this incredible town and you want to learn Russian?'

'Si, it's pissing down with rain. Why get soaked?'

'Yeah, but it hasn't stopped raining since we crossed the border.'

Ignoring him, I flick to the beginning of the book and glance down at the first page.

'Basic expressions,' I grin. 'That sounds good. I'll start with basic expressions, "Greetings and Apologies".'

'Yeah, I'd learn apologies first if I were you,' Si laughs. 'I mean, it'll come in handy for when you have to apologize to the pretty girls for having a pin dick.'

'Do you mind, I'm trying to submerge myself in a new

language here?'

'Ha, "submerge". You're only learning Russian because you think it'll help you get laid. You think that by slipping a few Russian phrases into the conversation, you'll have girls doing back flips onto your cock. Well, don't be surprised when they back flip out of the door.'

'Fuck off! I'm learning Russian so I can be a good ambassador for our country. You know, show the people of Russia that we respect their culture by at least giving their language a go.'

'Fair enough, Chris. I guess when we were in Mexico you did try and learn a bit of Spanish. Well, at least the words for "hey, beautiful, nice arse and two beers", but I was impressed.'

'You have to start somewhere when you're learning a new language. I mean, look what it says on the cover of this book. "Travel with ease and communicate with confidence". Now, that's exactly what I intend to do.'

Si frowns. 'Shouldn't you be learning Czech?'

I look up from the page. 'I'm sorry, what was that?'

'Shouldn't you be learning Czech?'

'Why?'

'What do you mean "why"? Call me a frigging idiot, but aren't we in the Czech Republic?'

'Yeah, but I just think the more Russian I learn now, the easier … hey! I don't need to explain myself to you. Get off my back, will ya.'

Si raises his hand. 'All right, all right! No need to get over excited. It just seems a bit stupid that's all. If you were in Spain you wouldn't be learning French.'

'OK, I get your point.'

After twenty minutes of learning a few Czech words and a few near impossible Russian phrases, it stops raining. We lock up the car and slip on our coats. Without a map of the town or a guidebook at hand, we head into the centre on foot and wander through the deserted cobbled streets in search of somewhere to stay. It isn't long before we reach the main square. Walking down a quiet alley, we stumble across a backpacker hostel called The Traveller's Rest.

'Here we go!' Si grins. 'A bed for the night.'

'What a shit hole! There must be somewhere better than this.'

'It'll be cheap.'

'It should be free!'

I poke my head around the door and peer inside a small, smoky room crammed full of young smiley faces. A large group of backpackers sit around a table in the corner, drinking beer and laughing in unison. 'The Red Hot Chili Peppers' blast from speakers as we make our way over towards a kid standing behind a small bar. The posh looking nerd, who's wearing a Red Bull T-shirt, appears to be eves dropping on the group drinking at the large table.

He finally turns to us, and smiles. 'All right, fellas.'

'Hey, you're English!' Si grins.

'Yes, born and bred,' he replies.

'Where you from?'

'Bristol. What about you guys?'

'We're from a small town called Daventry in the Midlands. You probably won't have heard of it.'

'Yes, I know Daventry.'

Si frowns. '*Really?*'

'Well, I don't know it as such. I'm sure I've seen a signpost for it on the M1. Is it nice?'

'Yeah, it's all right.'

'Cool. I'll tell you what, give me your mobile number or email address and I'll come and visit you guys. You can give me a tour of the town and introduce me to all of your friends. Yeah, I'd really like that … I've got a pen around here somewhere.'

'So what you doing working here?' I quickly ask.

The kid seems to immediately forget about the pen and

opens a bottle of beer.

'Well, I decided to work here because I thought it would be a good crack. I'm Inter-railing around Europe, you see. I'm on my gap year.'

'Nice one!' Si beams. 'Look, we want to stay here tonight. Can you tell us where the reception is?'

'This is the reception. It's the bar-cum-reception if you like. We're pretty full at the mo, though. Actually! Saying that, I think there might be two beds free in the dorm.'

I frown. 'Dorm?'

'Yes.'

'Dorm as in dormitory?'

'Uh-huh,' he nods. 'Don't look so upset they're mixed dorms, which is great! My advice is to sleep with one eye open, you never know what interesting things you might see, if you know what I mean?'

'Yeah, we'll remember that,' Si grins. 'You don't have any private rooms left?'

'Nope. Just the twelve-bed dorm, I'm afraid.'

'Twelve beds?'

'Yep.'

Suddenly, the big group of backpackers sitting at the table next to the bar roars with laughter, and begins to chant the name Snowdon. A blonde guy sitting at the head of the table, who's wearing a white England Rugby shirt and has an uncanny resemblance to Prince William, stands up and raises his drink.

'Thank you my good friends,' he bows. 'Thank you so very much.'

'Tell us another joke, Snowdon,' a small spotty kid sitting around the table cries.

'All in good time, Freddy,' he winks, 'all in good time. I think I'll let you all recover from the last joke first before I split your sides with another.'

'Who's the show off?' I ask.

'That's Snowdon,' the kid behind the bar replies. 'He's

probably one of the funniest guys I've ever met. He's a master at telling jokes. They're so funny and he's so cool. He's a natural. All the girls fancy him. He's on his gap-year and Inter-railing around Europe, too … just like me! Hey, Snowdon, that joke was hilarious!'

Snowdon stops laughing and looks over at the kid. 'Thomas, you lazy fuck. Eight more beers over here and make it snappy!'

'Right away,' Thomas salutes. 'Absolutely no problem!'

Si turns to me with a smile. 'What an arse-licker.'

'Hey, Thomas!' Snowdon yells. 'Do you know any jokes?'

Thomas drops his smile. 'Uh … no, I don't think I do. I mean, I did do once, but I've forgotten it.'

'Oh, I know the joke,' Snowdon smiles. 'Is it the one about some loser called Thomas who goes Inter-railing with a hair dryer?'

Everyone sitting around the table bursts out laughing. Thomas's face turns bright red with embarrassment. Snowdon sits back down in his seat and flashes him a smug grin.

Si turns to Thomas. 'That was a bit harsh, don't you think?'

'Nah, he doesn't mean it. He likes me. We're best buddies. It's just harmless fun. He's a very funny guy, and he respects me.'

'Are you sure?'

He nods vigorously. 'Yep! I'd bet my mother's life on it.'

'Come on, Thomas, tell us a joke!' Snowdon cries. 'OK, it seems quite obvious you don't have a funny bone in your body … is there anyone else here in the house tonight who knows a joke?'

'I know a joke,' I grin, raising my hand.

The backpackers stop laughing and look over at me.

Snowdon stands up and folds his arms. 'You do?'

'Yeah.'

Si turns to me, and frowns. 'You do?'

'Yeah, I know loads of jokes.'

Snowdon looks me up and down. 'Well, why don't you join our table and share this "joke" of yours with us? Come on … don't be shy, we don't bite.'

We both walk over and sit down at the far end of the table. Snowdon sits back down and takes a large gulp of beer.

'OK, let's hear it, then,' he mutters, wiping his chin. 'I can hardly contain my excitement. Actually, hold on a minute, I've got an idea that'll make this more interesting. Why don't we each tell a joke and the one that gets the biggest laugh wins, the loser has to buy the whole table a drink. What do you say?'

The little shit I think to myself. I can't stand fucking gap-year kids. They're young, naïve and most probably still sleep in their pajamas. This table is full of rich toffs on their once in a lifetime adventure before they skip off to University and become doctors and lawyers. They're so fresh faced and clueless.

A kid sitting next to Si raises his thumbs in the air and smiles. 'Yeah, I think it's a cosmic idea, Snowdon.'

'Yeah, me too!' A fat girl with a posh Edinburgh accent yells.

'Thanks Edward, thanks Lilly. So we're all agreed, then? This coin I have in my hand will determine who goes first. What will it be, heads or tails?'

'Uh … heads,' I reply.

'What the fuck you doing?' Si whispers in my ear. 'You don't know any jokes – let's get out of here!'

Snowdon holds the coin between his finger and thumb and spins it on the table. We all watch the coin intently as it whips around on its axis. Eventually, it begins to lose momentum and falling onto its side it rattles to a halt. Snowdon covers it with his hand and cautiously steals a glance.

'It's tails!' he cries.

Everyone lets out a cheer.

'Right, so that means I go first,' he grins. 'But, as I'm a bloody nice bloke, I'm going to let you go first.'

Resting my elbows on the table, I throw Snowdon a nod.

'Chris, this is stupid. Let's fucking leave!'

I ignore Si and clear my throat. 'OK ... uh ... why do the Irish keep empty milk bottles in the fridge?'

Everyone shrugs.

'...Just in case somebody wants a black coffee!'

Silence. Nobody laughs. There isn't one single smile - not one! The fat girl sitting next to me picks up her drink and drops her gaze, while Edward scratches the back of his head and looks over at Snowdon. Even Thomas, the guy who wants to be liked by everyone doesn't even back me up with a snigger.

'Well, well, well,' Snowdon grins. 'That wasn't very funny, was it? I don't want to jump the gun or anything, but I'd say that from the reaction around the table you might want to start ordering our beers. Oh, and by the way, I'm half Irish, so ... yes, I am a little offended by the joke.'

'Tell your joke, Snowdon!' Thomas yells.

'Right, OK,' he replies, straightening his posture. 'A horse walks into a bar and orders a drink. The barman turns to the horse and says, "hey, what's with the long face?"'

The table erupts with laughter. Thomas whistles, Edward stamps his feet, tears run down Lilly's face and everyone else just goes absolutely crazy. We sit dumbfounded and watch the gap-year kid's fall about in uncontrollable fits of laughter.

'What's with the long face?' Snowdon screams. 'Beat that, I bet you can't!'

'Si, for Christ sake, that has to be the oldest joke in the history of jokes. I've had enough of this shit, let's leave - school time over!'

'About frigging time, you idiot,' Si replies, rising out of his chair.

'Hey!' Snowdon yells. 'Where do you think you're going? You haven't bought our beers yet.'

I turn to Snowdon. 'Shut it!'

'I beg your pardon!' he snaps. 'You can't speak to me like that I'm going to Oxford University, you know.'

'Yeah,' Thomas shouts from across the bar. 'He's going to Oxford University.'

'Well, good luck,' I reply, slamming a couple of notes on the table, 'because you're gonna need it!'

* * *

'What a bunch of cock-heads!' Chris yells, stumbling out into the street.

'I did try to warn you, but you couldn't resist telling that joke, could you?'

'It's a very funny joke ... I love telling that joke ... it's a great joke ... why didn't they laugh?'

'It was crap, that's why.'

'Oh, and that posh twat's joke was funnier, was it?'

'Who cares?' I laugh. 'Hey, fuck this! Let's sleep in the car tonight. I really can't be arsed to spend all night looking for a place to stay.'

Heading back to the car via a pizza joint, we perch ourselves on the bonnet of the Sierra and look out over the river that sparkles in the moonlight.

'Well, it looks like we're going to be sleeping upright again,' Chris mumbles, taking a large bite out of his pepperoni pizza slice.

'It beats staying in that hostel any day. My days of sleeping in a dorm are most definitely over. I'd rather sleep in the car!'

'I suppose we'd better get used to it. I can't imagine there'll be many backpacker hostels in deepest Siberia. Actually, come to think of it, we must be insane!'

'I know, fucking exciting, isn't it? I mean, can you imagine that lad Steve from the freezer just dropping everything and chipping off to Russia for a few months.'

'Hey, leave Steve-o out of this,' Chris grins. 'He was a good lad. It was just a bit unfortunate he got his girlfriend pregnant when he was sixteen, and very unfortunate that it was the first time he'd had sex.'

'You what? Was it his first time?'

'Yep. It's sad, but true. Until the night he clapped eyes on Kaz outside the post office, he was indeed a virgin.'

'Imagine having to work all those hours in a freezer just to feed your girlfriend's fat ass?'

Chris shakes his head. 'Pure tragedy.'

'He must love her, though, mustn't he? He must be happy.'

'I bloody hope so, the poor lad's only twenty-one.'

'Who would your dream girl be, then?'

Chris frowns. 'Now there's a difficult question. I'd hope she'd be pretty – curvy, nice tits. Maybe someone like that glamour-model Jo Guest.'

'Jo Guest? But what about personality?'

'Personality? Hmm … mellow, but passionate about life. She'd have to want to travel like me, and yet still be secure enough for us not to have to be together all of the time. I need my space. Maybe an artist, what about you?'

I shrug. 'I haven't really got a specific type. Blonde, brunette, short, tall, none of that really matters to me.'

'As long as she's pretty, right?' Chris grins.

'You'd hope so! I wouldn't want her to be vain, though. There's nothing less attractive than a girl that's vain, I prefer girls that are naturally beautiful.'

'Who like?'

'Someone like Michelle Pfeiffer or Audrey Hepburn.'

'What about that Charlie Dimmock off the gardening program, Ground Force? She's pretty natural.'

'Earthy more like. What I mean is, I like a girl who's beautiful, but doesn't appear to know it.'

'Hang on, what's all this talk about dream girls, anyway? Are you getting lonely, Si? Scared of the future are you … scared of the future?'

'Piss off! It's just something you think about sometimes, isn't it?'

'Maybe you should've gone back to London and married Emily?'

'Don't be ridiculous!'

A couple of months after returning home from my travels in the US with Chris, I had arranged to meet my ex-girlfriend, Emily, in London one weekend. I had stayed in contact with her by email during the remainder of the trip and, feeling confident that I could handle seeing her again after our painful break up, I nervously got on the train and headed for the big smoke. Before I knew it, I was on Hampstead High Street for the first time since the day our relationship ended. Memories of our time together flooded into my mind, and I suddenly felt anxious as to how I might feel about seeing her again. Having arrived early, I decided to duck into a nearby pub to calm my nerves a little before meeting her, and sitting at the bar I sipped a pint and enjoyed the sensation of being alone with my thoughts. Sitting there I remember thinking how familiar it all felt, and it suddenly occurred to me that I'd spent many afternoons before perched on bar stools waiting for Emily. It had become a regular activity that I'd started to enjoy right from the early days when we'd first met, and for the years that followed I would often find myself arriving early to meet her and use it as an excuse to enjoy some time to myself. There was something deeply relaxing about waiting for her to arrive, and I realised that as much as I looked forward to seeing her, I enjoyed the comfort of being able to enjoy being alone just as much.

Mellowed by the alcohol, I made my way to the restaurant where we had agreed to meet and finding a space at the side of the street, I waited patiently for her outside. Watching the traffic pass by, I tried to guess which direction she might appear from and turning in the direction of her apartment, my heart skipped a beat when I saw her walking towards me with her big smile. Stamping my cigarette out on the floor, I looked up in time to receive her embrace.

'Simon,' she giggled breathlessly, kissing me on the cheek.

Leaning back, she looked at me anxiously and with wide eyes.

'Hey,' she laughed. 'Have you been drinking?'

'Just a pint,' I grinned. 'I got to Hampstead a bit early.'

'You piss head.'

'Come on, let's go inside.'

Taking her arm, we entered the restaurant and grabbed a free table by the window. I watched as she removed her coat and the long red scarf that I had bought for her 21st birthday. She looked as beautiful as ever, with her long shiny brown hair and clear skin and forcing myself to avoid admiring her familiar curves, I signaled to the waiter for the menu.

'Are you hungry?' I asked.

'Starving,' she beamed.

'Me too.'

Making herself comfortable, she rested her elbows on the table. 'So when did you get back? What was it like? I want to know everything!'

'It's been a few weeks now.'

'Was it amazing?'

'It was fucking insane!'

'I'm *so* jealous. You look fantastic.'

'Do I?'

'Yeah, you're tanned. You look more relaxed.'

'You're not looking too bad yourself.'

Reaching over the table we took each other's hand. I knew this was a bad idea. Chris had warned me not to get too close, but after four years together it just felt natural. We hadn't seen each other for nearly six months, we missed each other's company and finding ourselves in bed together later that afternoon, I put the consequences to the back of my mind and enjoyed the moment.

Lying next to her in bed after the best sex I think we'd ever had, I starred up at the ceiling. I felt incredibly happy, but simultaneously a strange sadness lay twisting in my guts. Finally, I knew it was over. I had needed to know that what I'd felt for her was something special, and feeling it more strongly than ever before I could also see that it could never work. We had grown apart. We wanted very different things, and in the pursuit of lasting happiness for ourselves I think we both realised that it was over. In the back of my mind, I'd hoped maybe we could find something that might hold us together, but kissing her before I left her apartment that day, I knew I would never see her again and I think she knew the same.

Walking through the streets of North London towards Camden, I'd felt strangely free as I made my way to a bar to meet my old friend Dermot. My life had changed direction for good and, although I felt nervous about what the future held, I felt as equally excited about the endless possibilities that lay in front of me. What I did with my life now was in my hands and my hands alone. I had nobody to blame for my frustrations. I could no longer use Emily or my career as an excuse not to pursue my dreams. For the first time in my life I was responsible for my destiny.

Bohemian Rhapsody

Embracing a half-eaten slice of pepperoni pizza, I open my eyes and glance sleepily up at the stone bridge that arches above the car. Blinking, I leap forward in my seat and glare open mouthed at the sight of a large group of Japanese tourists, with surprisingly small cameras, all pointing and nudging each other as they battle to take photographs of us both asleep in the car.

'Hey, Si, wake up!'

Removing his face from the passenger window, Si glances up at the tourists and shields his eyes from the bright flashes of light.

'Jesus Christ ... *HEY!*' he shouts, rolling down his window. 'What the fuck do you think you're doing? There's a thing called privacy, you know!'

The Japanese tourists ignore him, and continue to fight amongst themselves for that one special picture of two European street urchins sleeping rough at the roadside. I tear open my sleeping bag and quickly reverse the car out of view.

'Where's the respect? We're not a couple of animals in some frigging ... *BOLLOCKS!*' Si cries, screwing up his face. 'I've slept in my bloody contact lenses again. Why do I always do that? *WHY?*'

'Are you *OK?*'

'*NO!* Right, that's it, I'm going back to wearing glasses!'

'Glasses?'

'What's wrong with wearing glasses? I look cool in glasses.'

I laugh. 'Are you sure?'

'Yes!'

'But if you do that, I'll take the piss out of you and start calling you four-eyes.'

Si scratches his chin. 'Hmm ... that's true. Bollocks! Why am I so frigging blind?'

'You should have laser treatment.'

'It's too expensive.'

'Just get one eye done.'

'Chris, don't be ridiculous. Come on, let's get out of here I need to find somewhere to wash my hands.'

Waving goodbye to Cesky Krumlov, we return to the lush green countryside and pass through numerous villages that appear to be frozen in time. As we leave one particular town lined with Noddy cars and classic Skoda's, we drive beside an old mansion house covered in green vine and spot a huge stalk feeding its baby in a nest perched on a tall chimney top.

'Si, quick, pass me my camera! I can see a P.O. with my name on it. Quick! Quick!'

Si reaches down between his legs and fishes my Nikon FM2 out of his bag.

'What's a P.O?' he asks.

'A Photo Opportunity.'

'Oh, right...'

'This is incredible,' I beam, raising the camera to my face. 'Absolutely incredible! Have you ever seen anything so beautiful? It's a stork, for Christ sake. It's huge!'

'Chris, please don't think I'm criticizing your equipment, but have you ever thought about going digital?'

I lower the camera. 'You what?'

'Digital. You know, the future of photography.'

'Yes, I do know what digital is, thank you very much. Why?'

Si shrugs. 'Oh ... uh ... no reason. It's just I've heard you can take a good quality picture with them now, and they're coming down in price.'

'I do know about digital cameras. I'm a photographer, I read Amateur Photography.'

'Ooh ... OK, sorry David Bailey. What's your favorite digital camera, then?'

'Fuck knows. Look, Si, what's with all the questions? Are you purposefully trying to piss me off?'

'All right, calm down! I must've hit a raw nerve.'

'Are you saying my camera is shit and outdated?' I cry, waving the Nikon in his face. 'Is that what you're saying?'

'No.'

We sit in silence for a few seconds.

I place the chunky camera on my lap. 'I guess it is starting to look a bit old fashioned. But I like using film, I wouldn't use anything else.'

'Fair enough, Chris. As long as you take a good snap, who cares what you use.'

Purchasing a motorway pass from a post office in the city of Plzen, we find ourselves hurtling towards the capital city of Prague. Excited by the prospect of seeing the Bohemian architecture and experiencing a city that I've heard so much about in recent years, I blast up the volume on the radio and set to work at playing some serious air guitar.

Reaching the outskirts of the city, we spot a tourist information sign above a small grey portacabin. Pulling off the motorway, we follow the slip road and park up next to a shiny black BMW. An attractive blonde girl smokes a cigarette behind the wheel and flicks through a glossy magazine. Smiling in her direction, we climb out of the Sierra and make our way over to the entrance. The girl reluctantly tosses the magazine to one side and jumps out of the car. She babbles something at us in Czech, and smiling innocently she swings open the door to the portacabin and gestures for us to follow her inside. The office is tiny, with a flimsy counter and one chair. There are tourist posters pinned to the walls and a red folder on the counter. Grabbing the folder, she opens it at the first page and slides it in front of us. Flicking through the file, we study pictures of the large selection of kitsch hotel rooms on offer.

'Hey, Si, what do you think?'

'Yeah, she's pretty hot,' he whispers.

'No. The hotel rooms, you idiot.'

'Oh, I dunno. Bit basic, aren't they?'

'How much is forty euros?'

Si shrugs. 'About thirty quid, I think.'

'Hmm ... that's a bit out of our price range, maybe we should just head for the train station and see what we can find around there.'

'The train station? You're kidding, right?'

'No.'

'Chris, hotels around the train station in any city are notorious for being flea-bitten hellholes.'

'Well, they can't be any worse than the dives in these pictures, and at least they'll be cheap.'

Si turns to the girl standing behind the counter. 'Uh ... es gut, but nein danke,' he mutters, hoping she'll understand a little German.

Looking disappointed, the girl punches the number 30 into a calculator and then points to a page in the folder.

'She's knocked down the price,' Si grins.

I shake my head. 'Nah. We don't know where the hotel will be. It could be miles outside town.'

She slides the folder in front of us. We both peer down at the pictures and notice that it's student accommodation. She then points at a map of the city and indicates that it's in the centre.

Si turns to me, and nods. 'Sounds perfect! Let's book in for the night.'

Giving the girl the thumbs up, she grabs her mobile off the counter and begins to make a call.

'Hey, this is going to be fun!' Si cries. 'Maybe we should ask her if she'd like to join us for a few drinks tonight.'

I frown. 'Do you think so?'

'Yeah, why not?'

'She's probably got a boyfriend. A sexy girl like that always has a boyfriend.'

'Not necessarily. Ask her!'

'Why me?'

'I'm always doing it. Go on,' Si winks.

'I can't.'

'You're a wimp.'

'Piss off! Anyway, she doesn't speak English. It's pointless.'

'Chris, it's called the language of love, dear boy, the language of love. You don't need words.'

The girl finishes talking on the phone and blushes. She slides the address across the counter.

'Thank you, I mean dekuji,' I beam.

'You're welcome,' she replies. 'I hope you guys have a pleasant stay in Prague.'

Feeling deeply embarrassed that she speaks English, we grin falsely and return quickly to the car.

* * *

Reaching the centre of Prague, we drive across one of the impressive stone bridges that arches low over the Vltava River. Miraculously, Prague was completely untouched by World War II, and we're immediately wowed by the city's incredible bohemian architecture. Chris guides me through the busy tram infested streets, and pausing at a pedestrian crossing we watch the people of Prague rush by.

We arrive at the rather run-down student accommodation building and head straight for a nearby car park situated beneath a concrete fly-over. Waiting in a queue, Chris excitedly points out a GB sticker stuck to the boot of the car in front of us. Inching our way through the gate, we take a ticket from a friendly old man in the office and pull up in an empty space next to the blue Vauxhall Astra with the GB sticker. A smartly dressed guy in a suit climbs out.

'Hey, you're from Great Britain!' Chris smiles, pointing at the sticker.

'Yes, I am,' the guy replies, grabbing a laptop case from the boot.

'Have you driven all the way, too?'

'Sure have,' he smiles, rushing around to the passenger window. He cups his hands and peers through the glass before tapping his trouser pocket. He then urgently jabs his fingers inside his jacket pocket and pulls out a computer disc.

'Are you here on business?' I chip in.

'Yeah, I'm a journalist. I'm supposed to be interviewing someone in about...' he glances down at his watch, 'hmm ... half-an-hour ago. Whoops, I'm a bit late, but not bad considering I've just driven all the way from Surrey, I suppose.'

'Bliemey, you must be knackered,' Chris laughs.

'Well, I had a pit stop in Brussels and Dresden, so I don't feel too tired. Where are you guys staying?'

'At a hostel near here,' I reply. 'It's part of the University, I think.'

'The place around the corner?'

'Yeah.'

'That's where I'm staying,' he beams.

'Really?'

'Yes. Maybe later we could meet for a drink in the bar?'

'Good idea,' Chris nods enthusiastically.

'Does nine o'clock sound OK?'

Chris looks over in my direction, and nods. 'Yeah, nine should be fine.'

'Great. OK, I'd better be off. See you guys later.'

Storming off to his meeting with his laptop case tucked under his arm, we casually gather our bags together and head towards the hostel.

Checking into the student halls, we drag our bags down a dark corridor and enter our musty jail cell. Collapsing onto a lumpy bed, I stare up at the nicotine stained ceiling. The room is dark and cold with steel bars at the window. Tutting, I reach over for my cigarettes on the bedside table and turn on the lamp. The bulb flickers a few times before producing a dim orange glow. Sitting up, I lean against the cold wall.

'I bet Terry Waite had a better cell than this,' I mutter, glancing over at the antique radiator hanging from the wall.

'Stop complaining, it's not that bad. It's just somewhere to crash for the night.'

'It's a shit hole!'

'Yeah, yeah, whatever,' Chris mutters, as he rummages inside his rucksack. He looks up. 'Hey, have you got a towel?'

'Use your own.'

'I haven't brought one.'

'Why the fuck not?'

'I forgot it.'

'Well, bad luck It's not my fault,' I cough, swinging my feet off the bed. 'There's no way I'm using a damp towel that's just been used to dry your shitty arse.'

Collapsing onto his bed, Chris buries his face in the rock hard pillow.

'Oh yeah, and while we're on the subject you can stop using my frigging soap, too!'

Chris frowns. 'Why?'

'Because it's unhygienic, that's why. I really don't fancy waking up one morning with mushrooms growing off the end of my knob. All right?'

I'm awoken sometime later by a gurgling sound coming from the radiator. I rub my eyes and look around the room. Chris is sitting on the end of his bed and cleans his camera lens with a sock. He's showered and dressed to impress.

'What time is it?' I groan.

'About seven thirty, I think.'

Grabbing my towel and wash kit, I leave the prison cell and stumble down the dark corridor towards the communal bathroom. As I push open the door, I'm surprised to hear someone singing 'Lady in Red' in one of the shower cubicles. Steam fills the room and throwing my towel over the door to the adjacent cubicle, I step inside and begin to undress.

'*Lady-in-red!*' the guy shrieks, '*is dancing with meeee... cheek to cheek.*'

Smiling at this guy's awful singing ability I turn on the shower and quickly begin to apply shampoo to my greasy hair. The shower is surprisingly hot and powerful, it lifts my mood and I have to resist the desire to join in with the rest of the chorus. After applying soap to my body, I stand with my hands by my sides and relax for a moment beneath the warm blanket of water. I turn off the shower, wrap my towel around my waist and step out of the cubicle. Just as I'm about to turn and head for the sink, the guy in the cubicle opposite immerges at the same time as me. I'm surprised to see it's the journalist from the car park. He's bollock naked apart from wearing a pair of misted up glasses.

'Hey!' I cry, feeling extremely uncomfortable. 'How are ya?'

'I'm good. I feel as fresh as the morning dew,' he replies, throwing his towel over his shoulder. 'I was just taking a shower.'

'Yeah, me too,' I grin falsely.

'Great!'

We both stand in silence.

'So, how was your interview?' I quickly ask.

'Good.'

'Great!'

There's more uncomfortable silence.

'Well … uh, I'm going to brush my teeth,' I grin.

'Me too,' he replies, whipping off his glasses.

Walking over to a row of sinks, we both squeeze toothpaste onto our toothbrushes and begin brushing. The guy begins to hum 'Lady in Red', while I look down into the sink, trying desperately to avoid the grotesque sight of his flaccid penis in the reflection of the mirror. Catching his eye, we both nod before spitting the toothpaste simultaneously into the sinks.

'What room number are you in?' he asks.

'Thirty.'

'I'm in thirty-one, we're neighbours! I'll knock on your door instead of meeting you in the bar, shall I?'

I slip my T-shirt over my head and gather my things together. 'Sounds great … bye.'

'Wait a minute!'

I stop and peer over my shoulder.

'What's your name?' he grins, standing exposed with his hands on his hips. 'My name's Cliff.'

'Simon,' I quickly reply, and disappearing around the corner I hurry back to the room.

Cliff's Arse

There's a firm knock at the door. I take a peek through the spy hole and see Cliff's big head and bulging alien eyes glaring back at me.

'Anyone home?' he smiles.

I swing open the heavy door and invite him inside. Looking fresh and wearing a pair of perfectly pressed chinos and a white shirt, Cliff steps inside our cell clutching a bottle of wine.

'Goodness me,' he laughs, '...and there I was thinking my room was shabby. Never mind, I thought I'd tempt you guys with some of the finest white wine in the world.'

'Great,' Si beams, leaping off the bed 'I love wine!'

'Good, because this little beauty just happens to be from the steep slopes of the Mosel valley.'

I walk over and inspect the label. 'It sounds delicious.'

'Indeed it is,' he nods. 'Germany produces some of the lightest, most delicate white wines on the planet. You won't be disappointed.'

Whipping a corkscrew out of his pocket, Cliff extracts the cork and pours some into a plastic cup.

'Ah, piquant and racy,' he smiles, handing Si the cup.

Si sniffs the inside before taking a sip.

Cliff looks at him with keen interest. 'What do you think?'

'Yeah, not bad.'

He frowns. 'Can you taste the Riesling?'

'The Riesling?'

'The grape!'

'I think so,' Si replies, looking confused.

Shaking his head disapprovingly, Cliff snatches the cup out of Si's hand and takes a sip. He washes it around his mouth a few times before swallowing.

'Delicious!' he cries. 'It has that mouth-freshening enchantment that leaves your palate perky and your mind unfuddled.'

We both turn to each other and frown.

'Come on, guys, let's get the wine flowing here!'

He quickly fills two more cups.

'Yeah, bottoms up,' I grin. 'To fine German wine and to, uh...'

'The EU,' Cliff smirks.

'Yeah, to the EU! I'm Chris by the way and this is my brother, Simon.'

'We've already met. You're brothers, you say?'

'Twins.'

'*Really?*'

'Uh-huh.'

'Well I never. You don't look anything alike.'

'Yeah, thank God.'

'Do you always travel together?'

'We have been recently. We couldn't do it all the time, though.'

'Why not?' Cliff asks.

'Because if we did, Si would be six feet under by now.'

Si narrows his eyes. 'Uh ... I think you'll find you'd be the worm food, pal. Not me.'

'I sense a little tension between you two,' Cliff smiles.

'Nah, there's no tension. It's just sometimes I get the urge to tie Si's arms and legs together and chuck him in the canal.'

Cliff laughs out loud. 'Oh, brotherly love! So where are you guys heading after Prague?'

'Up through Poland,' I reply. 'I want to visit Auschwitz, the Nazi Germany concentration camp. It's supposed to be very – '

'Depressing,' Si butts in.

Cliff sighs. 'It sounds like you're really seeing Eastern Europe. I'd like to see more someday.'

'Why don't you?'

'Well, the thing is, I've got an eighteen-month old baby daughter, so I can't be away from home for too long. Otherwise I'd be heading that way myself. This is a working trip. I'm a freelance journalist, you see. I write articles for computer magazines.'

'That must be interesting.'

'Yes, it can be. I particularly enjoy it when I get the chance to go on a trip like this. When I was given the opportunity to interview the chairman of this big computer company here in Prague, I jumped at the chance, although, my wife wasn't too happy. "Can't you interview him over the phone?" she said, but I kept telling her it's not how it's done. I mean, OK, I could have interviewed him over the phone, but I find it's always best to see these fat cats face-to-face. Oh, and it's also a good excuse to go on a little road trip by myself, too. I could've flown.'

We both give an understanding nod. Cliff sits down on the bed and takes a sip of wine.

'It's crazy how fast your life can change,' he continues. 'Change without you even realising it. Anyway, listen to me drone on - I still can't believe you are *twins*! I bet you get into all sorts of trouble.'

'Yeah, not half,' Si winks.

I pick up the bottle of wine and refill the cups. 'How long are you going to stay in Prague?'

'A few days,' Cliff replies. 'There are one or two things I'd like to check out while I'm here.'

'What kind of things?'

'Oh, you know, this and that. What about you guys?'

'We'll probably leave tomorrow after a little sightseeing,' Si smiles. 'If you're interested we're thinking of going to this really good club later.'

Cliff shakes his head vigorously. 'Sorry, guys, but I'm going to have to take a rain check on that one. I'm way too tired. It's been a hell of a day. I think I'll just crawl into bed and read my book.'

* * *

We grab a taxi to the Charles Bridge in the Stare Mesto area of the city. The setting sun hangs over the beautiful church of St Nicholas, providing Chris with not only great light, but also great photo opportunities (P.O's). I stand and watch him dance around the tourists with his camera, poised and ready for action. For a brief moment I lose sight of him, but spot him crouched down behind a statue as he battles to find the best composition. Eventually, he staggers over to me with a big smile across his face and two film cartridges in his hand. I pat him on the back and suggest we find a bar and get drunk immediately. Crossing the Charles Bridge, we enter the Mala Strana area and within seconds we stumble across a drinking hole away from the tourists. Sinking four glasses of excellent Czech Budvar beer with a rather mature crowd of hard drinking locals, we leap to our feet and make our way excitedly to the Roxy Nightclub.

Joining the queue outside, we pay at the small window and descend a flight of stairs into an enormous venue that's jam-packed with the young and fashionable. Dance music blasts out across the club as we squeeze through the crowds and head for a circular bar. Grabbing a couple of drinks, we head up to the next level where we find comfy seats overlooking the dance floor. We peer down over an ocean of gyrating bodies.

Chris lights a cigarette and smiles. 'Dancing is weird,

isn't it?'

'What do you mean?'

'Well, imagine if you turned on all the lights and stopped the music - everyone would look like freaks. Hundreds of nutcases jerking from side-to-side, waddling around in circles and punching the air.'

'I hadn't really thought of it like that before, but now you mention it.'

'Why do we do it?'

'What, dance?'

Chris nods. 'Yeah. I mean, what makes us want to move our bodies whenever we hear a funky beat?'

I consider this for a moment. 'It probably stems all the way back to primeval courtship, I suppose. You know, similar to the way swans have evolved to perform a kind of courtship dance to attract a potential mate.'

'I guess so,' Chris replies, sipping his whiskey.

'If you think about it, Chris, one of the main reasons a bloke stumbles onto the dance floor in the first place is to go in search of the ladies. It's all about showing the girls some moves and seeing whether they respond positively before moving in.'

'Is that what you're supposed to do? I just thought people liked to get-on-down and shake-their-thing.'

'Oh, I'm sure they do, but apparently the action of dancing also releases some natural chemicals in the brain that make you feel horny.'

Chris's eyes light up. 'Really? I wonder why that is, then?'

'Well, for some reason, natural selection has favored humans who get a buzz from prancing around to a funky beat. It must have benefited us at some time in our evolution. Maybe the strongest and most agile males were more likely to be successful breeders.'

'Do you reckon?'

'Uh-huh. It's all in a book I've been reading called 'The

Selfish Gene' by some dude called Richard Dawkins. I'll lend it to you if you like. Have you finished reading 'Peter and Jane go to the Seaside'?'

'Piss off, I'm reading 'The Rats' by James Herbert at the moment.'

'Hmm, I'm not really into horror.'

'You're a pussy that's why ... a natural born ... hey! Check out that goof in the middle of the dance floor.'

'The guy dancing next to the group of girls in white tops?'

'Yeah, the lanky lad with his short-sleeved shirt tucked into his jeans. What's he doing?'

'I think he's dancing,' I snigger. 'Either that or he's having an epileptic fit.'

Chris slaps his thigh and stubs his cigarette out in the ashtray. 'Jesus Christ, now that is a classic example of what not to do. That guy is going to spend his entire evening dancing to impress but will sadly go home alone. If he wants to get some action, he'll have to improve on his moves. Girls like a guy who can dance, it's a fact!'

'At least he's giving it a go. Actually, come to think of it, I haven't exactly seen you cut a rug on the dance floor in a while. In fact, I can't even remember the last time I saw you dance.'

Chris frowns. 'Can't you?'

'No. Why is that?'

'I do dance.'

'Really?'

'Yes.'

'Naked in front of the mirror, perhaps.'

'Piss off, Si! I had a little jig at Gary's wedding last year. Besides, I haven't exactly seen you dance for ages, either.'

'True. Although, when I was in London I would often shake a leg, especially at the weekend.'

'I got tired of it, to be honest with you.'

'Yeah, I suppose you never really were into the clubbing scene.'

Chris shrugs. 'I much prefer sitting at the bar and having a chat.'

'Like an old man?'

'Yeah, like an old man.'

Consuming a few more cocktails from the bar, Chris falls into conversation with a couple of lads from Amsterdam while I purchase an ecstasy tablet from a dodgy looking Czech guy in a baseball cap. Within minutes, I'm rushing my tits off and gurning like a trooper. Unable to resist the lure of the music I spring board myself into the crowd, and with a grin the size of Siberia I begin to cut shapes into the air and dance like I've never danced before. Finding some space by a group of girls near to the DJ booth, I quickly light a cigarette and lose myself in the music. I glance up in the flickering strobe light and catch the eye of a girl dancing a few metres away. She tosses her head back and flashes me a sensual smile. Inspired by her energy and rhythm, we find a connection and I immediately know that for the rest of the night she will be mine.

When I first arrived in London, the club scene exploded in a cloud of ecstasy and more than happy to go along for the ride, I would hit the town most weekends with my new student buddies. Until then, I'd lived a pretty quiet existence in Daventry, smoking a few joints and getting pissed with my friends in the local pubs. The club scene was something new to me and discovering the pleasure of Love Doves, my world was to rapidly change. Around that time, I had never considered myself to be a good mover on the dance floor. Dancing was not in our culture, girls danced. Most guys just stood around the edges, drinking heavily and eyeing up the talent. Ecstasy changed all this for me, and using the drug to break down those self-conscious barriers, I was surprised to learn that rhythm was something quite instinctive to a human. There was something tribal about dancing in an ocean of perspiring bodies. The DJ was our leader and taking us on a roller coaster ride of hedonistic pleasure for those hours on the dance floor, we felt united and free.

All of a sudden a hand slaps down on my shoulder. I spin around and see Chris fighting to squeeze his stiff body through the hoards of spaced out clubbers.

'Have some water,' he yells, patting me on the back.

Putting my arm around his shoulder, I give him a loving squeeze. 'I love you, man!'

'Yeah, whatever, mate,' Chris sniggers.

He hands me a cigarette and receiving a light from a sweaty guy gurning next to me, I admire the beauty of a flame.

Grabbing my arm, Chris tries to regain my attention. 'Those dudes from Amsterdam are going to another place.'

'What place?'

'I don't know, they didn't say. Another club near here, I think. They're nice guys. Are you coming?'

'Nah, I'm staying here.'

'Are you going to be all right on your own?'

I spin around and shake my ass. 'No problemo!'

* * *

Ivan and Petre are twenty-six year old pleasure seekers. Living in Amsterdam for most of their lives, they have a very liberal attitude to life – a Dutch attitude, which in many ways I can relate to. Petre isn't shy in telling me that he has slept with prostitutes in the Red Light District, and Ivan ... well ... let's just say he isn't shy. They seem like nice guys, harmless and only interested in making sure that my night in Prague is one to remember.

'Have you been to Amsterdam, Chris?' Ivan asks, handing his ticket over to the girl in the cloakroom.

'No, but I've heard shit loads about it.'

'Amsterdam is the best! You should make a trip.'

He takes his coat and winks at the girl. She blushes and turns away. Petre is waiting for us outside. We hail a cab and head to the club.

'Hey, Chris, you like to schmoke?' Ivan grins.

'Yeah, sometimes.'

'In Amsterdam you can schmoke the best. One puff and you are in fucking cuckoo land.'

They both laugh.

The cab quickly pulls up outside a large building about five minutes away from the Roxy Nightclub. There's no name above the entrance, just a stocky guy standing in front of a closed door.

'How do you know about this place?' I ask Ivan.

'Surfing the internet,' he replies with a grin. 'Like I said, it's the best place in Prague.'

We all jump out of the cab and walk over to the guy dressed in black. Petre hands him a pile of cash, and with a smirk the guy swings open the door. On the internet, I think to myself as we step inside. We walk into a luxurious room that's flooded in red light. The air smells sweet and there's a small fountain in the corner surrounded by many large tropical plants. Two men sit on a white leather sofa accompanied by a girl wearing a blue glittery dress. Petre sits down on another sofa while Ivan drags me over to the bar.

'What do you think?' he asks, raising his blonde eyebrows. 'There are four other rooms, one large room with a dance floor and three ... more private rooms.'

I order a vodka and lemonade, and nearly choke when I find out how much it costs.

'Come on!' Ivan yells. 'Let's go to the dance room!'

We walk behind a red velvet curtain and then behind

another curtain leading into a fairly large room. Candles flicker on tables and a disco ball hangs from the ceiling. Colourful lights spin across the room to the sound of cheesy Britpop, and two girls flirt with three drunken businessmen standing in the middle of the dance floor. Four more girls sit pretty at the bar.

'Where's Petre?'

Ivan shrugs. 'Don't worry about him, which girls do you like?'

Avoiding eye contact with a brunette at the bar, I turn to Ivan.

'You what?'

'Which girls?'

Suddenly, Petre bursts into the room in fits of laugher with two pretty girls wrapped around him. I acknowledge him with a nod, and watch as he takes turns kissing them both on the lips.

'In London you'd pay twice as much for this quality, wouldn't you?' Ivan grins. 'Especially for a threesome.'

'A threesome?'

'Ya.'

'I don't know, I've never had one.'

Ivan looks shocked. 'You have never had a threesome? Me and Petre like to do this very much, but in Amsterdam it is a little expensive.'

Ivan pushes me over to the bar.

'I am having those two on the left, OK?' he smiles. 'You have the other two.'

What am I doing? I shouldn't be doing this. More to the point, I can't afford to do this.

'Buy them each a drink,' Ivan whispers in my ear.

'Both of them?'

'Ya. The more drinks you buy them, the better time you will have.'

Ivan nudges my arm, and winks.

Feeling well out of my depth, I begin to think of Si in the

Roxy Nightclub shaking his booty on the dance floor and having a good time.

'I'm leaving!' I yell to Ivan over the music. 'This really isn't my scene.'

Ivan looks surprised, but shrugging his shoulders he reaches out and shakes my hand.

'Are you sure?' he smiles.

'Yeah, I'm a bit short of cash.'

'No problem, Chris, It was nice meeting you.'

'Yeah, you too, have a good time!'

'This will not be difficult here,' he grins, turning to the girls.

I walk past Petre, who is too busy getting his balls squeezed to notice my goodbye wave, and head straight out of the room, but I get confused and step behind the wrong curtain into one of the private rooms. I'm suddenly shocked to see a naked man lying face down on a heart shaped bed. A topless woman with enormous breasts kneels beside him, and proceeds to spank his bare bottom with her white stiletto. They both turn and look at me, and I gasp as I realise the guy peering over his shoulder is none other than Cliff! Cliff the journalist from our hostel - the journalist with a wife and an eighteen-month old baby ... the journalist, who was supposed to be crawling into bed and reading his book! Leaping back in horror, I fall through the curtain and crash to the floor. I quickly clamber to my feet and sprint for the exit.

Hailing a cab, I burn back to the Roxy Nightclub. It doesn't take me long to find Si's big mop-head bobbing up and down on the dance floor. Fighting my way through the sweaty bodies, I grab his attention and wave him over to the side.

'Cliff was getting his bottom spanked with a stiletto?' Si smiles, and spins around. '*Awesome!*'

'Uh-huh, I saw it with my very own eyes.'

'Fucking hell, are you sure it was Cliff?'

'Of course I am! It was definitely him, I didn't imagine it.'

'The dirty little toe-rag, you wait till I tell his wife.'

'It's not funny.'

'Yes it is,' Si laughs. 'It's pissing hilarious, "Uh … sorry, guys, I'm tired. I think I'll just crawl into bed and read my book" – yeah right! You caught him red handed in some hooker joint.'

'Shit, I hope we don't bump into him at the hostel. He saw me. He knows that I know what he was doing.'

'Don't worry about it. We'll avoid him. Look, forget about that for a second, what happened to you?'

'Well, before I had the unfortunate pleasure of seeing Cliff's butt cheeks being spanked, I was minutes away from having a threesome with two blondes.'

'*No way!*'

'Yes way! But I decided not to.'

'Why, you crazy fool?'

'It would have cost shit loads. And, anyway, I don't need to pay for it.'

'Bollocks! You chickened out, didn't you?'

'Fuck off! I've got to be careful with my money. Let's change the subject, shall we?'

'Pussy!' Si shouts.

I knock back my drink. 'Step aside, hippie boy, it's my turn to dance!'

'You?'

'Yeah, you didn't think I was just going to stand at the side and look moody all night, did you?'

'Yes!'

'Well, you were wrong. My night isn't going to be ruined by seeing Cliff's arse.'

With a yeeeeeehaaaaaa! I leap onto the dance floor and begin reinventing my best moves; flying a kite, shadow boxer and making a sandwich. We dance until the end. Si gets a kiss from some girl and I, for once in my surreal life, discover that dancing is actually quite fun.

Arbeit Macht Frei

Swinging my heavy rucksack over my shoulder, I turn towards the door and accidentally hit Chris in the face.

'Careful, you idiot!' he snaps, rubbing his forehead.

'It was an accident.'

Muttering to himself, Chris battles to close his bag that bulges at the seams.

'Quick, it's ten minutes past ten. We're supposed to be out of the room.'

He looks over at me and sighs. 'Hold on!'

I spin around and bump into Chris a second time.

'*FOR FUCK'S SAKE!*' he yells, giving me a hard shove.

I stagger backwards and lose my balance as the weight of my rucksack pulls me to the ground. I lie helplessly on my back with my feet in the air like an overturned turtle.

'*YOU BASTARD!*' I cry, wrestling to get my arms out of the straps.

Jumping to my feet, Chris looks worried by the psychotic expression on my face.

'Don't do anything silly,' he mutters, edging back towards the window. 'We're both very tired after last night.'

'Don't you fucking push me over!' I spit.

Chris presses a finger to his lips. 'Shush, listen.'

I refrain from punching him in the arm. 'What is it?'

'I think Cliff's in his room.'

'So?'

Chris grabs a plastic cup off the bedside table and places it against the wall. 'I can hear movement.'

'My God, you're a twat.'

'Shush, he'll hear us.'

'I don't give a flying fuck. Who cares about Cliff, anyway? It was you who saw him … not me!'

'Come on, Si, let's get the hell out of here.'

Poking our heads around the door, we peer into the dark deserted corridor.

'If I see him, I'll fucking die,' Chris whispers.

'I wouldn't worry about it. He's either hiding in his room or exploring other dark corners of the city.'

'OK. Well, let's just go for it.'

Chris follows close behind as I tiptoe out into the corridor. I pause outside Cliff's room.

'What you stopping for?' he snaps.

'I can hear movement. Yes, you're right. Cliff is definitely in his room.'

'Si, keep moving, you prick!'

'Shush…'

All of a sudden, we hear a key rattling in the lock. Chris shoves me out of the way and sprints over to the stairs at the far end of the corridor. I lose my balance and crash against the wall. Cliff swings open the door to his room and peers out.

'Hello, Simon,' he smiles.

'Cliff, hey! How are ya?'

'I'm great. Are you leaving so soon?'

I glance down at the straps on my shoulders. 'Yep, it certainly looks like it. It's … uh … time to hit the road jack. Time to motor on to pastures new.'

Cliff leans against the doorframe and folds his arms. He's naked apart from a small yellow towel wrapped around his waist. Feeling extremely uncomfortable, I dart a quick glance up and down the corridor.

'Is everything all right?' he asks.

'Uh-huh,' I quickly reply. 'Everything is cool in the gang. Sorry, but I'm in a bit of a rush. Chris, the idiot, left his credit card in the club last night, so we have to go back and get it. That's why he's not with me at the moment. He's … uh … gone.'

'Oh, I hope he finds it.'

'Yeah. I hope so, too,' I grin falsely.

Cliff frowns. 'Simon, are you sure you're all right? You seem a little flustered.'

'Yes, I'm fine,' I nod enthusiastically. 'OK, I really better be going, have a great time in Prague.'

I turn and make my way down the corridor.

'Simon, wait!' Cliff shouts. 'We haven't swapped email addresses!'

I close my eyes and release a deep sigh.

'We have to exchange emails,' he beams. 'I want to know how your trip is going.'

Cliff disappears inside his room and returns with a business card.

I peer down at the card, "Cliff Barnes, Journalist - likes his bottom being spanked." I slide it into my back pocket. He hands me a piece of paper and a pen. I scribble down my email.

'Excellent! Thank you, Simon.'

We shake hands. Suddenly, a young couple carrying rucksacks appear at the top of the stairs. They both stare at Cliff standing in the corridor in his towel. Embarrassed, I acknowledge them with a smile.

'OK, Cliff, I'm off. Mustn't keep those gas chambers waiting.'

'Of course not, good luck. Oh, and say hi to Chris for me.'

'Sure.'

I turn on my heels and quickly head down the stairs.

Dumping our rucksacks in the boot of the car, we decide to grab something to eat in an attempt at sobering ourselves up a bit. Walking towards the train station, we find a coffee stand in the park outside. Buying a cinnamon-laced coffee and a couple of chocolate-coated doughnuts from a scruffy teenager, we plonk ourselves down on an empty bench facing a water fountain. Stressed out, white-collared businessmen with black briefcases rush to work, while chilled out students slowly stroll to university with their colourful folders. Devouring the coffee and the doughnuts, I begin to feel human again and reaching for my cigarettes, I pause as an old homeless woman staggers towards me. Reaching out her hand she grins a toothless smile, and feeling in a good mood and humbled by her cheerfulness, I offer her one. Beaming, she snatches the entire packet out of my hand and starts to cackle as she places a cigarette between her cracked lips. Amused by her reaction to my generosity and despite losing all of my cigarettes, I watch with satisfaction as she shuffles away.

With new energy, we race back to the car and crawl through the rush hour-traffic. Heading north out of the city, I grab the map and begin to study it with keen interest.

'Hey, Chris! There's a place near the Polish border where you can see strange rock formations.'

'Rock formations?'

'Yeah, the Ayers-Teplice Rocks. We should check it out.'

Chris frowns. 'But what about Auschwitz?'

'What about it?'

'I thought we were heading there next?'

'We are, but what's the rush? We have to pass by the place anyway, so we may as well make an afternoon of it. You'll regret it if we don't.'

'Uh ... no I won't. I don't give a shit about a bunch of frigging rocks. Once you've seen one rock you've seen them all.'

* * *

In a bid to quench Si's bizarre new thirst for geology, we arrive at the Teplice Rocks in the early afternoon. The main road leading to the entrance point is lined with tour buses and turning left into the main car park, I stupidly pull up beside a coach full of screaming school kids. A swarm of excited brats leap off the bus and hover around the Sierra. Their teacher, who looks flustered and extremely disorganised, dashes off the coach after them. She tries in vain to round them up, but fails miserably. A little kid with curly black hair stares at us through the window and sticks out his tongue.

'Charming,' Si smiles.

The kid runs off and joins his friends beside the coach, whilst their teacher tries desperately to order them into single file.

'Si, are you sure this is a good idea?'

'Of course it is, it's supposed to be incredible! According to this leaflet there's a big waterfall inside a cave.'

'Yeah, but there's nothing worse than trying to take artistic photographs when you're surrounded by irritating little squirts, how am I supposed to concentrate?'

'Chris, don't worry, 'oh, great master of photography', we'll jump ahead of them.'

'OK, but I warn you now, if they get in the way of my shot I won't be responsible for my actions.'

Waiting in the queue at the ticket office, two kids standing in front begin to pull faces at us. Si smiles back, but I ignore them and peer anxiously over at their teacher.

'Come on,' I mutter. 'How long does it take to buy a frigging ticket?'

'Chris, chill out would ya! What's your problem?'

'It's these bloody kids. They're a pain in the ass!'

The two kids in front continue to pull faces and giggle. One of the little rug-rats stamps on my foot, while the other pokes me in the stomach and sticks out his tongue. This is the last straw. I peer down at them with an evil stare and release a low monster-like growl. They stop giggling, and with frightened faces they quickly push their way to the front of the queue. We finally reach the counter and enter the park.

Studying a map of the area stuck to an information board, we decide to follow a 5km trail looping around the national park. Striding ahead of the school kids, we weave through a forest and quickly reach an impressive group of bizarre rock formations. They reach for the sky from the forest floor, some over a hundred metres tall. I feel inspired to take a few photographs, but just as I'm about to start snapping away, a million excited school kids run into the frame. They swarm around me like flies around shit. The teacher stumbles around the corner, shouting at the kids in Czech. They ignore her and continue to race around in all directions. I take a disappointing picture before urging Si to press on.

Once again, we escape the chaos and quickly make some distance. We eventually arrive at an incredible natural stone archway, which leads into a passageway between the rocks. Beaming with joy, I look through the viewfinder and just as I'm about to take a beautiful picture, a large group of pensioners begin to file out of the archway. They gather in a huge semi-circle at the entrance, all thirty-six of them. A geeky tour guide babbles facts at high volume through a crackling megaphone. Seeing there's no way to squeeze past, we wait impatiently for the tour guide to end his spiel. I look over my shoulder and notice the school kids are catching up fast.

'We're surrounded,' Si grins.

'This is ridiculous!' I scream.

Marching over to the tour group, I take a step forward

and squeeze through the crowd. I make it past the first O.A.P and even manage to weave around the second, but as I fight to push past the third, the gap suddenly closes behind me and I find myself surrounded. Si pokes his head in between the pensioners, who seem to have collapsed into a state of rigor mortis.

'Entschuldigung Sie bitte,' he mumbles, turning sideways and using his slim build to slip past.

Standing on tiptoe, I look over the white perms and shiny baldheads and see the school kids racing towards the tour group.

'Right, that's it! Out of my way!' I command, moving a sour faced old codger to one side.

Charging through the crowd to the sound of cursing and grunting as I step on fragile toes, I eventually make it to the other side. Standing in the entrance of the archway, I lean against the moss covered rock face and catch my breath. Si suddenly slides up next to me.

'Hey, how did you get through so quickly?' I laugh.

'Years of practice in the mosh pit,' he smugly replies. 'These old dudes should hold the brats up for a while ... come on, let's keep moving!'

We high-five and disappear through the archway.

After a few hours of walking around the trail, taking pictures of waterfalls, dramatic views and the tops of people's heads, we both agree that we have severe 'rock formation' overload. Deciding to head back to the car, we fight our way through the ever-increasing crowds and eventually find ourselves hurtling down country lanes towards southern Poland.

It isn't long before we approach a long queue of stationary trucks at the Polish border. A hard-faced Polish truck driver peers down at our car as we crawl towards passport control. I look up and grin. He doesn't smile back; he just continues to stare at us with a look of hostility in his eyes.

Joining a shorter queue of cars, we crawl towards the blockade that stretches across the width of the road and grabbing my camera, I quickly snap a picture of the sign for the Polish Republic and a flag that flaps proudly in the breeze.

'Careful,' Si whispers, 'we don't want to draw any unnecessary attention to ourselves.'

'We're tourists ... tourists take photographs!'

'Yeah, but they probably don't get many young travellers passing through this way.'

'Si, you're talking shit. Stop being paranoid, just act normal.'

A stern faced officer approaches the car and peers through my open window. We smile nervously and hand over our passports. He flicks through them and without saying a word moves onto the red transit van behind. We eventually reach the front of the queue and wait at a small traffic light. It turns green, so we pull up beside two more uniformed officers. One of the guys opens my door and gestures for me to get out of the car. He takes my documents and walks slowly around the Sierra. Pointing at the boot, I assume he wants to take a look inside. I remove the small piece of metal that we've been using as a rather ineffective ariel for the radio and, much to the official's amusement, I use it as a tool to open the lock. As with all used cars, our Sierra had a slight imperfection when we purchased it. The lock on the boot had been drilled out, possibly by some well equipped thief, and unprepared to spend money on a new one, we had resigned ourselves to levering it open with our handy double purpose ariel, or, piece of metal that Si found in the garden shed. Standing back, I wait patiently for the official to rummage through the trash in our boot. Content in his mind that we're not criminals (even capable of being criminals) he waves us through to the next stage. Without any fuss they check and stamp our passports before raising the barrier. We pull over by a row of shops and cafes on the other side of the border.

'So this is Poland!' Si cries.

'It sure is, hippie boy!'

'Hey, we need to change some Traveller's cheques into zlotys.'

I frown. 'Zlotys?'

'Yeah, it's the Polish currency.'

'It's not the sexiest sounding currency in the world, is it?'

'As long as it buys me a few beers, Chris, they can call it whatever they like.'

We make our way over to an exchange shop where we change two hundred euros into zlotys, and then pop to the shop next door where we insure the Sierra third party for two weeks. Skipping back to the car, we feel ready to explore the depths of southern Poland.

Si seems happy for me to drive and passing through a number of small grey towns, we observe dozens of shaven headed youths hanging around bus stops and drinking cans of super strength lager at the side of the road. It reminds me of England in the 70's and 80's, with the skinhead culture that had become a fashion amongst the unemployed and disgruntled youths of the time. Concrete tower blocks fill the suburbs like monuments to the communist era, and feeling unable to just pull over and grab something to eat without our car being vandalized or stolen, we push on into the night.

Spying a 24-hour petrol station that serves fast food, we decide to take a break. Asking a young lad inside the shop for directions to the town of Oswiëcim, he rather over-enthusiastically opens a huge road map out on the counter in an honorable attempt to practice his English. Patiently playing along with him, he gives me a long series of completely incomprehensible directions, which I immediately forget. I thank him anyway, in the hope of encouraging him to learn more, and return to the car with a couple of giant sized hot dogs and two cups of piping hot tea.

Picking up road signs for Oswiëcim, we're eventually directed off a motorway and find ourselves weaving through the countryside. Wisps of fog glide over the bonnet of the car like spirits in the night – ghosts of the Auschwitz victims haunting our path. We eventually reach the suburban town of Oswiëcim, a place with little character and we follow an old train line, which leads us all the way to the gates of Auschwitz. Parking up at the side of the road, we decide to sleep in the car outside the concentration camp. Wrestling to get comfortable, I glance out of the window at the large wall that surrounds the camp. I find it impossible to remove the thought from my mind of the horrors that must have been committed inside. During Hitler's reign of terror over 6 million Jews were exterminated. Both Auschwitz and Birkenau are living museums to one of the worst atrocities of humanity in modern history. As a child, I had studied pictures in history books of the naked twisted bodies of Auschwitz victims piled high in mass graves. It made me realise humans are simply flesh and bone, hair and teeth and that all of the dignity and fear we feel in life will eventually be stripped away.

* * *

The sound of a truck's horn wakes me with a start. Striking the engine, I switch on the window screen wipers and wait for the blades to remove the film of water covering the glass.

'Chris, we need to move the car!'

'What?'

'The car! We need to move it!'

Trucks roar past on the busy main road, the swooshing of their tyres against the wet tarmac frightening us into action.

'Bad place to park, or what?' Chris mutters.

'It seemed quiet last night.'

Waiting for a gap in the traffic, Chris swings the car out onto the main road and turns into the gateway of the Auschwitz car park. An attendant dressed in jeans and wearing a high-visibility vest waves us through the barrier, and crossing the empty car park I pull up beneath a giant oak tree. Taking a moment to get my head together, I open the car door and feel drops of rain on my face. I sit motionless, allowing the water to refresh my tired eyes. Ruffling my hair I climb out of the car and touch my toes, my back aches and my neck feels stiff from resting my head at a strange angle against the window. Collecting the empty crisp packets and sweet wrappers stuffed into every available orifice of the car's interior, I empty the ashtray and begin to fill an empty Tesco's carrier bag with rubbish. Chris begins to fold up all of the loose items of clothing - coats, damp socks and jumpers strewn across the back seat. Tying up the plastic bag, I walk over to a bin beneath the large oak tree and toss it inside. The lid closes with a satisfying clang. Feeling the heavy droplets of water falling into my hair from the branches of the tree, I take a deep breath and watch in amusement as Chris struggles to change his T-shirt in the small confines of the car. Deciding to freshen up a bit before heading off to the museum, I rub some toothpaste on my teeth and change my socks and T-shirt. In an attempt at looking a bit smarter and possibly more studious, I dig out my blue roll-neck jumper from the bottom of my rucksack.

'I think we must be the first ones here,' Chris mutters, peeling a banana.

'Yeah, I suppose it is only eight-thirty.'

Switching on the radio, we listen to some soothing classical music on a polish station and munch happily on some stale crackers. Seeing the first tourist coach arrive in the car park, we decide to go and check things out. I step out of the car and look up at the sky. It's stopped raining, but thick black storm clouds hang menacingly overhead. We walk across the car park adjacent to the high perimeter wall, and quickly reach the main entrance to the red brick building. Poking our heads inside, the main foyer is empty apart from a girl wiping trays behind the counter of a small cafeteria. Standing in the empty foyer, we study black and white photographs hung in a line along the walls. Suddenly, a well-groomed middle-aged woman in a long black raincoat enters the foyer. She shakes her umbrella and smiles over at us.

'Hallo,' she beams. 'I'm sorry, but you are a little early. Please take some time to read the information.'

'Thank you,' I reply.

The information on the boards has an English translation, and we mill around the room devouring facts. A coach party files into the building and they greet us as if they were entering our home.

After sometime, the lady with the raincoat informs us that we can now purchase a ticket for the museum and also watch a short film in the cinema. Following her instructions, we quickly find ourselves being herded into a small cinema at the end of the hall. The place quickly fills up with people all chaotically trying to find a seat in the dark, and hearing the projector whir into life we watch an emotional fifteen-minute documentary about Auschwitz and Birkenau.

Exiting the cinema we're led into a quad. Looking around, I recognize it from the documentary and I feel the hairs on the back of my neck stand up on end. Nothing has changed. It all looks exactly the same as it did in the film, and seeing where the prisoners were executed by firing squad on the grass adjacent to the sinister looking barbed wire walkway, the harsh reality of what happened here is made immediately clear. Breaking away from the other tourists, we pass a tall watchtower and I find myself giving it a wide berth. The spotlight on the top follows us around like a large eye, and I try to imagine how terrible it must have been to be imprisoned like this - to live in fear of being shot by a bored SS guard with a rifle who's watching your every move.

Chris nudges me. 'I think that building over there is one of the gas chambers.'

'How do you know?'

'I recognize the tall chimney from the film.'

Walking cautiously over to the small grey building, we peer inside. I feel a little shaken by the thought of what happened here. It was mostly women, children and the infirm that were murdered ... the ones who couldn't work.

'This is sick,' Chris whispers, as we enter the cold, dark building.

I walk over to the window and peer out through the metal bars. We're stood in the room where they had been ordered to remove their clothing, believing they were going to take a shower and be disinfected. I feel physically sick as I follow Chris into the main chamber. Dim orange lights hang from the ceiling, and a vase of flowers has been placed in the middle of the concrete floor. I touch the damp walls and can hear the screams of the thousands of men, women and children who perished in this very room. I can see the terror in their eyes as the Zyklon B pellets, a crystallized form of hydrogen cyanide, fell around their feet from vents in the ceiling - killing them not instantly, but after fifteen to twenty painful minutes. I feel suddenly nauseous and follow Chris through an open doorway into the next room. The sight of the two furnaces is too much to take in, and I find myself backing away. All I can think about is how anybody could think it was right to do this. How could they physically put it on themselves to extract gold teeth, collect rings, jewelry and even shave the corpse's heads before burning the bodies in the furnaces? On average 8,000 people were gassed everyday at Auschwitz and Birkenau. By the end of the Holocaust, a horrific six million people had been murdered … six million innocent lives taken away.

Making our way outside, the clouds burst open and the rain thunders down on Auschwitz. We run across the courtyard and shelter beneath a doorway opposite the firing range.

'This place is truly horrendous,' I shout to Chris over the noise of the rain.

A man stood next to us smiles. 'Expect to see what Hitler called 'ethnic cleansing',' he bellows in a broad Yorkshire accent.

'We've just been to the gas chamber,' I reply, shaking my head. 'It's a deeply disturbing experience.'

'Yes, that it is. I've been here before, you know. I'm a history teacher at an inner city comprehensive school in Leeds. Coming to a place like this helps me to appreciate what I teach my students. I'm here with my wife and children, Amy and Ben.'

The two young kids look wet and miserable. They peer up from beneath the hoods of their orange raincoats.

'Say hello, kids.'

They look shyly away.

The guy's wife forces a smile, but the man either forgets or doesn't think to introduce her.

'They're all a little tired,' he continues. 'It's been a busy few days. We flew into Warsaw on Wednesday and I hired a car. Poland is a very interesting country, but Auschwitz was on the top of my…' he turns to his wife, 'sorry … our holiday itinerary. The kids wanted to go to Spain like last year and play on the beach for the whole holiday, but I thought I'd introduce them to history and what better than to start with the Auschwitz concentration camp.'

Chris nods. 'Oh, I see.'

'They might not appreciate it now, but they'll benefit from this someday.'

He turns to his wife again. She opens her mouth to say something, but misses her chance.

'When they go to comprehensive school and do projects on the Holocaust, they'll be the best in their class. Gold stars all round. Well, looks like the rains slowing down,' the guy observes, peering up at the sky. 'Come on, folks. We'd better be going!'

We watch as he marches off across the quad with his family trailing reluctantly behind. Turning on his heels he calls over in our direction.

'Make sure you stop by the medical rooms. It's where they used to carry out the sterilization experiments.'

'OK ... thanks, we will,' Chris waves.

Giving it a few more minutes, we eventually walk over to the main gates where all of the prisoners were kept. Above the gate is the sinister motto: "Arbeit Macht Frei" (work makes one free). We walk along the main street past brick buildings or 'Blocks' where the prisoners slept. The buildings look fairly modern and are in surprisingly good condition, making the recentness of this atrocity seem even more horrifying. All of the photographs I had seen in history books had been in black and white – images from a time before, when the world was different, but seeing the place in 3D and in colour makes it all seem suddenly very real. We pass the 'Death Block' where prisoners who caused trouble or tried to escape died from starvation, firing squad or lethal injection. Next we examine the actual wooden beam where twelve Polish prisoners were hung, in the biggest public execution in the KL Auschwitz. Januz Pogonowski, Leon Rajzer and Tadeuz Rapacz are just three of the twelve men who died right here on this very spot.

Behind glass in another block, mountains of hair, false

teeth, shoes and suitcases are on display. Their belongings were stored in giant hangers, nothing was wasted – even lamps were made out of skin cut from the dead. In the next block, framed photographs of people imprisoned at Auschwitz hang on the wall in a long line on opposite sides off the corridor. I'm shocked by how similar they look to people I know at home, how similar they look to the young guys with shaved heads we saw on the way up here. The pictures are so clear and sharp they could've been taken yesterday. I stare into their eyes, they stare back blankly at the camera in their stripy prison uniforms. Under each photograph there is a date of how long they lasted at the labour camp. Some died after two years, some after only two weeks.

We leave Auschwitz and drive the 3km to the vast Birkenau camp, a sub-camp of Auschwitz, where the largest numbers of Jews were exterminated. With 300 prison barracks and 4 gas chambers, which were able to hold 2,000 people, the camp could facilitate in total up to 200,000 inmates. When the trains arrived, the Jews were separated into two lines and endured what was known as the 'selection process'. The chosen ones went to work, while the others were sent immediately to the gas chambers at the end of the line. We look around the appallingly cramped conditions of the barracks where the prisoners lived. It's a large area, and we find ourselves weaving between bunk beds and standing at cracked washbasins.

Returning along the train track to the gates, I look over my shoulder at the camp one last time. I had never had much faith in humanity - Auschwitz and Birkenau only confirm this to me. As a species, it seems clear we have a long way to travel along the evolutionary chain before reaching anything close to what we might call perfection.

Fresh Fish

I feel fresh. My clothes smell clean, my hair has been washed with the finest Polish shampoo and my armpits are dancing the Salsa. With a skip in my step, I make a tasty salt and vinegar flavoured crisp sandwich while Si merrily sucks the vitamin C out of a big juicy orange. With breakfast out of the way, we hesitate no longer than necessary and waving farewell to the trucker's café outside Oswiëcim, we head north for the Great Masurian Lakes.

By-passing Warsaw, we race across the flat open countryside and begin to see where the wealth of Poland hides. Large houses with acres of land and expensive 4x4's litter the roadside. Even the girls working in the petrol stations look cuter and less repressed somehow, which is great!

'Right, that's it!' Si smiles. 'I'm gonna do it!'

'Do what?'

'I'm gonna catch my dinner.'

I turn to him and laugh. 'Catch your dinner? You're joking, aren't ya?'

'Nope.'

'You mean by using traditional hunting methods such as trapping a wild pig or spearing a deer?'

'Uh ... no, I'm talking about grabbing a rod and going fishing!'

'Si, the last time you tried to catch a fish you fell in the canal.'

'I slipped.'

'You tripped more like, you dumb ass. My God, if you think about it, we wouldn't last five-minutes in the wilderness without food, would we?'

Si shakes his head. 'Probably not. In fact, I'd give us two days max before we'd be heading off in search of the nearest McDonald's. It's mad really, you'd think it would be a necessary part of a child's education to learn how to survive in the wild.'

'Yeah, but then I suppose in our society it's not really seen as relevant anymore. I mean, why waste valuable time learning to fish or hunt, when you can just pop down the local fish 'n' chip shop and buy yourself a nice piece of battered cod.'

'Chris, fishing today isn't just about obtaining food for survival, it's a sport and a hobby as well, you know. It's about keeping the skills alive. Remember that kid at school, who used to jump lessons so he could fish pike down the reservoir. His fishing knowledge was passed down to him by his old man, just as his father had taught him.'

'So, fishing isn't just an excuse to get away from your nagging wife, then?'

Si nods vigorously. 'Oh yeah, of course it is, but some people just love to fish all the same.'

Grabbing the pocket SAS Survival Guide from his bag, Si flicks to the first page. 'Listen to what John Wiseman says here, "survival is the art of staying alive. Combine the instinct for survival with knowledge, training and kit and you will be ready for anything."'

I peer down at the book. 'Who's John Wiseman?'

'The author of this book,' Si replies. 'He served in the SAS for twenty-six years.'

'Hardcore. I bet he's seen a bit of action in his time.'

'Damn right, you don't make it into the SAS unless your balls are made of steel.'

'Heavy.'

'Chris, do you think you could make it into the SAS?'

'No problem! Might have to quit the fags first, though.'

'Oh yeah, you'd have too. I'm telling ya, those boys can trek for weeks with a pack the weight of a baby elephant.'

'Bollocks!'

'It's true! It's all about training. If you put your mind to it you can accomplish anything.'

'What, even if you're a natural born pussy like yourself?'

'If it's a matter of life and death, then, yes,' Si grins.

'Shit, maybe we should study this book a bit more before we get to Russia. I've got an awful feeling we're going to need it.'

'Study all you like, but don't worry too much.'

'Why not?'

'Well, some things are just out of your control.'

I frown. 'What do you mean?'

'Well, take death for example.'

'Jesus Christ, Si! Enough about death, I'm still traumatized by our little visit to Auschwitz.'

'Death affects us all, my friend. There's no point ignoring it.'

'"Ooh, hello everyone, my name's Simon and I'm here to *liven up the party!*" You prick.'

'Hey, cut the piss-take. This is serious shit.'

'You could've fooled me, hippie boy.'

'Don't get me wrong; I'm not purposefully trying to sound morbid here. Its just death is a reality we have to face everyday. There's so many ways it can happen there's no way you can ever totally prevent it. Sure, you can limit your chances of it happening by living a safe, healthy life and by teaching yourself a few basic survival skills. But at the end of the day, when that large piece of masonry from the roof of a church comes crashing down on your head and squashes you into the pavement, there ain't a hell of a lot you can do about it.'

'I guess you're right.'

'Chris, don't let that put you off, though, it's still good stuff to know. All I'm saying is there's no point living in fear of what might happen, because ultimately it's not in your control.'

As I drive cautiously over an old disused railway track, I can see the sparkling blue water of Lake Wigry flashing past through the trees. Pulling off the road, we crawl down a bumpy path leading to the water's edge and ditch the car close to a wooden jetty that reaches out across the flat surface of the lake. Walking cautiously over the wooden slats, I squat down at the end of the platform and glance out across the tranquil view. I hear Si clomping clumsily behind me, and brace myself as he pretends to push me off the edge. Disturbed by the commotion, a large Canada goose hiding in the dry reeds beats its wings and lifts itself a few feet into the air, before crashing clumsily back into the water. It disappears with a honk.

'This place is perfect,' Si smiles.

'It's beautiful!' I sing, dipping my fingers in the water.

Ripples suddenly appear all around the platform. '*Hoooha, ride the ripples!*'

'Shush!' Si hisses. 'You'll scare the fish away?'

Pausing in thought, I furrow my brow. 'Do fish have ears?'

Si shrugs. 'Fuck knows, but I'm sure you're supposed to be quiet. Maybe they feel the vibrations.'

Climbing slowly to my feet, I tiptoe back along the platform and sprint across the grass to the car. Popping the boot with the ariel, I rummage through the junk and grab hold of the fishing rod that we'd thrown in at the last minute - along with a load of other crap we thought might come in useful. I untie the faded plastic bag wrapped around the reel and extend the telescopic rod, a revolution in fishing equipment introduced sometime in the 1980's, and untangle the line. Inside the faded carrier bag, which has probably been tied around the rod since we last went fishing about ten years ago, I find some spare hooks and more line. Placing them on the ground next to the rod, I scratch my head in the heat and try to think what else a man needs in order to catch a fish.

'Bait!' I grin.

Reaching deep inside the boot, I manage to grab hold of a small shovel wedged underneath our bags. Pulling it free, I stumble backwards and accidentally step on the rod lying on the ground. I hear it snap.

'*FUCK!*' I cry, glancing down at the broken pieces.

Removing the broken end from the line, I real in the hook and hold what's left of my rod in the air. It looks ridiculous, a mere stump compared to the length it should be, but tossing the broken end back into the boot I'm keen to get my hook in the water while the fish are still visible. Slamming the boot shut, I walk back down the path and notice Si waving vigorously from the bank.

'There's shit loads of fish!' he cries. 'You can see the bubbles! Here's three worms, I'll dig up some more. Go on, get fishing!'

With the tangled ball of worms in my hand, I smile at Si's enthusiasm as he eagerly digs a hole by the water's edge. I find a suitable spot at the end of the platform and crouching down on my hands and knees, I thread a nice juicy worm on the end of the hook and make a float from a discarded lollypop stick. Weighing the bait down by tying a stone to the line a few inches above it, I remove the spare reel from the plastic bag and attach a hook to the end. Following the same process, I make another float, but this time from a piece of bark that I manage to peel from one of the wooden planks used to make the jetty.

'Good lad,' Si smiles, admiring my handy work.

Opening his hand he reveals another seething mass of worms.

Keen to try his luck, I offer him the rod and he makes his way excitedly to the far side of the jetty.

Squatting down, I extend the fishing line and carefully lower my worm into the water. Happy with the length, I toss the stumpy rod over my head and catapult the bait a good four metres away. Watching the stick bob up and down on the surface of the water, I feel instantly relaxed. Glancing over at Chris, I watch as he swings his hook backwards and forwards like a pendulum, and gathering enough momentum he lets go of the line and casts it rather unsuccessfully into the lake. I lean back against a wooden post and smile. Like Huckleberry Fin and Tom Sawyer, minus the straw hats and dungarees, we bask in the sunshine at opposite ends of the jetty. Persuading myself that it's unlikely we'll catch anything, particularly as neither of us had managed to in our lives before, I close my eyes and enjoy the peace and quiet.

Around the same time I had said my final farewells to Emily in Hampstead, I returned to London a few times during my time in Daventry. On one such occasion, I drove to Queen's Park for the weekend to visit my good friend Dermot. Dermot lived in north London with his girlfriend in a flat overlooking the Salisbury Road. We would drink in his local pub, The Salisbury Arms, and then stumble back to his place after closing for a good old fashion smoke and a singsong with his guitar called Gareth. Waking up on his sofa one morning with a killer hangover, I decided to head out and grab something to eat from the Organic Café around the corner. Walking into a blustery winter's day, I wrapped my scarf tightly around my neck and half-ran, half-jogged down the quiet main road. Making myself comfortable inside the busy restaurant, I ordered the eggs benedicts from the menu and a large cappuccino. I grabbed a newspaper and waited patiently for my food. Just as I was about to read an interesting article about Colombia, I suddenly noticed a guy enter the café with a very familiar face. I peered over my newspaper and watched as he stormed across the restaurant - it was none other than my ex-boss, Lawrence Cox! This was a man who had made the early years of my career a misery, and was an individual who can only be described as a complete and utter tosser. Ducking behind the newspaper, I closed my eyes and prayed for him to pass by. He didn't. I lowered the newspaper and we made eye contact.

'Simon!' he grinned, looking surprised.

'Lawrence!' I beamed, trying to look even more surprised.

'How are you?'

'Great!'

I stood up and we shook hands.

Lawrence grabbed a chair and swung it over to my table. 'Mind if I join you?'

I rolled my eyes, and sighed. 'Of course not.'

A waitress walked over and took his order.

'So you're back from your travels I see?'

'Yeah, I got back a couple of months ago.'

'That's fantastic. How was it?'

'Incredible. A real adventure.'

'You went to the States, didn't you?'

'That's right, and to Mexico.'

'What was Mexico like? I've always wanted to see the cliff diving in Acapulco.'

'I didn't go that way, but the Yucatan is beautiful.'

'Sounds fabulous,' Lawrence smiled.

'Yes, it was. How's Global?'

'Wonderful! We've just finished a complete redesign. It looks fantastic! A lot has changed since you left. I've been promoted, actually. I'm now the Production Manager, overseeing the development of all new content. Big step, but I'm enjoying the challenge.'

'Congratulations.'

'Thanks. So, now you're back what are your plans?'

'Well, I was thinking –'

'We'd love to have you back at Global, Simon, but I'm afraid there isn't the head count right now,' Lawrence interrupted.

Stunned by his assumption, I tried to remain calm.

'Oh, really?' I replied pretending to sound disappointed.

'I'm afraid so.'

'Well, it's a fucking good job I wasn't planning on coming back, then, isn't it?'

Lawrence's face dropped. 'Oh, I just assumed you wanted … so, where are you working now?'

I hesitated before answering. 'I'm working in the Midlands at the moment.'

He frowned. 'What are you doing in the Midlands?'

'I'm working in distribution.'

'Distributing internet software?'

'No, frozen food.'

Lawrence smiled. He wasn't sure if I was being serious or not. 'Frozen food?'

'Yep, I help distribute frozen oven chips and pizza to the nation. I'm working temporarily in a freezer-packing warehouse for Tesco's.'

'Golly. Quite a change from Global.'

'You could say that.'

'Why on earth would you choose to do that? Didn't you want to move back to London?'

'I'm happy in the Midlands at the moment, thanks.'

'Where are you based?'

'Daventry.'

'Don't know it. Got a flat?'

'No, I'm living with my mum at the moment.'

This is almost too much for Lawrence. He busts out

laughing and slaps his hand on the table.

'With your mum?' he coughed.

The waitress arrived with his order and placed the plate of food in front of him. I began to feel a little stupid. Why did I tell him I lived with my mum?

'Oh, dear,' he beamed, wiping a tear from the corner of his eye. 'I haven't laughed like that for ages. Sorry, I don't mean to be rude – it must be hard sliding down the career ladder like that. You're certainly putting on a brave face. I'm just sorry I can't do anything to help you out.'

I suddenly felt my blood reach boiling point. He had pushed me too far this time, and without warning I exploded in a torrent of rage.

'Listen here, you cock sucker,' I hissed, grabbing his shirt and pulling him close to my face. 'I wouldn't waste another minute of my life working with you, even if you paid me a million pounds a year and lent me your ugly whore wife to fuck over my desk all day. You may think behaving like a cunt is an acceptable existence, but believe me, buddy boy, there's a whole world out there that's passing you by.'

Jumping to my feet, I snatched a sausage off his plate and took a large bite. He looked up at me in stunned silence.

'So long, Cox.'

Storming out of the café, I could feel the adrenaline pumping through my veins. The next chapter of my life had definitely started and there would be no turning back now.

Disturbed by a splashing sound, I open one eye and see bubbles on the surface of the water. Following the line from the end of my rod, I notice that it has gone taught and jumping into action my instincts take over. Chris leaps to his feet.

'You've bloody got one!' he cries.

'Have I?'

'Yes! *Quick*, reel the damn thing in!'

Leaning over the side, I grab hold of the line and give it a firm tug. I can feel the weight of the fish as I begin to slowly reel it in. Standing up, I'm able to lift the hook out of the water and seeing the white belly of the fish thrashing against the surface, we release yelps of excitement.

'Don't lose it, Si!'

Tugging at the line, I heave the fish out of the water and swing it through the air into Chris's hands.

'FUCK! IT'S A FISH, SI! IT'S A FISH!'

Crouching down, Chris brings it close to his chest and wrestling to get a grip on its slippery body, he removes the hook from its mouth and drops it into the faded plastic carrier bag. Deep green in colour, the fish lies motionless on its side and gasps for air. Prodding it with my finger, I jump back in surprise as it appears to find a final burst of energy and flipping into the air it leaps out of the bag and lands on the wooden jetty. We both pounce on the fish, head butting each other on the way down. Rubbing our temples, we suddenly notice the fish is making its escape over the edge.

'*NO!*' Chris screams.

I dive on top of the fish, but it slips through my fingers and flips off the side. It disappears into the lake with a satisfying plop.

Chris peers over the edge and drops his head. 'Bollocks! We finally catch a fish after all these years … and then you let it get away!'

'*ME?* It was slippery, you little shit, there was nothing I could do!'

Chris turns away and walks sulkily over to his line. Frustrated, I squash a fresh worm onto the end of my hook. I lower it into the water and just as I'm about to reel in the line a little, I watch in amazement as another fish leaps out of the water and takes hold of the bait.

'*I'VE GOT ANOTHER ONE!*' I yell, swinging the silver fish through the air.

'No way!' Chris hollers, and looking over at his line he realises he has one too.

For the next hour, we hook fish out of the lake with as much ease as Fat Larry serving up cod in Buster's Chip Shop on the High Street. The excitement of catching a fish is overwhelming, and despite struggling at first with the guilt of killing a living creature, we quickly get used to the idea - particularly the hungrier we become.

Returning to the car with our catch, we feel like proud hunters returning to the village with a feast. The bag slung over Chris's shoulder contains twelve little fish, and excited by the idea of tasting fresh fish caught with our very own hands, we immediately find the small camping stove and heat up the frying pan on the boot of the car.

Chris pours a drop of oil into the pan. 'What does it say in the SAS Survival Guide about cooking them?'

Thumbing through the pages I find the 'Fish and Fishing' section. 'Now, let me see. It says here that all freshwater fish are edible. Those fewer than five centimeters long need no preparation and larger fish must be gutted. Perfect! All of ours are tiddlers so we don't need to gut them.'

'Yours might be tiddlers, pal. This last one I caught is massive.'

He turns the fish over and opens its mouth. 'Look at its teeth. It was a fierce battle catching this giant.'

'Chris, it's tiny! My dick's bigger than that.'

'Yeah, right! In that case you must be hung like Dirk Diggler.'

'Hey, nobodies that big.'

Following the guidelines in the book, we scrape off the scales and place a couple of the fish in the hot pan. We watch excitedly as they sizzle and curl up in the heat. I pick out some flesh and pop it into my mouth. It tastes of blood ... truly disgusting. We try adding some salt and a shit load of ketchup, but the taste doesn't improve.

Tossing the fish into a bush, we climb into the car and munch on the last remaining crackers, which have gone stale. Turning off the torch, Chris falls immediately into a deep sleep and smiling to myself, I feel satisfied that although our cooking skills might need some improvement, tonight at least we had proved to ourselves that we could survive in the wild.

The 80's Coming Back

My fingers smell of fish. The inside of the Sierra smells of fish, my T-shirt smells of fish and as I swing my legs out of the car I nearly step on a charred frying pan full of … uh … fish. Fish is everywhere! It's up my nose, it's in my hair and as I sit up I hear a low growl in my stomach and fear it's the fish taking their revenge. Si is nowhere to be seen; only his sleeping bag lies unzipped on the passenger seat. Grabbing a tissue from the glove box, I blow my nose really hard and scan the area for any traces of his where-abouts. He doesn't seem to be anywhere insight. He's most probably gone for a long walk to get rid of the smell of fish, or he was dragged out of the car last night by mummy fish and eaten alive, hmm … maybe not.

'Chris!'

I look over my shoulder and see Si walking from behind a bush close to the edge of the lake, with his shorts on and top off. I wave back and watch as he makes his way over to the car clutching a toilet roll in his hand.

'Are you all right?' he grins.

'Yeah, apart from the disgusting smell of fish,' I grumble, forcing a tissue up my left nostril.

Si slaps a hand on my back. 'Got off with this girl once who smelt of fish.'

I throw him a look of disgust.

'What's the matter with you, you grumpy fuck? Can't

hack the smell of fish?'

'For fuck's sake, Si … *please!* My stomach feels like it's about to explode. Are you sure we cooked them properly? The last thing I need on the road is to feel like I'm going to throw up after every mile.'

Si leans against the car and folds his arms. 'John Wiseman said you don't need to gut fish under five centimeters long, remember? Well, the fish we caught were about two centimeters long so don't panic.'

Waving goodbye to Lake Wigry, we head further north past the town of Suwalki and up to the Polish-Lithuanian border. It's such a relief to smell fresh air again. I stick my head out of the sunroof and make a promise to myself that I will never smell of fish again.

Reaching the Polish border at Budzisko, we cross with ease into the Lithuanian town of Kalvarija and continue north along a brand new stretch of highway that carries us towards the city of Kaunus.

'Hey, Si, did you know the Lithuanian forests played an important role in regional folk tales?'

Without taking his eyes off the road, Si grabs a mint off the dashboard.

'Did they?' he nods.

'Uh-huh. According to this guidebook, during times of war the forests were a safe haven for those in danger. The oak tree was worshipped during pre-Christian times and today represents longevity and strength. Lithuanians often plant oak trees to mark important occasions. Pretty interesting stuff, don't you think?'

Si ignores me and continues to stare at the road.

'Also, in Lithuania until May 2002, the Soviet-era rules required women to undergo gynecological examinations to qualify for a driving license.'

He stops sucking on his mint and turns to me. 'You what?'

Suddenly, a horse and cart veers across the road in front of us, forcing Si to brake sharply and swerve to the left.

'*SHIT!*' he cries, narrowly avoiding the back wheels of the cart.

The old couple driving this ancient mode of transport bounce up and down in their seats as they hang on for dear life. The guy wearing a flat cap thrashes the horse with a whip while the old gal, who has a face like a slapped arse, looks sternly at us.

'*FUCKING IDIOTS!*' Si shouts, blasting the horn. 'They're gonna get themselves killed!'

Dropping down a gear, he composes himself and picks up speed. The horse and cart veers off the highway and flies down a steep embankment before disappearing through the gateway to a field.

'Idiots!' Si spits. 'What the hell are they doing trying to cross a motorway on that?'

'I suppose it used to be just farmland around here, until they plonked this bloody great big motorway right in the middle of it.'

'Well, somebody's going to get killed. They need to build a frigging bridge!'

Heading for the Baltic Sea, we turn west onto the A1 and cross the Nemunas River. Reaching the industrial city of Kaunas, we avoid the centre and continue on, hurtling past a large industrial power station that bellows thick black smoke into the atmosphere from towering red and white-stripped chimneys. There's little to capture the imagination, and after a few hours we reach the outskirts of Klaipeda on the Baltic coast.

Si pulls into a petrol station adjacent to a large industrial estate.

'What a shit hole,' he mutters. 'We're not staying the night here, are we?'

'No way! How about we go to that sandy spit.'

Si frowns. 'Sandy spit?'

'Uh-huh. It's near some lagoon. There's a load of giant sand dunes, apparently.'

'Umm ... I'm sure it's beautiful, but the last thing I want to do right now is spend the night on a sandy spit.'

'Actually, neither do I. In fact, I'm hungry.'

'Me too! Hey, Chris, why don't you grab something from the shop.'

I glance out of the window at the uninviting petrol station forecourt outside. 'Can't you go?'

Si pauses for a moment, then sighs. 'Oh ... OK, you lazy fuck.'

As Si scurries off across the tarmac it begins to rain. Adjusting my seat, I make myself comfortable and pass the time by observing the local Lithuanians outside. Suddenly, just as I'm about to drum a tune on the dashboard, a huge truck, minus its load, roars into the car park and screeches to a halt opposite the Sierra. I watch with intrigue as a man wearing a blue pinstriped suit, white shirt and grey tie jumps out of the driver's cab clutching a briefcase. He races across the car park and disappears inside a brand new BMW X5 with blacked out windows. Surprised to see someone so well dressed behind the wheel of a lorry, I eye him suspiciously.

Si quickly leaps back into the car and passes me a can of Coke and a dumpling, which is an unhealthy yellowish colour.

'Sorry, that's all they had.'

'What is it?'

'A Lithuanian dumpling,' he smiles. 'It's got meat inside. Might as well try the local dish.'

'Yeah, but not from a smeggy petrol station.'

'Food's food, fat boy.'

I keep my eye on the BMW.

'Fucking weather,' Si grumbles, as he picks at his dumpling.

'Hey, you see that lorry over there?'

'Uh-huh.'

'Some bloke in a pinstriped suit just jumped out of it holding a briefcase.'

Si shrugs. 'So?'

'Don't you think that's a bit odd?'

'Why, because a lorry driver is wearing a pinstriped suit?'

'Uh ... yeah!'

'Maybe he's on his way to a wedding.'

'In a great big dirty lorry?'

'He could be,' Si nods. 'They might do that around these parts.'

'Open your frigging eyes, will ya! There's definitely something going on. He looked suspicious. I wonder what's inside the briefcase?'

'Who knows, Inspector Columbo. Probably his sandwiches, a calculator and a photograph of his wife.'

'Si, don't be a dick, I'll bet it's full of money. He's probably involved in smuggling cigarettes, or some other dodgy shit.'

'Cigarettes?'

'Yeah, cigarette smuggling is big business around these parts. Those cheap boxes of two hundred we were getting from the Kurdish guys in the freezer were probably from here.'

'Nah, they were coming from Romania.'

'Well, he's definitely up to something. These guys make millions selling contraband on the black market. Look, he's getting out.'

The black 4x4's passenger door swings open. The guy in the suit immerges without the briefcase this time. He races back to the lorry with a concerned look on his face and climbs quickly into the driver's cab. Striking the engine, he accelerates at great speed out of the car park. Through a gap in the window of the 4x4, I notice a man of Middle

Eastern appearance starring suspiciously in our direction. Looking down at our crotches and in any other direction but his, Si nervously stubs his cigarette out in the ashtray.

'This place is fucking dodgy,' he mutters.

This time the driver's door swings open, and we watch as his shiny black leather shoes step down onto the tarmac. We see this as our signal to leave.

'Let's get out of here,' I grin, spinning the car out onto the main road.

'Good plan,' Si replies. 'The sooner we get to Estonia the better. We'll be nice and close to Russia, and we can relax a little before...'

'Before what?'

'Before the real journey begins!'

Peering out of the window, I scan the horizon in the hope of catching a glimpse of the Baltic Sea. On the map we appear so close, but looking out of the window it's nowhere to be seen.

'Where the hell is it?' I cry.

'Where's what?' Si frowns.

'The ocean, you fool. It should be within pissing distance.'

'Maybe it's behind those trees on the horizon.'

'Si, it's not a glass of water we're talking about here ... it's the Baltic Sea! Seventy-two percent of the Earth's surface is covered by water. Where the fuck is it?'

Feeling irritable, I turn up the music on the radio and listen to an orchestra belt out what I think might be Beethoven's Fifth Symphony, although, I could be wrong.

'This classical music malarkey is pretty good, isn't it?' I smile.

'I guess it is pretty relaxing,' Si replies. 'The music goes with the countryside. It makes it look more beautiful. In fact, I'm glad the tape player doesn't work.'

'Why?'

'Because I'd have to listen to your Guns N' Roses tape all of the time.'

'There's nothing wrong with 'Guns N' Roses', pal. Those boys know how to rock!'

'Yeah, but it's so bizarre you've only just discovered them.'

'Come on, Si, you know I've never been very up on my music.'

'You came to see a few bands at the Roadmender when we were at school, didn't ya?'

'Nah, I drove you and that weird friend of yours to see a few bands, then me and my girlfriend, Lucy, would go to the cinema or have a pizza.'

'Oh yeah, you were like a married couple at the age of seventeen, weren't you! Bloody hell, Chris in love! It's hard to imagine now.'

'What do you mean?'

'Well, you were so different back then.'

'Was I?'

Si nods. 'Uh-huh, you were so … sensible. What happened?'

'Dunno? I was young and in love. I'm probably a bit more cynical about the whole cabuddles these days. I've learnt a lot since then.'

'From watching daytime television?' Si smiles.

'No, from life.'

'Cynical you say? Why?'

'I've had some pretty messy relationships. Oh … I don't know. Maybe it's because I haven't met the right girl, or I'm having too much fun to settle down and become involved in something serious right now.'

'Or maybe you're just afraid of getting hurt again?'

'Fuck off, Si! Are we talking about you or me here? You're the one who's afraid of getting hurt again after Emily. Anyway, the whole relationship process just seems a bit false to me at this moment in time. Unless you're ready to fully commit, what's the point? You're living a lie.'

'Yeah, I guess at the end of the day if your hearts not in it, it can only end in disaster.'

It's surprisingly quiet as we approach the Latvian border. Si pulls up at customs control and a round, jolly gentleman with rosy cheeks appears from a booth. He looks a bit like the laughing policeman, only he's dressed in a tight green uniform. He beams a smile and gestures for us to drive on.

It begins to get dark as we push on into the evening. We head directly for the capital city of Riga, which is close to the border with Estonia and is where this year's 2003 European Song Contest is to be held tomorrow night.

'You can't beat a good old fashioned European Song Contest,' Si smiles.

'Yeah, maybe one day we'll find someone with a bit of talent, who might actually win a point.'

'I wouldn't hold your breath.'

'Maybe we should try and get a couple of tickets?'

Si shakes his head. 'Nah, I'd rather watch it on the telly.'

'OK, let's wait until we get to Estonia. We'll book into a hotel and make a night of it.'

The city lights of Riga twinkle in the distance, as we cross an impressive suspension bridge that carries us over the river Daugava. Surrounded by grand architecture with examples of all styles from Middle Ages to modern times, Si sticks his camera out of the window and attempts to grab a few shots of the city, which I predict will be blurry images of ... uh ... the passing traffic. Even though the idea of necking a couple of the local Latvian Aldaris Zelta beer sounds tempting, we try to stay focused and leave Riga in a bid to move closer to Estonia.

After what feels like an eternity, we eventually find our way out of the city and onto the motorway via a very confusing diversion. Seeing a service station up ahead, I realise that I'm starting to lose concentration, so turning off the motorway I find an empty space behind the petrol station and we immediately collapse into a deep sleep.

* * *

I'm rudely awoken by the fantastic smell of freshly cooked bacon. Leaping out of the car, I find Chris hunched over the frying pan and flipping greasy rashers with his penknife.

'Morning!' he cheerfully sings. 'Yesterday Latvia, today Estonia!'

'Good lad, where did you get the pig?'

'From the petrol station, these Latvians love their meat.'

'Smells delicious, I'm starving! I could eat a horse and chase the jockey.'

'Patience, dear boy, you can't rush a man when he's cooking bacon.'

'Very true! Hey, Chris, I can't wait to check out the girls in Estonia. According to the legend, they're supposed to be the hottest honeys on the planet.'

'Where did you hear that?' he replies flicking a rasher of bacon onto a plate.

'On the wind.'

Chris frowns. 'On the wind?'

'Yeah, you know, on the grapevine.'

'Oh, I thought Venezuela had the hottest girls in the world. I'm sure they've won Miss World four times.'

'Who cares! Maybe it's a folklore that has been passed down through generations from father to son, or a sailors tale that has been whispered in taverns and spread across oceans.'

'Bollocks,' Chris laughs. 'You saw a program about the country on the Travel Channel, didn't you?'

'Well, yes, that might be true, but this time we're going to see it for ourselves. The program I saw focused on a university in Tallinn, the capital of Estonia, and boy-oh-boy from the girls I saw in the program are we in for a treat!'

Before we know it, we're back on the road and heading along the A2 towards the city of Valmiera. Passing through the Gauja National Park, I whistle a tune as Chris merrily steers the car towards the small town of Valka. The warm morning sunshine streams through my window and I smile as we pass through another border control, which takes us into the northern Baltic State of Estonia.

Chris whacks the Sierra into fifth gear. 'Right, where shall we head first?'

'To the ocean!' I smile. 'There's a small seaside town in the south west called Parnu.'

'Parnu? It doesn't sound very exotic, does it?'

'Nope, but it's where the party's going down.'

'All righty, then, Parnu it is!'

Heading west across the country, we weave quickly through the pretty little towns and villages of southern Estonia. We stop for lunch along the way, and devour a mean burger from a bar-cum-restaurant with a ship theme. The gaunt skinny girl behind the counter is dressed in a navy blue sailor suit and white naval cap. Trying not to laugh as she slides the menu over the counter, which is shaped like a ship's wheel, we begin to feel like we've finally arrived on our holidays.

We reach the outskirts of Parnu in the early afternoon and pass billboards advertising campsites, restaurants, bars and an endless list of holiday activities.

'This place is great!' Chris smiles. 'It's so...'

'Tacky.'

'Yeah, tacky.'

Finding a cheap hotel in the centre of town, we park the Sierra in the car park around the back and head up the stairs to the reception desk. Pushing through the heavy glass doors, I smile at the attractive woman sitting behind the counter. She is of Scandinavian appearance with blonde shoulder length hair and beautiful blue eyes. In my finest Estonian I ask her for the price of a room. The woman doesn't appear to understand, so I resort to pointing to a sentence in the phrasebook. She nods and calmly makes her way around the reception desk. As she fiddles with a large bunch of keys, I'm surprised by how tall she is. I nudge Chris and he grins in recognition. Following her down the corridor, she unlocks one of the doors and swings it open.

'We pay now?' Chris asks, showing her his wallet.

She shrugs her shoulders and smiles sweetly. With her hair practically brushing against the ceiling, she turns and heads back to reception. Throwing our bags into the room we immediately celebrate our arrival, and crack open the bottle of red wine that has been rolling around in the car since we left England.

I spark up a cigarette.

'Si, you can't smoke in here!'

'Why not?'

'There's a no smoking sign on the door.'

'OK, I'll have it out of the window.'

'You'll set the smoke alarm off.'

'Chill out, will ya!'

Kneeling on the bed, Chris joins me and we both lean as far out of the window as possible.

'We made it!' Chris smiles, peering down at the cars on the busy main road. 'Estonia! Think how far north we are now. We're right near Finland, aren't we?'

'Yep, not far, Helsinki is just across the water from Tallinn.'

'Not bad for a three hundred pound Ford Sierra. It'll get us to Vladivostok no problem!'

I snatch the bottle of wine out of Chris's hand. 'I wouldn't count your chickens. We're not even sure if the highway in

Siberia is passable yet.'

'That's true.'

'Did it say on the internet when the road would be finished?'

'Yeah, sometime in 2005, but I don't reckon it'll be one hundred percent complete until the year 2008.'

I frown. '*2008?*'

'Yep.'

'But that's in five years time.'

'Don't panic,' Chris smiles. 'I read on this official road website that they only have a three hundred and fifty kilometre stretch of highway left to complete, between the Siberian cities of Chita and Khabarovsk.'

'Have they started building it? I mean, is there actually a road?'

Chris shrugs. 'Dunno. I guess that's what we're gonna find out.'

Taking a well-earned shower in the communal bathroom, I return to the room looking as soft and pink as a newborn baby. Fishing out my finest glad rags, I quickly get dressed while Chris scurries off to disinfect himself. Peering out of the window, I look past the road and over the small park behind the hotel. A group of lads in baseball caps congregate around a skate ramp beneath the bright blue sky. It feels like the middle of the afternoon, but guessing that it must be closer to nine o'clock in the evening, I'm suddenly made aware of how far north we are.

Bursting through the door with a towel wrapped around his waist, Chris races across the room and switches on the TV.

'The Eurovision Song Contest is on!' he cries.

Glancing over my shoulder, I take a swig from the bottle of wine and watch Marie Naumova and Renars Kaupers present the 2003 Eurovision Song Contest live from Riga.

'Three cheers to Terry Wogan!' Chris sings, as he wrestles to pull his boxer shorts on beneath his towel.

'Wogan won't be commentating on this channel, you dumb ass. He only does it for British TV.'

'Bollocks! It's Terry's armchair wisecracks that make it funny.'

Watching the titles, I can see that it promises to be a night of the usual cheese with dance numbers, power ballads and weird entries that involve attractive dancers removing their clothes. A group of lads dressed in black suits and colourful chunky knotted ties march across the stage.

Chris falls onto the bed. 'Which country is this?'

'I dunno?'

The four-piece band burst into song, which surprisingly breaks all Eurovision traditions by providing virtually all instrumentation, as they perform a Britpop-style number called '*The 80's coming back*'. I find myself tapping my fingertips on the windowsill.

'They've got to win!' Chris smiles.

'Do you reckon?'

'Definitely… "*I've got a feeling the eighties are coming back*",' he sings, grabbing his jeans off the bed. '…Hey, Si, do you think he's singing about your hair?'

'Fuck off!'

Giving my bouffant a quick flick, I draw my hair back in a ponytail.

'It'll never win,' I mutter aloud.

Chris frowns. 'Why not?'

'It's not cheesy enough.'

'*HEY!*' he suddenly cries, applauding excitedly. 'It's Estonia's entry! Come on Estonia!'

'My God, they'll be a party in town tonight if they win.'

'Chrissy boy, they'll be a party in town tonight if they don't.'

Fun Lovin' Criminals

Heading out into the street feeling good and buzzing from the wine, we storm through the centre of Parnu in search of a bar. Turning left, we spy a pub full of holidaymakers sitting at tables outside.

'Hey, can you hear that?' Si smiles, as we approach the pub.

'Hear what?'

'I think it's Roy Chubby Brown ... it is! It's Roy Chubby Brown!'

Grinning, I look eagerly around. 'No way! Where?'

'He's not actually here, you idiot,' Si snaps. 'Listen to the music coming from those speakers.'

'Oh yeah, it bloody is as well! Who'd have thought it? Britain's crudest seaside performer has made it big on the Baltic. Have you ever heard him do the routine about the cup of tea and the used tampon?'

Si shakes his head vigorously. 'No, and I really don't need to hear it now.'

'Why the hell are they playing, "*Alice? Who the fuck is Alice?*" in a family pub, anyway?'

'They probably don't understand the words.'

As we pass a young couple and their two children eating a meal at a table outside, fat Roy belts out the chorus, "*ALICE? WHO THE FUCK IS ALICE?*" from the speakers positioned directly above their heads. I glance over at the parents and wait for their horrified reaction, but there isn't one - they seem totally oblivious to the bad language and continue to tuck innocently into their dinner.

'Excellent!' I chuckle. 'Roy Chubby Brown in Estonia.'

Si skips inside the pub. 'Makes a change from Britney, I suppose.'

Toasting the night, we sink a couple of delicious Estonian beers to the, uh ... delightfully repeated vocals of Roy Chubby Brown. Tables of merry holidaymakers provide a vibrant atmosphere, and feeling well oiled we go in search of the nightlife of Parnu.

The queue outside the Mirage nightclub contains a bizarre mixture of characters.

'Hey, Si! Check out the dude with the orange mullet and green crocodile skin loafers ... nice!'

'You think that's bad,' he smiles. 'What about Betty Boop over there in the white fur coat?'

'Bloody hell, and I thought there were some freaks in Vegas.'

Handing over our jackets in exchange for a plastic token, we race up the stairs and enter the club. Turning left into the main room, the dance floor is already crowded with an interesting mixture of smiley, eccentric looking individuals. We find a spot at the end of the bar and order a couple of whiskeys. To the right of the bar a group of girls dance in a circle around their handbags ... Essex style.

'Hot potatoes!' Si yells. 'Check out all the women!'

We slam back a few more drinks before finding the confidence to explore.

'Head for those tables at the back!' Si yells over the noise of the electronic dance music.

As I push my way through the middle of the dance floor, I suddenly hear Estonia's Eurovision Song Contest entry, 'The 80's coming back' burst from the speakers. Everybody dancing instantly goes crazy, and a saucy looking blonde girl in a short yellow skirt grabs Si by the hand and begins dancing around him in circles. Swept away by the crowd I'm pushed towards the edge of the dance floor, and grabbing hold of the wall I feel relieved to have escaped the humiliation of being forced to dance. Amusing myself, I watch Si from a distance as he tries to impress the girl with some of the new moves he had been working on in Prague. Chuckling, I turn to the guy in a black leather jacket standing next to me.

'All right, mate,' I smile.

Ignoring me, the guy licks his lips and continues to drill holes into the butt cheeks of a girl dancing nearby. He suddenly turns to me.

'You Arab,' he grunts with a strong Russian accent.

'Arab? No, I'm English.'

'You look like Arab.'

He throws me a cold stare.

'I from Chechnya,' he snaps, pointing proudly at his chest.

Removing a small bottle of vodka from his jacket pocket, he unscrews the lid and pours some into my glass.

'Nastrovia!' he nods, slamming back his drink.

'I'm Chris,' I grin, stretching out my hand. 'What's your name?'

'Sergei. I from Grozny.'

'Are you on holiday?'

'Holiday? Nyet, I live here five years.'

'Oh, I see. Do you work here? You have job?'

'Nyet. I Chechen criminal,' he replies sternly.

I flash a smile. 'You're a Chechen criminal?'

He nods. 'Everyone think Chechens are criminals, so I criminal.'

Offering Sergei a cigarette, I listen with intrigue.

'Very very bad in Chechnya, too much guns, so I leave. I come to Parnu ... why you here?' he asks, lighting my cigarette.

'I drove here from England with my brother. We're heading to Vladivostok.'

Sergei laughs out loud. 'Vladivostok?'

'Yeah.'

'You drive to Vladivostok?'

'Yep. In our Ford Sierra.'

'Ah, you make joke.'

'No, it's true! We're on our way to Vladivostok.'

He laughs again before refilling our glasses.

'Impossible!' he cries. 'Not even Chechen soldier do this.'

'Why not?'

Sergei draws a finger across his throat. 'Too dangerous, many bandits ... you will die!'

Suddenly, a guy in a grey roll neck jumper appears next to Sergei, and I quickly discover that Azamat is also from the city of Grozny in Chechnya. Sergei talks to him quickly in Russian, and they both turn to me and laugh.

'You will die,' Azamat repeats, tossing his head back and roaring with laughter.

Desperate to change the subject, I interrupt the laughter and ask Azamat what he is doing in Parnu.

'I Chechen criminal,' he replies proudly.

'You as well?' I smile.

He frowns and turns to Sergei. Sergei turns to me, and nods.

I clear my throat. 'Oh, uh ... cool!'

Across the crowded dance floor I suddenly spot Si pushing his way towards the bar, so I quickly offer my new criminal friends a drink.

'You want vodka?' I ask, knowing that this is a stupid question.

Grinning at me insanely, Sergei pats me hard on the back. 'Da. Spaceeba, Chris from England, spaceeba.'

* * *

As I wait patiently at the bar, Chris suddenly leaps onto the stool beside me.

'Hey, hot shot! How's it hanging?'

'Chris, you numb-nuts! Where did you disappear to?'

'I got swept away by the crowd.'

'Bollocks!'

'I *did*!'

'Of course you did. I forgot you're a pussy when it comes to dancing.'

'No I'm not.'

'Stop being so self-conscious and just ride the music.'

Chris laughs. '"Ride the music", you cheesy git. I'm quite happy chilling out on the sidelines, thank you very much.'

'OK, fair enough. Right, Chris, its drinks time! I need to order a cocktail for the cutie on the dance floor.'

'The girl in the yellow skirt?'

'Yeah.'

'Good lad, she's fit as fuck!'

'I know. I think I'm in love.'

'Not again!'

I frown. 'What do you mean by that?'

'Si, you fall in love with all the girls.'

'No I don't … hey, why don't you come over? I'll introduce you to her mates.'

'No way, they're all fat.'

'I thought you liked a girl with a bit of meat around the hips.'

'Yeah, but not half a fucking cow! Besides, I've been chatting to these two Chechen criminals.'

'*What?*'

'Yeah, Sergei and Azamat, they're both criminals from Grozny in Chechnya. I'm gonna buy them a drink!'

'Wait a minute … back up, buddy boy. Chechen criminals, as in criminals from Chechnya?'

'That's what I said.'

'What kind of criminals?'

Chris shrugs. 'No idea, I didn't ask … I'll ask them!'

'Noooo … don't be a twat, they could be dangerous. Use

your noodle. I'd stay well away from them if I were you, it can only lead to trouble.'

'Nah ... they seem OK. Well, as OK as two Chechen criminals can be.'

Ordering a round of shots from the bar, Chris balances them on a small tray and shuffles over to his new friends. Leaving me with the bill, I hand over the cash and dance with my cocktails over to Eva and her weighty chums. Approaching her from across the dance floor, I'm immediately reminded how beautiful she is. Taking the drink out of my hand, she leans over and kisses me softly on the cheek.

'You very good boy, Simon.'

'Thanks,' I smile. 'You very good girl.'

She reaches over and puts a finger to my lips. 'Nyet good girl, Simon, I am naughty girl.'

'Really, why?'

'I will not tell you,' she grins cheekily.

I raise an eyebrow. 'Now I'm really intrigued. Come on, why are you a naughty girl?'

Looking unsure whether to tell me her secret, she tries to distract me by pushing her firm breasts against my chest in an effort to get me to dance. It works, but only for a brief moment.

'OK, don't tell me, then.'

'If I tell you, you not like me anymore.'

'Yes I will.'

'I have baby,' she whispers, dropping her gaze.

'A baby?'

'See, now you don't like me.'

Drawing Eva close, we begin kissing passionately in the middle of the dance floor. Grabbing my arm, she leads me across the club to an empty booth at the back of the club. Pushing me inside, she follows close behind and jumping across my lap she begins kissing me wildly. Surprised at first by her enthusiasm – I quickly relax, and tenderly caressing her soft thighs beneath the hem of her skirt, I feel bizarrely like I'm fourteen years old again.

* * *

I stumble out of the club and onto the wet pavement. A police car with its blue flashing lights is parked on the curb outside. Two cops leaning against the bonnet laugh at the pissed up clubbers, and eye up the girls as they dance around in their high heels. Spinning around, I see Si wave a hand in the air as he disappears around the corner with the blonde girl he'd met on the dance floor. I consider chasing after them, but decide to leave them to it. I lost Sergei and Azamat somewhere between going to the toilet and chatting up Betty Boop, who turned out to be a freak from the dark corners of Berlin. I try to stay focused despite feeling severely mashed. Everybody standing outside the club begins to either climb into a taxi, or disappear on foot down the main shopping street. Not wishing to be left alone with two bored policemen, I follow their lead and head off in search of the hotel. Staggering through the dimly lit streets, I turn left and then right in the direction of a big road, which I think is near to where we're staying. Within minutes I'm lost. The wind starts to pick up and a large spot of rain splashes across my forehead. I scan the area for any recognizable landmarks, but there aren't any - not one. A brightly painted church on the corner looks vaguely familiar, although, I can't be sure. Breaking a smile, I begin to laugh.

'Ha-ha! Where-am-I?' I sing out loud.

I stop laughing.

Taking a few deep breaths, I try to think clearly and decide to turn around and walk back to the main shopping street. The last thing I need is to end up in some fucked up crack estate on the outskirts of town. Rubbing my eyes, I focus on the pavement in front of me and begin zigzagging back through the streets. All of the buildings on either side of the road are in darkness and, apart from the occasional swoosh of a car going by on the road or a dog barking far away in the distance, it's eerily quiet.

I reach a crossroads and stop at the corner as I try to retrace my steps. How difficult can this be? This is ridiculous. I just walked down here a few moments ago. Suddenly, I notice a guy in a brown bomber jacket walking towards me up the street. I straighten my shoulders and try to look as though I know where I'm going. He reaches the crossroads and shouts over, but I don't understand what he's saying. He crosses the road and walks up to me. I stand my ground, annoyed with myself for not paying more attention to Jackie Chang's karate moves in the movie 'Rumble in the Bronx', which I saw recently on DVD. The unshaven guy looks at me suspiciously. He then says something. I shake my head and shrug my shoulders.

'Woman,' he laughs.

I frown. 'Woman?'

He nods. 'You want woman?'

'No, thank you,' I reply in a slow, clear tone.

He laughs. 'Jiggy-jiggy, da?'

I smile nervously. 'Nyet.'

His face falls and his eyes are drawn to my jacket pocket. I start to feel a little uncomfortable and take a step back, but he steps forward - his eyes still firmly fixed on my jacket pocket. Distracted by a passing car, I look away from the guy for a second and before you can say 'Jackie Chang', he reaches inside my pocket and grabs a couple of notes I'd stuffed in there for safe keeping. I'm completely shocked, and freeze as I watch him run off down the street. How did he know I had money in that pocket? That's not important, my immediate concern should be to get my money back, so I do ... well, I try. Chasing after him, I shout really scary things like "I can use a gun, you know!" and "The police are coming!" but he finds my threatening words rather amusing and just laughs over his shoulder instead of stopping and handing back my cash. After a hundred metres, or so, the shock of what's just happened slowly begins to subside, and it suddenly occurs to me that pursuing this thief might actually be quite a bad idea. There can't have been more than ten quid in my pocket. I'm certainly not going to be knifed to death, or shot in the head over such a small amount of money. I skid to a halt and watch as the thief disappears out of sight.

Feeling a little foolish and annoyed with myself for getting into this dangerous situation in the first place, I pick up pace and eventually find my way back to the main shopping street. It's deserted. After walking thirty yards, I suddenly see a guy who looks remarkably like Sergei, the Chechen criminal from the club. He's standing under a shop awning with his head hanging down and his hands in the pockets of his black leather jacket. At first I think he's starring down at his boots, but as I walk over to him I see the poor guy is fast asleep. I don't want to wake him up so I creep by, but I accidentally kick an empty Coke can across the ground. Sergei's eyes spring open, and his head slowly lifts up like a zombie rising from the dead. He doesn't move for a few seconds; he just stares at me intently before cracking a smile.

'Chris!' he grins, his eyes struggling to focus on my face.
'What you doing, Sergei? It's raining. Were you asleep?'
He shakes his head. 'Not asleep.'
'You were asleep.'
'Nyet. I wait for friend,' he replies.
'Azamat?'
'Nyet, other friend.'
I offer him a cigarette. He pulls his collars up and takes a lighter out of his pocket.
'Where you go now?' he asks, cupping his hands around

the lighter.

'To my hotel.'

'You want vodka? We drink more vodka.'

'No, I go to my hotel. I'm very tired.'

He points up the street. 'We go drink.'

'I go home,' I reply. 'I sleep.'

'OK. You crazy, Chris!'

On that note, Sergei drops his head again, closes his eyes and goes back to sleep.

* * *

Walking through the dark streets of Parnu in the early hours, with an Estonian blonde in one hand and a vodka and tonic in the other ... I feel like a God. All I had managed as a way of goodbye to Chris was a weak wave over the crowd, but he knows the score. I've learnt over the years that slipping away after the club closes is always a wise thing to do, especially when there's a girl involved. Passing a newspaper stand, I buy Eva a coffee and with a look of mischief in her eyes, she drags me down towards the river. We find a bench close to the bridge and sit with our arms around each other, watching the boats chug slowly by in the dark. Deeply feminine, Eva looks at me with her small soft features and long delicate eyelashes. She doesn't speak very good English, and as she tries to explain something to me about herself, I interrupt her by gently taking away her coffee and launching it into the river. She looks surprised by my spontaneity, and grinning wildly I take her in my arms and begin kissing her passionately. Pausing for a moment she looks at me with wide eyes, and greatly turned on we pull at each other's clothes and make love right there on the bench.

It begins to grow light. We rearrange our clothes and sit on the bench in comfortable silence, which is a relief considering we've just had sex in a public place. Eva rests her head on my shoulder and caresses my chest. I feel so relaxed, a little cold, but relaxed.

I escort Eva along the river to the entrance of a high-rise tower block. She doesn't invite me inside, but I guess it's understandable particularly if she has a young child. She scribbles down her mobile number on my hand in eyeliner. What an amazing night …what an amazing girl. I look down at her number on my hand and smile. We kiss before breaking away, and smiling at each other one last time, I float across the grass as she disappears out of sight.

Catching a taxi back to the hotel, I skip up the stairs and sing a good morning to the tired looking woman sat behind reception. Gliding down the corridor, I pause outside our room and feel vaguely surprised to see the door slightly ajar. It's not like Chris to leave the door open. I enter the dark room. I don't want to turn the light on and disturb him as he snores loudly beneath his sheets, so I fumble my way over to my bed on the far side of the room. Whipping off my T-shirt, I collapse onto the bed and lie in the darkness. All of a sudden, the door swings open and I sit up in surprise. A beam of light from the corridor blinds my vision and, through half-closed eyes, I can just make out a silhouetted figure in the doorway.

'Chris?'

The room light flicks on and I'm surprised to see an elderly woman in a nightgown stood in the doorway. Her eyes widen, and she releases a bloodcurdling scream when she sees me lying on her bed with my top off. Scrambling off the bed, I pull my T-shirt over my head and immediately try to calm her down, but she continues to shriek insanely. She begins shouting at the lump in the bed, and I turn and see the frightened face of a man with a baldhead peering cautiously over the duvet. The woman continues to scream while the bald guy continues to cower beneath the covers.

'I thought he was my brother!' I yell. 'I thought this was my room!'

The woman on reception suddenly appears at the door and barks at me in Estonian. I quickly try to explain that I've made a mistake. She doesn't seem to understand. The old lady in the nightgown clutches onto the receptionist's arm and begins to pant breathlessly. She seems to be on the verge of hyperventilating, so the receptionist helps her onto a chair in the corner of the room. I try to explain to the receptionist what has happened, but she just scowls at me as she tries to calm the old woman down.

'*Wrong room!*' I shout. '*I got the wrong room!*'

Chris suddenly pokes his head around the door. 'What the fuck are you doing?'

'I got the wrong room! This isn't our room!'

'I know it's not. Our room is next door, you idiot!'

'Fuck! Chris, it wasn't my fault! I thought this was our room. All the doors look the same in this place. I thought it was you in the bed.'

'I've only just got back to the hotel myself, you prick.'

'*HELP ME, YOU MOTHER FUCKER!*'

The old lady begins to scream again, but we eventually manage to calm everyone down and explain exactly what has happened. From the way the receptionist scowls at us, you can tell she thinks we're little more than two stupid drunken tourists with no consideration for other people, whilst the old couple glare at us with disgust. With bright red faces, we edge our way out of the room. Nosy guests in their jim-jams poke their heads out into the corridor as we return shamefully to our room.

'What the fuck!' Chris laughs, falling onto his bed.

'Oh my God,' I cringe, biting my fingernails. 'Did that really just happen?'

'I'm afraid so, hippie boy.'

I pace up and down the room, sweating profusely. 'Christ, I feel so bad.'

'I can't believe you got the wrong room! Your face was hilarious.'

'We need to get the hell out of here … yeah, that's what we should do … shit, I'm still pissed.'

'Chill out! We're all right for a few more hours.'

'I thought it was our room. You were snoring. I thought it was you beneath the covers. Fuck, this is bad, so very-very bad. I feel really guilty. One of them could've had a frigging heart attack. Right, we have to leave, Chris. I'm not staying around here … no way! They probably thought I was robbing them. Oh, that poor woman's face when she saw me.'

'Come on, Si, people must make the same mistake all of the time.'

'Do you reckon?'

'Actually … probably not.'

'*BOLLOCKS!* We need to leave immediately.'

'Si, relax. It wasn't your fault. Come on, it must be after seven, let's grab some breakfast. I think we both need it.'

Racing frantically around the room, we throw everything into our rucksacks and make our way cautiously towards reception. We make our final apologies and head sheepishly for the exit.

Unavailable Funds

After a hearty breakfast and two hundred cups of coffee, we flee Parnu and arrive in the capital city of Tallinn around noon. Finding a car park near to the Ferry Disaster Memorial, we smarten ourselves up and go for a stroll through the enchanting Old Town. Desperately trying to avoid the hoards of tourists, we wander around the castle walls and admire the tall church spires and restored medieval buildings, which spring out at every turn. Si takes my photo in front of the Alexander Nevsky Cathedral, and we watch playful actors dressed in 14th century costumes entertaining the crowds in the colourful Town Hall Square. Shattered from lack of sleep, Si quickly develops sightseeing overload, and happy to drive I let him snore away in the passenger seat as we leave Tallinn and head closer and closer to Narva - the gateway to Russia.

Hurtling along the Tallinn-Narva highway through the Lahemaa National Park, I begin to feel nervous as we approach a country that conjures up a million images of Lenin and Stalin, the cold war, the KGB, Red Square, concrete tower blocks and freezing cold weather. When I was a kid I remember watching Boris Yeltsin on the news climb on top of a tank during the coup in 1991, and seeing footage of the queues of people in Moscow as Russia opened its first McDonald's. Throughout my life Russia has been a place of danger and mystery, and approaching the border myself for the first time absolutely scares the living shit out of me.

We arrive in Narva, Estonia's easternmost border town, just as it's beginning to get dark, which seems incredible considering it's nearly eleven o'clock at night. Si spots a 24-hour petrol station on the edge of town, and we park up for the night next to a Russian articulated lorry.

Snuggling inside my lovely warm sleeping bag, I find myself worrying about money. This is a very rare occurrence for me. In fact, it's something I don't do enough.

'Hey, Si,' I whisper into the darkness.

'Yeah?'

'Money!'

'What about it?' he grumpily replies.

'How much have we got?'

Si opens one eye. 'What are you talking about? Go to sleep.'

'No, it's important. How much money have you got on you?'

He stirs. 'Don't know.'

'Check.'

'Why?'

I sit up and flick on the interior light. 'We can't cross into Russia without money.'

'Turn off the bloody light. I'll check tomorrow.'

'Best do it now.'

'Chris, sort it out tomorrow, you annoying prick!'

'We have to be prepared if we're going to cross the border early. I'm going to get some cash out now, I can see an ATM just over there.'

'Do what you like.'

Unzipping my sleeping bag, I fall out of the Sierra and gently close the door behind me. It's cold outside and extremely quiet. There's no one around, just five rusty lorries parked up nearby. I fold my arms and make my way quickly across the forecourt. Approaching the cash machine, I reach inside my pocket and slip my bankcard out of my wallet. The Cirrus logo glows above the keypad as I feed my card into the slot and glancing quickly over my shoulder, I speedily enter my pin number. On the display it prompts me to select the amount I wish to withdraw, I choose 3,000 kroons, which is approximately one hundred pounds. Starring at the display, I wait impatiently for the machine to kick-start into life and spit out my cash, but nothing happens. I continue to wait, but it seems to be taking longer than usual. My heart begins to beat faster and suddenly my worst fears are presented to me – fears that haunted me throughout my college days. The words "*UNAVAILABLE FUNDS*" scream out at me.

'*Unavailable funds!*' I spit. 'What the fuck?'

I look over my shoulder again before pressing the cancel button. My card pops out and I try once more – slowly this time. The same thing happens. I glaze over and my legs turn to jelly. Something must be wrong with the machine. Maybe it doesn't accept Cirrus? But it says it does. Maybe it's my card? Maybe my bank has fucked up? Maybe someone has got hold of my bank details and stole all my money? Maybe ... and this is just a wild guess, maybe I've spent it all? Shit! Yeah, that must be it. I've spent all of my fucking money. Sliding the card back into my wallet I return to the Sierra, feeling totally confused. I climb into the car and stare out of the window.

Si turns to me, and frowns. 'What's the matter with you?'

'You're not gonna believe this.'

'What's the matter?'

'It's my money.'

Si whips off his woolly hat and sits up. 'What about it? Oh, shit. You've just checked your bank balance, haven't you? What's the damage ... five hundred quid left?'

I shake my head. 'Not quite.'

'How much, then?'

'Uh...'

'You're not at your limit already, are ya?'

I look away.

'*What?* Couldn't you get any money out?'

I shake my head. 'Nope.'

'But I thought you'd paid off your overdraft?'

'Yeah, I did.'

'Well ... where's it all fucking gone, you idiot?'

'I don't know, do I? I've got seven-hundred quid of it in Traveller's cheques.'

'And what's your limit?'

'One thousand five hundred pounds.'

'Well, that should leave you with eight hundred quid.'

'Yeah, but there were a few costs before we left and we've been spending quite a lot, haven't we?'

'Chris, you can't have spent eight hundred quid!'

'Hmm ... I could have.'

'You dumb-ass! Will you ever have any money?'

'Fuck off, Si! At least I'm not a tight arse like you, counting every penny like an old miser.'

'Hey, I'm not shy getting it out when the moments rocking.'

We sit in silence for a second.

'Well, I'm not lending you jack shit,' Si mutters. 'This is what happened in Mexico, remember?'

'Keep your mullet on! You lent me two hundred quid and I paid you back immediately.'

Si winds down his window and takes a deep breath. 'You should keep an eye on your finances.'

'Don't lecture me!'

'I'm not.'

'It's none of your business, anyway.'

'It is my business, especially when I'm the one who has to bail you out all the time.'

'You don't have to give me a penny. I'm fine!'

'I don't believe it, Chris. We're not even in Russia yet and you've already run out of money.'

'I haven't run out of money! I've got seven hundred quid in Traveller's cheques.'

'Doesn't that have to get you back home as well, though?'

'I suppose, but I'll worry about that when we get there.'

'What, when you get to the other side of the frigging world?'

'Uh ... yeah.'

* * *

The alarm on Chris's watch wakes me with a start. It's 4:30am and it's starting to get light. I drive through the deserted streets and follow signs to the border, which annoyingly take us on a five-mile diversion around the outskirts of town. Dipping under a low bridge, we burn past a large factory before picking up the signs again. Weaving through the back streets of Narva, we eventually approach an official checkpoint. Jumping out of the car, I walk over to a small booth and proceed to have a very confusing conversation with the woman sat inside. She waves to her colleague, who dashes over and explains to us that we need to go to another place to get a form. Making some space for him on the back seat, we feed the dude sweets as he directs us to a small brick building at the far end of a car park. We queue up behind a dozen old Larda's, and he leads me across the car park to the office. The official inside the small office stamps our documents and gives me a receipt of some kind. Our personal escort chats to the official and they both begin to laugh. I get the distinct impression they're laughing at my hair.

Back at the other checkpoint, our documents are stamped and we're pushed right through. We proceed to drive onto the Friendship Bridge, which stretches across the Narva River, and join a long queue behind the same Larda's as before. We look in awe as the sun begins to rise over the Russian town of Ivangorod. I climb out of the car and admire the two huge castles that face each other on either side of the river. It's an amazing sight to see and a clear reminder of Estonia and Russia's medieval past.

After about twenty minutes, car engines begin to splutter into action along the line. We jump back in the car and inch slowly towards the barrier. It isn't long before we reach the front of the queue. Popping the bonnet, I wait patiently for the official to inspect our vehicle. Everything seems to be in order, and waving us through we pull up at yet another booth, where our passports and customs declaration form for the car are checked over. The stocky woman behind the counter shouts at me in Russian, but I don't understand what she's saying. Pointing aggressively at the entry stamp, she looks at her watch and points back in the direction of Estonia. Realising she wants to know when we will be leaving the country, I quickly scribble down a rough date of about two months. She mutters something and sends me away with a flick of her wrist.

Exiting the final barrier we crawl along a bumpy road, and as if by magic we suddenly find ourselves on Russian soil.

We made it!' Chris laughs, swinging his door open. 'We're in bloody Russia!'

'Don't get out,' I cry, grabbing his arm.

'Why not?'

'There's probably bandits hiding around here somewhere, waiting for dumb-ass tourists to cross the border with all of their cash.'

'What cash?'

'OK, all of *my* cash.'

Ignoring me, Chris jumps out of the car and begins dancing around. An old man cycles past on a rusty bicycle and stares at him suspiciously. He looks like a peasant farmer from the 1800's.

'We're in *Russia!*' Chris sings spinning around and touching the ground.

'This is going to be well and truly fucked up!' I shout out of the window. 'What the hell do we do now?'

Chris jumps back into the car. 'Head for St Petersburg, of course. We have to register our visas within three working days.'

'How far is St Petersburg?'

'About a hundred miles.'

'We're a hundred miles away from St Petersburg?'

'Uh-huh.'

'Excellent!'

PART 2

Land of the Tsars

Feeling brave, I shove Si into the passenger seat and take the wheel. We quickly find the M11 and experience Russian roads for the first time, with a quiet country drive along a potholed stretch of tarmac that is in urgent need of repair. A white Larda suddenly appears in the rear view mirror. It seems to be quite a distance behind us, but when I look again I notice it has picked up speed and is now kissing our bumper. With a sharp swerve it overtakes, I dab the brakes and let it pass. The driver slows down again and chasing its rear-end for a while, I wonder if the dude is playing some sort of a game. Perhaps he wants to check out this foreign machine with the strange license plates, or he's just intrigued to see the faces of the people inside. Not wishing to disappoint him, I put my foot to the floor and begin to overtake the little car, but the driver of the Larda begins to speed up. Head to head, I'm forced to either drop down a gear and give it some welly or slow down. I choose to give it some welly, and impressed by the Sierra's monstrous acceleration we zoom off into the distance. I watch with satisfaction as the little car shrinks in the wing mirror. All of a sudden, I see a car heading towards us with its headlights flashing.

'Oh shit, it's the GAI!' Si screams, as the driver of the car waves a black and white baton furiously out of his window.

'The G.A.Y?'

'The GAI, you idiot! They're the traffic police … they're corrupt as fuck!'

'What shall we do?'

Si shrugs. 'How the hell should I know? Where are the documents?'

'In the glove box.'

Slamming on the brakes, I swerve to the side of the road and park up next to a goat in a field. The police vehicle swings around and comes to a halt behind the Sierra. The officer climbs out of the tiny vehicle, which is also an old box shaped Larda, and approaches the car. He's incredibly short and has a scary moustache.

'Dobraye ootra,' he mutters, peering through my open window.

Si flicks through the phrasebook and stops at a page. 'Dobraye ootra … dobraye ootra? Ah-ha, he's saying good morning!'

We both turn to him and flash a smile. 'Dobraye ootra,' we sing in unison.

The officer frowns before indicating for me to get out of the car. Si hands me the phrasebook. Feeling a little nervous, I peer down at the guy who begins to rant at me in Russian. Trying to look as confused as possible, which isn't difficult, I point at the phrasebook and shrug my shoulders. The officer stops talking and studies the GB sticker and the registration plate at the back of the car.

'Kooda vi eedyotye?' he mutters.

I shake my head and shrug my shoulders. He sighs.

Si sticks his head out of the window. 'Tell him you don't speak Russian.'

I flick through the phrasebook. 'Ya plokha gavaryoo parooskee.'

The officer nods and pulls a map of Russia out of his jacket. He shows it to me and I quickly point to St Petersburg.

'Spaceeba,' he smiles, slipping the map back into his

pocket. 'Passport.'

I unzip my money belt and hand him my passport. He studies my visa for a moment before passing it back. Waving me over to the cop car, he indicates for me to get inside. I'm not scarred for some reason, and as I squeeze my body inside his dwarf-mobile I smile at the other officer sitting in the front passenger seat. I try to get comfy in the back and battle to push my lanky legs behind the driver's seat. My new GAI buddy proceeds to show me a series of cards displaying speed limit signs. I nod and try to look serious, which is virtually impossible when it feels like I'm having a driving lesson with two dwarfs in a noddy car. After a few minutes the lesson is over, and as a kind gesture they make me pay fifty dollars for driving 55mph in a built up area. Reluctant to pay, I can't see anyway out without being dragged down the station, so I return to the car and fetch the money. With huge grins, the officers don't hang around to socialize and speeding out onto the highway, they leave me at the side of the road in a cloud of dust.

'Bastards!' I cry, climbing behind the wheel.

'Fifty dollars!' Si replies. 'If that happens to us everyday, we're fucked! Did you try and negotiate? Did you get a receipt?'

'Si, I haven't just bought a pair of slacks, we've been fined!'

'I know, but you're supposed to get a receipt.'

'Well, I didn't get one. Oh, fuck it, I was speeding in a built up area, anyway. They caught me red handed.'

Si looks around, and frowns. 'A built up area? What, two sheds and a goat?'

We look over at the goat and burst out laughing.

'You should have seen your face in that little car, it was hilarious!' Si laughs. 'You looked like a naughty giant being told off by two gnomes.'

Pissed off, but amused, we head back on the road feeling

bar

135

much wiser about the importance of sticking to the road rules. As we draw closer to St Petersburg, the conditions of the highway improve - unfortunately the traffic doesn't. Wary of the speed limit, we approach a GAI checkpoint in the suburbs of the city. Half a dozen officers stand at the roadside with their batons at the ready, but much to our relief we skip by without being stopped.

'Phew, that was lucky,' I grin. 'We'll have to make sure we keep an eye out for them. It's going to get hard now, so plenty of team work, OK?'

'No worries, Maverick,' Si salutes, 'I'll be your wingman anytime!'

We high-five 'Top Gun' style.

'Thanks, Iceman.'

Si frowns. 'I thought Goose was Maverick's wingman?'

'Nah ... Goose was Maverick's co-pilot, but he dies.'

'Yeah, but isn't Iceman his wingman at the end?'

I shrug. 'Fuck knows. "Maverick's a wild card, he flies by the seat of his pants"'.

'Well, I don't want to be either of them, anyway. I want to be Maverick. Pull over and I'll take the hot seat.'

I'm surprised by Si's request. 'You want to drive through St Petersburg?'

'Yeah.'

'Are you sure?'

He nods enthusiastically. 'Sure I'm sure.'

We quickly switch places.

'Right, Chris, you are now the navigator. Your job is very important, the smallest mistake and who knows what could happen. My life is in your hands. I trust you, so make me proud.'

'You what?'

'Just read the map. All you have to do is keep your eyes peeled for the street names and a big river.'

'Yes, sir!' I salute.

Relaxing, I sit back and enjoy the view as we roll

through the industrial suburbs of the city. Concrete tower blocks and rusty railway tracks stretch in every direction, and as we head closer to the city centre we begin to see the European architecture that had once given the city its reputation. Crawling through the traffic, Si does well to match the aggression of his fellow road users and working hard as his second pair of eyes, I point out trams hurtling in our direction or traffic lights that have suddenly turned red. Somehow Si's determination to push on into the heart of the city pays off, and stumbling across the main shopping street named Nevsky prospekt, we find ourselves driving through St Petersburg.

'No one's going to fuck with me in this car!' Si cries. 'I mean, who's going to come off worse in a battle between a Larda and a Ford Sierra. They've got no chance!'

'Hey, look! McDonald's in Russian.'

Si steals a quick glance. 'Cool!'

We decide to stay the night at the HI St Petersburg Hostel, which is located a few streets back from Nevsky prospekt and the train station. In the guidebook it says that the staff are 'preternaturally friendly' and all prices include breakfast … perfect! What more could two knuckleheads want?

Chasing a Ghostbusters style ambulance, Si turns right and hurtles down a back street.

'That's the road we want,' I cry. 'Take another right.'

Crawling down a residential street, Si pulls over at the side of the road and snatches the guidebook off my lap.

'The HI St Petersburg Hostel,' Si mutters. 'It's number … there it is!'

'Good lad, I'll go and check it out. Stay with the car.'

Racing inside the tatty building, I slide up to the reception desk and make my presence known to the middle-aged woman, who's wearing a burgundy-coloured jacket with enormous shoulder pads.

'Dobraye ootra,' I smile.

The woman looks down at her watch.

'Dobriy dyen,' she replies sternly. 'It is the afternoon.'

'So it is. Doesn't time fly when you're having fun.'

The woman frowns. 'How can I help you?'

I whip my passport out of my money belt. 'I'd like a room for two people, please.'

'Yes, that is no problem.'

'Great. We also need to register our business visas.'

She drops her smile. 'No business visas, only holiday visas.'

'Oh. Not even if we stay in the hostel?'

'No business visas.'

'I see. Well, can you recommend a hotel in the area that does?'

She shakes her head. 'Nyet.'

Her rudeness surprises me. Why is a business visa such a taboo? I mean, what's the big deal? The woman turns away and begins shuffling bits of paper on the desk. So much for being "preternaturally friendly", I've got a good mind to stuff her shoulder pads up her frigging arse. I leave the building and run back to the car.

'What'd you mean she wouldn't do it?' Si cries.

'As soon as I mentioned business visas she went all weird.'

'Why?'

'Dunno.'

'Fuck it, then. We'll just have to find somewhere else.'

Scanning through the guidebook, the only place that promises to register business visas is one of the larger hotels. Si selects a hotel nearby and we head through the streets to the Hotel Oktyabrskaya, a grand white building situated opposite the Moscow train station on Ligovsky prospekt. We pull up outside.

'Oh, come on!' I cry. 'Look at it! This place is going to be well expensive.'

'Well, what else are we gonna do?' Si replies. 'Let's at

least check it out.'

Si dashes inside the hotel and returns ten minutes later with a skip in his step.

'We got a room!' he grins.

'How much?'

'Ah … uh … you're not going to like it, but I had to take an executive decision on this one.'

'Si, how much?'

'One hundred and twenty pounds.'

'*What?*'

'Don't panic, big guy, think about it. If we'd stayed at that other place our own room would've been at least twenty or thirty pounds and they would have charged another twenty to register the visas. They do it for free here. Also, we probably would've had to pay another twenty pounds for parking the car somewhere safe overnight, so there's sixty already. This is an extra thirty each on top and we get to stay in luxury for once in our lives.'

'But a hundred and twenty quid, that's shit loads!'

'Chris, think of it as set up costs. After tonight we can sleep on the road. It didn't help that she made me take the executive suite. She probably thinks I'm here on business because of my business visa.'

'Ha, that's a joke! You look more like a student. I really don't think she would've mistaken you for being here on business.'

'Piss off! I could work in the music industry for all she knows.'

'The music industry? I don't think so somehow.'

Grabbing our bags from the boot, we race up the wide concrete steps and shuffle through the revolving doors. The reception area is huge, with grand chandeliers hanging from the enormous decorative ceiling. Two meathead doormen watch us suspiciously as we make our way over to the enormous marble reception desk. We sign-in, and the receptionist hands over the room key. Bumbling inside the plush lift, we make our way to the second floor and find our room. It's a huge suite with a separate lounge area, and bouncing on the beds we celebrate our arrival in the land of the Tsars.

* * *

Leaving Chris to chill out in the room, I skip out of the hotel and go in search of food. Marching through the busy streets of St Petersburg, I cross ploshchad Vosstania and stubble across a large outdoor market. Small kiosks selling beer, cigarettes and fast food run down the centre of a pedestrian street. I notice a stand selling whole roasted barbecued chickens, and after watching them for a moment turning on their skewers I dive inside my pockets and claim the largest bird. It only costs a few pounds, and happy with my purchase I grab some beer and cigarettes before returning to the hotel. Passing the Sierra, I smile at the sight of our old banger parked up outside the grand entrance to the hotel. It looks so out of place next to the brand-spanking new vehicles parked either side. Trotting up the steps I nod at the mean faced doorman, who proceeds to eyeball me all the way over to the elevator with my greasy chicken. Choosing the stairs for fear of stinking out the lift, I propel myself to the second floor and make my way quickly down the corridor. Pressing the bell outside our room, I hear Chris fumbling with the lock. He swings open the door.

'What did you get?' he beams.

Stripped down to his pants, he stands in the doorway covered in sweat. Following him inside, I stand at the bathroom door and watch in amusement as he begins dunking a T-shirt in the gigantic bathtub.

I frown. 'What the hell are you doing?'

Chris laughs like an excited kid at bath time. 'I'm washing me clothes!'

Scratching the back of his head with irritation, he leaves a crest of soapsuds in his hair.

'It's fucking hard work. I'm boiling!' he cries.

'Jesus Christ, the pikey brothers stay in a posh hotel.'

'Well, what else am I supposed to do?'

'Use the hotel laundry service, you freak.'

'Fuck off, Si! Have you seen how much they charge for laundry? It's about fifty-pence a sock.'

Laughing, I walk from the entrance hall into the extravagant main room and place the chicken on the glass coffee table. Chris appears a few minutes later and begins draping his wet clothes around the room; hanging them from every chair, door handle and window catch in sight. He flicks the sweat from his forehead before plonking himself down on the large corner sofa.

'This is great,' he grins, dabbing his face on one of the hotels fluffy white towels. 'Luxury at last!'

Tucking into the chicken, I grab a couple of chunky glasses from the bathroom and crack-open the two-litre bottle of beer.

'Not bad, hey?' I smile, pouring some into a glass.

'Nice one, Si. Where did you get all this from?'

'There's an outdoor market around the corner.'

'Cool, a feast fit for a king.'

'I still can't believe this room.'

'Worth every penny,' Chris beams. 'Look at it … it's *huge*!'

Running over to the towering windows, Chris throws open the floor-to-ceiling drapes. 'You can see the Sierra from here.'

'This is what it must be like to be a rock star.'

Chris frowns. 'What, eating a greasy chicken and drinking cheap beer?'

'No, you twat! I mean, hanging out in a glamorous hotel

room. We should make the most of tonight - invite some sexy honeys back to our suite and snort cocaine off their butt cheeks.'

'Do you reckon?'

'Why not?'

Downing the entire bottle of the super strength beer, we hang around the room all afternoon pretending to be rock stars. We make plans to "tear this city apart", but switching on the TV we stretch out on our comfortable beds and within seconds we're both fast asleep. Rock 'n' Roll!

Sunlight streams through the window. I climb out of bed like an old man and flick on the TV. It's 6:27am. I haven't slept this well for years. It almost feels quite strange to experience such comfort. The soft texture of the white cotton sheets remind me of a woman's bed, and I begin to realise that my circumstances of late have driven me to lead a very basic existence. I had by no means ever lived in extravagant luxury. In fact, since leaving home the only furniture I had bought was a broken futon and a wobbly table from Ikea. Until recently, my bed sheets were the same ones I'd used since I was a teenager, and since travelling I had even exchanged those for a tatty sleeping bag.

Making my way into the bathroom, I pull the chunky brass lever at the end of the bathtub. Water gushes from the large showerhead. I take Warren's advice and quickly check it for any brown scuffmarks before slipping off my boxer shorts. The water engulfs me, and using the free exfoliating shower gel supplied by the hotel in a small plastic bottle, I pour some into the palm of my hand and rub it over my body. Washing away the soapy grit I feel like a snake that has just shed its skin, and dancing across the heated marble bathroom floor, I'm embraced by the warmth of an enormous bath towel. Slipping on a robe, I brush my teeth and shave my patchy stubble in the large mirror. Studying my face, I grin at the fresh faced boy staring back at me and realise that a touch of luxury every now and then certainly rejuvenates the soul, although, the satisfaction of getting dirty first makes it all the more enjoyable. Disturbed by my cheerful whistling, Chris grumpily makes his way into the bathroom and returns seconds later humming the same tune.

We step into the elevator and make our way down to breakfast. I feel clean and powerful and arriving in the dining hall on the ground floor, we gasp at the sight of the banquet of food laid out in front of us. Chefs wearing tall white hats cook everything from omelets, sausages, bacon and fried bread on command. There's an entire table dedicated to an enormous selection of cold meat and cheese and another piled high with fresh fruit and juice, French bread, croissants, toast, five flavours of jam, honey, marmalade, cereals, tea, coffee and hot chocolate.

Chris looks at me in utter bemusement. 'Is this all for us?'

'Yes indeed, fat boy. Tuck in, we need to try and get our money's worth.'

Loading up our plates with a full English breakfast, we return for the continental. Chris piles a plate high with meat and cheese, and carefully manages to balance a couple of yogurts on top. Returning for seconds and thirds, we eat and eat and eat and pausing only for a cigarette, we find room for more sausages and bacon before loading up our pockets with packets of biscuits and fruit.

Feeling a little nauseous, we waddle out of the dining hall and return to the room to let our food digest. We hang around in luxury for a few more hours before checking out at 12 o'clock midday on the dot. The slim, assertive girl on reception hands back our passports and informs us that our business visas are now valid. Dumping our bags in storage we use the free one-hour internet voucher, which the receptionist gave us on arrival when checking in, and quickly let our family and friends know we've arrived. After checking our emails we exit the revolving doors and head out into the street.

'Wow, St Petersburg!' Chris cries. 'Here there shall be a town.'

'You what?'

'It's what Peter the Great said when he first set foot on the Baltic coast.'

'Done your homework, then.'

'Absolutely.'

Trying to gauge our bearings on a tourist map, I flip it upside down and identify the direction we need to go.

'Right, Chris, if we cross this mother of a road we'll be on Nevsky prospekt where all of the shops and monuments are.'

'Sounds good to me.'

Waiting for a gap in the traffic, we make a run for it and skip quickly past the ploshchad Vosstania Metro Station. Elegant buildings, five to six stories high, tower above us on either side of the street, and picking up pace we observe the Russian street life all around us. Smartly dressed women hop on and off trams and serious looking men rush by in the street, with their hands in their pockets and a cigarette protruding from their mouths. Crossing the Fontanka Canal, we pass the Catherine the Great Statue and eventually come to the huge Gostiny Dvor Department Store where we buy a road atlas that covers the entire road network for Russia and Siberia. Chris stocks up on camera film and deciding to do a spot of sightseeing we head further up Nevsky prospekt, which was once one of the grandest boulevards in the whole of Europe. Passing a stream of colourful shops, galleries and banks, we turn left and pause outside the Grand Hotel Europe, one of the most lavish hotels in Russia. A beautiful reconditioned racing green Auston Martin is parked outside. A banner draped across the hotel's main entrance reads "The London to St Petersburg Classic Car Rally". Looking up at the elegant balcony, a group of well-dressed gentlemen in tweed chatter and laugh noisily as they smoke cigars and drink champagne above our heads.

'I wonder if they've just arrived?' Chris mutters.

'Dunno. It's surprising we didn't see them on the road.'

'Maybe they only got here this morning.'

'Which means we beat them!' I smile.

Chris draws an invisible banner in the air. '"The Daventry to Vladivostok Ford Sierra Rally".'

I smile. 'Hmm ... it doesn't quite have the same ring to it.'

Through the open doorway of the hotel, I can see a sweeping marble staircase and a reception filled with highly polished antique furniture. Everything gleams.

'It's mad to think they're celebrating the end of their journey already, isn't it?' Chris smiles. 'I mean, they've only just got here. What about the rest of Russia?'

I shake my head. 'Rich fools.'

We continue further along Nevsky prospekt and quickly come to the Griboedova Canal. Looking down the street, we gasp at the sight of the multi-domed Church of the Resurrection of Christ, which sits in its entire splendor on the banks of the canal. Chris whips out his camera and takes a few snaps of the gold, blue and white patterned onion domes on top of the towering Cathedral, apparently designed to imitate the romance of a candle flame.

'What an amazing city,' I sigh. 'Do you think the rest of Russia will be anything like this?'

'I flipping hope not,' Chris frowns. 'We've spent a shagging fortune!'

'I'm sure once we're away from the main cities things will be a lot cheaper. Vologda sounds interesting - we should head there. What time is it now?'

'It's nearly three o'clock.'

'We need to get moving, there's no way we can afford to stay here another night.'

'Yeah, you're right. Come on!' Chris waves. 'To the Raven Mobile!'

Animal Farm

Like Batman and Robin, we leap into the Sierra and speed off through the heavy traffic. Before we know it we're on the M18, a three-lane highway that carries us out of the city and over the Volga River, the longest river in Europe. The road quickly becomes a potholed nightmare as we skim alongside the enormous Lake Ladoga.

'Hey, let's go to the Arctic!' Chris cries, as he swerves dangerously around a deep crater in the tarmac.

'You what?'

'If we drive for eight hundred miles up this road, we'll end up at the Barents Sea in the Arctic Circle.'

'Really?'

'Uh-huh. Imagine how cool that would be? At this time of year it's daylight pretty much twenty four hours a day - we could ride reindeers at two o'clock in the morning!'

'That's impossible.'

Chris shakes his head. 'No it's not, there's loads of reindeers around Murmansk.'

'No, I mean it's impossible to drive to the Arctic Circle and to Vladivostok, there's no way we can do both.'

'Come on! Where's your sense of adventure?'

'Chris, we'll be lucky if the Sierra makes it past the Ural Mountains, let alone all the way up to the frigging Arctic Circle.'

'OK, but imagine in forty-years time, my Grandchildren

sitting on my knee in front of the open fire and asking, "Grandfather, why didn't you go to the Arctic Circle? You were so close - why didn't you go?" and I'd reply, "Well, kids, because your Great Uncle is a fucking idiot!" and they'd reply, "What's a fucking idiot, Grandfather?"'

'Forget about it, Chris. The Arctic Circle will still be there in a few years time. You can do it then. This time round our mission is Vladivostok.'

Feeling happy that we're making tracks, I munch on a bruised apple and watch the pine trees flash by as Chris turns onto the A114. It's still light at ten o'clock and even though the sun has been setting around eleven thirty for the past few days, I'm still not used to it yet. We spend the night in the car outside an old petrol station and exhausted after our day in St Petersburg, I zip my sleeping bag up to my neck and drift off to sleep.

The sound of a truck's engine wakes me with a start. I poke my head out of my sleeping bag and look at the time. It's seven o'clock and I'm ready for breakfast. The truck parked up on the forecourt cuts out, and a man in a blue shirt and jeans begins to fill it up with diesel. An excited kid jumps around in the driver's cab, maybe the guy's son who has joined him on one of his journeys. After taking a look under the bonnet, the guy slams it shut and jumps back into the truck. He cranks it into gear and roars off. The kid excitedly presses his face up against the window and stares at me as they pass by.

Falling out of the car, I stretch my aching body and rub my sore eyes. Chris tears open a packet of biscuits and quickly butters some rolls. The petrol station is eerily quiet, there doesn't seem to be anyone around. Pulling up by a petrol pump, we decide to grab some fuel before we head back on the road to Vologda. Grabbing the hose I feed it into the tank. Nothing happens, so I hook it back in place and walk over to the little brick building with blacked out windows. Cupping my hands I peer through the glass, but all I can see is my puzzled face looking back at me in the reflection. Noticing a metal pole with a plastic handle jutting out from below the window, I take hold of it and find it's attached to a metal tray. It looks as though this might be how you pay for your petrol without having to see or speak to the person inside. You pull out the tray, put your money inside and slide it through the gap in the window. Now, if I'm not mistaken, this kind of set-up is either for really unsociable petrol station attendants, who can't be arsed to deal with customers face-to-face, or it's to prevent bloodthirsty bandits from robbing the joint. Deciding to give it a go, I place a 500-rouble note in the metal box and slide it inside. I'm surprised to hear a woman shouting at me from behind the glass, and a few seconds later the metal box comes flying back out at me. Leaping to one side, the metal bar misses my groin by a few millimeters. Confused and slightly offended by the attendant's aggression, I grab my money and return to the car.

* * *

We arrive in Vologda in the early afternoon to the sound of the Russian composer Yelena Firsova. It seems strange, but even though we're only a day's drive from the tourist hotspots of Moscow and St Petersburg, it already feels like we're deep within this alien world. The city of Vologda was the playground of Ivan the Terrible and is our first introduction to the Soviet years. The Kremlin with its silver onion domes dominates the skyline, as does the nearby golden spire of the St Sofia's Bell Tower. The Vologda River cuts through the city, and crossing town we pass the statue of Lenin close to the Market Square.

'What a beautiful place,' Si beams, as we make a loop

around the city.

'Yeah, this is the real Russia. Most tourists only see St Petersburg, Moscow and Red Square ... this is the real deal.'

It feels like the 1940's as we pass soldiers in full military uniform strolling down the street in the sunshine, with their oversized hats and long coats. The people look so different to anyone I have seen before, and I feel a rush of excitement as I drive through a city most people back home probably don't even know exists.

We go in search of the Sretenskaya Church Dorm, an old 1700's church that has been converted into a dormitory for students in the Ministry of Culture's study program. Recommended by the guidebook as the coolest and cheapest place to stay, it sounds right up our alley. Si directs me down a bumpy dirt track that runs parallel to the river, and in no time at all we pull up outside the old church. The building looks impressive from the outside with its whitewashed walls and grey domes.

'Chris, are you sure this is right?'

'I think so. On the map it's directly across the river from the Kremlin.'

'Great location.'

'Yeah, it looks a bit creepy, though, don't you think?'

We both look over towards the large wooden door at the bottom of the bell tower.

'Go and ask if there's a room for the night,' Si grins.

'Why me? You go.'

'Maybe we should look somewhere else. It's probably run by a bunch of religious freaks.'

'Yeah, sex starved nuns who haven't had any action for years.'

Si frowns. 'Do nuns have sex?'

'Russian nuns do, I'm sure of it.'

Locking up the car, we make our way over to the entrance of the church. The door creaks open and we step inside.

'Scooby-fucking-Doo, or what!' Si whispers, looking

nervously up the dimly lit staircase.

'Scooby-fucking-don't,' I reply, hesitating in the doorway.

Si pushes me in front. 'After you my good man, I'll be right behind ya.'

I shake my head and reluctantly begin to make my way up the narrow flight of stairs. It's dark and deafeningly quiet. Si hugs the wall as he follows close behind, and turning the corner at the top of the stairs I nearly shit my pants as a woman in a long blue dress jumps out in front of me.

'Kak deela?' the woman cries, her hair sticking up wildly.

'*JESUS CHRIST!*' I gasp, clutching my chest.

Si lets go of my hand and straightens his posture. 'Shit ... uh ... sorry, we've left our phrase book in the car.'

The woman frowns. 'Ya nee paneemayoo.'

'I'm-sorry-we-don't-understand,' he replies in a slow clear tone.

Suddenly, a tall guy with a neatly trimmed beard steps out of a room at the end of the corridor and walks over to us. He's dressed in a red roll neck sweater and beige corduroys.

'Would you like some help?' he asks with a French accent.

'You speak English, that's great,' Si beams. 'Thank God for that.'

'Yes, I speak a little English.'

He turns to the woman and says something to her in Russian. She nods and disappears down the stairs.

'You speak Russian, too!' Si grins.

'Of course,' he replies abruptly. 'We are in Russia. You are looking for a room?'

I nod. 'Yeah, just for tonight.'

'There are two beds free, please follow me.'

We follow him down the wooden corridor and turn into the first room on the left-hand side. We peer around the door into the … uh … kitchen-cum-dining area. It's a small room with two single beds - one against the wall and the other positioned under the window. The light isn't on and there are net curtains in front of the small window, so the room is dark and cold.

'Is this the room?' Si frowns.

The French guy nods. 'Yes. As you can see it is also the communal kitchen.'

A painfully skinny girl stands hunched over an ancient stove as she waits for the kettle to boil, and a man sits at a small table in the middle of the room and tucks into a plate of what can only be described as yellow vomit.

'Please, come inside,' the French guy smiles, waving us into the room.

We walk around the table and sit on the bed under the window. I glance over at the light switch and consider turning it on, but decide not to. The gaunt girl sits on the other bed and begins to merrily pick her toenails. The French guy with the beard grabs a chair and swings it over to us.

'So where have you come from?' he asks, wiping his mouth with a hanky.

'We've just driven here from St Petersburg,' Si replies.

'Formally known as Leningrad,' the guy quickly informs us. 'My name is Jon-Pierre by the way and these are my friends from the Russian Studies Program, Barbara and Carlos.'

The girl smiles vacantly, while the guy eating the vomit simply nods his head.

'What brings you to Vologda?' Jon-Pierre asks, stroking his facial hair.

'We're on our way to Vladivostok,' Si replies.

He laughs out loud. 'That's very funny … but seriously, what brings you here? Do you want to join the program?'

'No, we're on our way to Vladivostok,' Si repeats.

Jon-Pierre continues to stroke his beard, unsure if we're being serious or not.

'So, anyway, you like it here?' he asks changing the subject.

'Yeah, it's a beautiful city,' I reply.

'No, I mean Russia. You like it here in Russia?'

Si nods. 'Of course we do! I've never been anywhere like it before.'

'Do you know the history of Vologda?'

'Not a great deal,' I reply. 'I'm reading bits here and there in the guidebook.'

Jon-Pierre leans forward. 'Do you know about the history of communism?'

We both shrug.

'Only the basics,' Si smiles. 'We learnt a bit about it at school, and I've read Animal Farm.'

'Animal Farm?' I laugh. 'What's that got to do with communism?'

'Not *that* Animal Farm,' Si whispers. 'It's a novel by George Orwell.'

Jon-Pierre doesn't look impressed. 'I cannot believe you come to Russia and you do not know anything about its history.'

'Uh ... I beg your pardon,' Si snaps. 'I'm sorry, but it's none of your bloody business what we know and what we don't know about Russia. I mean, who the hell do you think you are?'

Jon-Pierre looks shocked by his reaction.

I nod in Si's defense. 'Yeah. Surely the best way to learn about a place is to go there and to see it with your very own eyes - absorb yourself in its culture.'

Jon-Pierre sighs. 'I meet many tourists who come to Russia, and their ignorance about its history offends me. I have been studying the end of communism for many years now; I can connect with the people. For example, what do you know about Boris Yeltsin?'

'He was a piss head,' I grin, hoping to spark a reaction.

Jon-Pierre doesn't smile.

'You see Carlos,' he calls over his shoulder. 'This is the kind of ignorance I was talking about. Yes, he liked a drink, but he was a great dictator. Boris Yeltsin ended communism. He said during a visit to the US in 1989 "Let's not talk about Communism. Communism was just an idea, just pie in the sky". He banned Communist Party cells from government offices and workplaces in Russia. He made Russia a free-market economy. His changes included the wiping out of state subsidies, freeing of prices, reduction in government spending and privatization of state businesses, housing, land and agriculture. He was committed and fought for the people of Russia and fought to make it a country of great visions. He created a path through the darkness and made it strong, so the people of Russia could eat bread, have fuel, sleep safely in their beds and be free.'

John-Pierre stares at us intently. The girl sitting on the bed continues to pick her toenails, and Carlos raises his bushy eyebrows at us before shoveling more of the vomit into his mouth.

Si applauds mockingly. 'Ooh, well aren't you clever. Which textbook did you memorize that from?'

Jon-Pierre looks outraged.

'I have read many books.'

'There's more to travel than history and politics, you know. Do you think the people of Russia really give a shit about how much you can tell them about their political history? It's what's happening in their lives now that really matters. Yes, we can see Russia is changing, yes, it's important to know what has happened in the past, but chill out, would ya. There's nothing more irritating than an intellectual with a chip on his shoulder - just be yourself!'

Clearly offended by Si's response, Jon-Pierre slams down his mug and exits the room. Relieved to see the back of the French twat, I take the opportunity to draw the net curtains away from the window. Sunlight floods into the room, and I sit back on the bed feeling finally relaxed. Carlos looks up from his plate and blinks in the light. Barbara just sits on the other bed and smiles.

'Would you like something to eat?' Carlos asks coyly.

'Oh, no thank you,' Si replies looking down at his plate. 'We've just eaten.'

'Sorry about Jon-Pierre, he's very passionate about his studies.'

'Yeah, so I see.'

'Have you seen much of Vologda?'

'No, we thought we'd find somewhere to stay first.'

'You should visit the St Sofia Cathedral, or stop by Stalin's Apartment where he once stayed. It's a pretty interesting city.'

'Oh, definitely,' Si nods. 'Where are you from, Carlos?'

'I'm Portuguese, but my mother is Russian. I thought it would be interesting to spend some time here and learn about where she is from.'

'Good idea, are you enjoying it?'

'Yes, I like it very much, although, the Russians are crazy people.'

Carlos walks over to the sink and rinses his plate under the tap. 'Well, we have to go now,' he grins, running his fingers through his black scruffy hair. 'We have an exam today.'

Barbara climbs off the bed and walks lazily over to the door.

'Good luck, it was nice meeting you,' Si waves.

We wait for them to disappear out of sight.

'What a fucking nightmare,' he cringes, looking around the room. 'They're all a bunch of frigging freaks!'

'Shall we leave?'

'There's no point, we're here now.'

'What's that Jon-Pierre's problem?'

Si shrugs. 'I don't know, but I was close to whacking the guy.'

'The dude's fucked in the head, isn't he?'

'Uh-huh, he's probably struggling to come to terms with his sexuality.'

I nod. 'Yeah, there's definitely something going on there, and that Barbara! She's got some serious issues. Not bad looking, though.'

Si screws up his face. 'You must be desperate, she's rank!'

'A bit crusty maybe, but nice titties.'

Si looks at me strangely. 'We must get drunk immediately!'

Coffee with the Cops

Disturbed by the clatter of pots, I open my eyes to a room buzzing with activity. Jon-Pierre butters toast by the sink, Barbara sits at the table picking her toenails and munching on a grape, Carlos is hunched over a plate of vomit and some other guy with long hair and glasses, who just looks weird, stares at me from the doorway. It takes me a few seconds to work out what exactly is going on, then, it suddenly occurs to me that I'm lying practically naked in a bed in the kitchen-cum-dinning-room, surrounded by a bunch of freaks. It's cold and dark in the room, but I can just about see daylight through the net curtains.

Jon-Pierre looks over at me. 'Hello, Chris, how are you this morning?'

I sit up and lean against the wall, feeling a little uncomfortable. 'Uh … yeah, I'm fine.'

'You sound a little croaky,' he mumbles, taking a small delicate bite out of a piece of toast.

'We had a few drinks last night at the Vologda Hotel.'

'I know. My room is next door to the kitchen, you were very noisy.'

Ignoring Jon-Pierre, I turn and catch Barbara looking at me strangely. All of a sudden the events of last night come flooding back. We had drunk far too much at the Vologda Hotel yesterday evening. Si had befriended a group of Russian businessmen at the bar and challenging them to a game of ten-pin bowling, one of the hotels many activities, we had quickly become involved in a highly competitive drinking game. We lost pretty severely and stumbling back to the church dorm around midnight, we crashed through the main door and proceeded to play a few 'Guns N' Roses' tunes with the creaky floorboards. If this wasn't bad enough, sometime in the small hours, Barbara had crept into the kitchen in her nightgown and climbed into bed with me. At first I'd tried to send her away, but she dipped her head under the covers and persuaded me otherwise.

I struggle to pull on my jeans inside my sleeping bag. It's all very embarrassing, and I smile as everyone in the room eats their breakfast and watches the circus monkey getting dressed. I eventually manage to get myself looking semi-decent, and despite my T-shirt being the wrong way round and inside out, I stumble across the room and wake Si up.

'Nice tits,' he groans, as I shake him from unconsciousness.

Carlos and Jon-Pierre snigger, both clearly enjoying the mornings free entertainment. We quickly gather all of our stuff together and head for the door. Clearing my throat, I squeeze past Barbara in the doorway and bidding our student friends farewell, Jon-Pierre smiles falsely as we head down the stairs to the car. Carlos, Barbara and the weird dude with the long hair and glasses follow us outside. Tossing my bag in the boot, I turn and jump in surprise as I see Barbara stood directly behind me. She looks extremely pale and thin in the daylight. Her eyes begin to well up and she suddenly leaps at me with both arms. Hanging around my neck and burying her head into my chest, she begins to make strange whimpering noises. I pat her lightly on the top of her head before gently loosening her grip. She won't let go of me, so I'm forced to grab her by the wrists and push her away. She stands back and glares at me with vacant eyes.

'I've got to go,' I smile awkwardly.

Tears begin to roll down her face.

'You've got my email address, right? Email me!'

She slowly nods her head and wipes a tear from her pale cheek. I run around to the passenger door and leap into the car.

'What the fuck was that all about?' Si cries, revving the engine.

'Shut up and drive!'

Si toots the horn, and releasing the handbrake we accelerate away. I feel immediately guilty as I see Barbara disappearing in the wing mirror.

'You didn't fuck her, did you?' Si asks suspiciously.

I choose to ignore the question.

'You did, didn't you!' he shrieks. 'You fucked her!'

* * *

With messy hair and puffy eyes, Chris sits in silence as we head south towards Yaroslavl on the M8. Driving deep into the rural countryside of European Russia, we pass through many small villages along the way. Pretty blue and green Hansel and Gretal style houses (made from wood rather than gingerbread) litter the roadside, all with intricately carved shutters around each of the many small windows. Hard-faced women wearing headscarves and flowery patterned dresses covered by a cardigan, gossip at the side of the road while carrying heavy buckets of grain and water for the life-stock. With their thick black stockings and wellington boots, they look like peasant farmers' wives from an age gone by. At this time of day there are very few men around, apart from the odd old boy staggering along the roadside all hunched over and wearing a suit jacket that certainly pre-dates World War II.

After a few hours on the road we eventually reach the

city of Yaroslavl, which sits to the east of the golden ring surrounding Moscow. We see more domed churches as we pass by, but keen to push on we cross the bridge over the Volga River and head east towards the industrial city of Ivanovo. Winding down some very narrow country lanes, we chase an old fella on a rusty moped and find our way back onto a red road. Fiddling with the radio, Chris finds a station playing Russian jazz and losing myself in the drive, I finally begin to feel more relaxed than I have since leaving England. Our worries of getting the Sierra into Russia are no longer a concern, and with thousands of miles of tarmac ahead of us before we reach the frontier of our journey, there is little left to do except switch off and simply enjoy our existence.

Driving for much of the day, we eventually reach Ivanovo in the early afternoon. Passing a large industrial power plant as we roll through the ugly concrete suburbs, I lose my bearings and become confused by the lack of road signs directing us through the city. Approaching a busy junction I hesitate for a second, unsure whether to turn left or right.

'Go!' Chris shouts. 'There's a police jeep next to us.'

'But which way?' I yell. 'Left or bloody right?'

The impatient driver of the car behind blasts his horn.

'Left ... *NO* ... right!'

'Right? It's one way, isn't it?'

Chris shrugs. 'I don't know!'

The commotion draws the attention of the police officer sat behind the wheel of the jeep, and he immediately signals for us to pull over.

'Not again!' Chris yells. 'There goes another fifty dollars down the pissing drain.'

I get out of the car and brace myself for some trouble. The police officer swaggers towards me and barks something in Russian.

'I'm sorry I...'

I look over my shoulder, expecting Chris to be stood behind me, but he's not and I quickly realise that I'm on my own. Snatching the documents out of my hand, he begins flicking through my passport. He finds the page with my photograph and makes brief eye contact before asking me another question in Russian.

I shrug my shoulders and grin helplessly. 'Nyet Rooskey.'

Shaking his head, he gestures for me to follow him over to his police vehicle. Opening the door to the old jeep, he flips the front seat forward and I climb into the back. He climbs behind the wheel and mutters something to the young cop in the front passenger seat. They both look at me and continue to exchange comments to each other in Russian. While the officer studies my papers, I take the opportunity to flick through my pocket phrasebook and turn to the page of useful phrases. He waves my passport in the air and starts speaking to me in Russian again, but I can only look at him blankly as he begins to laugh. Taking a wallet out of his pocket, he shows me a fifty-ruble note and I assume he wants money. Unprepared to argue I hand one over, which is approximately one pound sterling. This appears to relieve the tension a bit. Showing him the phrasebook, I point to the word for 'tourist'. He laughs again, and the young fresh-faced rookie sitting next to him looks at me with intrigue. The older cop's face is weather-beaten and from the many deep lines running across his forehead and across his cheeks, you can tell he likes to smoke the occasional cigarette. He looks stressed and tired, but drink probably helps him through the day. It seems immediately clear to me that fining people is a normal thing to do in this country, but then I guess who can blame them when they probably only get paid a few hundred dollars a month. Snatching the phrasebook out of my hand, the cop points to the word "nationality".

'Oh ... uh ... English,' I reply.

'Ah,' he laughs. 'Britaniya. How-do-you-do?'

Cracking a smile, I reach over and shake his hand. 'Yes, how-do-you-do, too?'

This breaks the ice and we all begin to laugh.

'David Beckham,' the young cop chips in.

'Yes! David Beckham,' I reply.'

Looking around the car, the older guy grins psychotically. 'Rooskey Jeep.'

'Da,' I nod, pressing the soft-top hood. 'Rooskey Jeep.'

He ejects a tape from out of the cassette player.

'Rok moozika!' he beams, handing it to me.

'For me?' I reply, pointing at my chest.

'Da, da!'

'Spaceeba,' I smile.

This sparks off the young lad, who reaches inside the glove box and fishes out a packet of banana flavoured condoms. He hands them to me and I study the packet with keen interest.

'Boom-boom,' the older officer nods, thrusting his hips back and forth.

This really amuses them and we all begin to slap our thighs and laugh in unison. I flick my wallet open and whip out two condoms, which I keep in the secret pocket at the back.

'For you,' I grin.

Fascinated, they both look at the writing on the packet and return grateful smiles. I can't believe I'm sitting in a police jeep in Ivanovo swapping condoms with a couple of Russian cops.

'Rooskey lady,' I grin, outlining the hourglass shape of a woman. 'Sexy!'

The young cop turns red and shyly avoids eye contact. The boss looks at me. 'Britaniya?' he replies making the sign for 'OK' with his fingers.

'Da...' I grin. 'Not bad.'

He turns to the kid, who continues to blush. All of a sudden another police vehicle pulls up beside us, and the older cop looks serious for a minute as he talks to his colleague out of the window. He starts the engine and moves the jeep closer to the Sierra.

Pointing at me and then at our car, he suggests we follow him. Opening the door, I jump out and hop back into the Sierra.

'What the fuck's going on?' Chris frowns.

'It's OK they're not the GAI, they want us to follow them, I think they're going to help us get out of the city.'

'Really?'

'Yeah, look! They gave me a packet of banana flavoured condoms.'

Chris's eyes light up. 'Excellent!'

Striking the engine, I indicate right at the junction and the cop overtakes me and pulls out into the road. He puts on his blue flashing lights and we're given a police escort through the city.

'This is insane,' Chris beams. 'I've never had a police escort before.'

'Hey, they gave me a Russian rock music tape, too. Try and remove that Cruising Tunes tape that's stuck in the tape player.

Chris forces a pen inside the tape slot, and wiggling it around vigorously he manages to pop it out. Following the cop's lead, I turn left into a small car park next to a run-down café.

Chris looks worried again. 'What's going on? I thought they were taking us out of the city?'

I shrug. 'Fuck knows. Maybe it's their local diner.'

We pull up next to the police jeep and jump out of the car. The cops walk over to the Sierra and study our vehicle.

'Ford,' the older cop smiles as he peers through the window.

Grabbing the Cruising Tunes tape from the dashboard, I hand it to the younger cop.

'Spaceeba,' he replies.

He slots it into his stereo and turns up the volume. 'Black Velvet' blasts from the speakers and the two cops bob their heads in time with the music. After walking around the Sierra a few times, the older cop points at the café and we lock-up our vehicles and head over to the run-down building. Stepping inside the small canteen, the cop walks up to the counter and greets the woman on the till. Everyone stops talking and looks over at us, but I feel safe in the company of the policemen. Following the young cop outside, we sit at a picnic bench beneath a green tarpaulin roof. Seconds later the waitress appears from the canteen with a tray of hot dogs and coffees. I whip out my wallet, but the older cop raises his hand and insists that he pay. Squirting mayonnaise onto our hot dogs, we all look at each other between mouthfuls of food and nod in agreement that it tastes good. Opening up the atlas on the table, Chris shows them our route from England on the map. They're fascinated by our journey and seem puzzled as to how we got the car across the water from England to France. Picking up the phrasebook the older cop studies it for a moment before pointing to the word "destination".

'Vladivostok,' Chris replies, sipping his coffee.

They look at each other in amazement.

The older cop points to Vladivostok on the map. 'Da?'

I nod. 'Da.'

They grin at each other and exchange comments. I find the word "married" in the phrasebook and point to the cops. They both nod. The young rookie has a baby and the older guy has three daughters. I offer cigarettes around the table and we all spark-up.

'Brother,' I enthusiastically announce pointing to Chris.

I quickly look up the word for "brother". 'Brat!'

'Brat?' The young kid smiles.

'Da.'

They both look surprised. I consider telling them we're

twins, but decide not to over complicate things.

Finishing our coffees we return to our vehicles. The older cop quickly fetches something from the police jeep. Overwhelmed by his generosity, he presents us with half a bottle of Russian vodka and his policeman's hat. The younger guy follows suit and removes his police tiepin and clips it to my fleece. Chris digs out a few English coins and a postcard of our hometown of Daventry from his rucksack. He writes a message on it thanking the cops for their hospitality. The older cop responds by taking the pen and writing down the side of the bottle of vodka in Russian "from the Ivanovo police department". Putting on their blue flashing lights again, the cops escort us out of the city and reaching the outer limits, they encourage us to fill up an empty bottle from an ancient water pump. Shaking their hands in turn we bid them a final farewell. Buzzing from drinking coffee and eating hot dogs with two Russian cops, we sound the horn and wave frantically out of the window as we head off on our journey once more.

With fresh legs we head east on the P152. Chasing the Volga River all the way to the city of Nizhny Novgord, we pass through its bustling streets and observe its inhabitants milling around the shops and market stalls. It feels cleaner and less repressed than Ivanavo and surprised by the abundance of attractive women with shoulder length blonde hair, I make a promise to myself to return here someday. Finding our way onto the M7 we continue along the Volga, passing through countless villages and tiny rural communities. Grumpy old ladies sell apples in multi-coloured plastic buckets at the roadside, and we avoid horse drawn carts as the farmers make the journey home after a long day at the market.

As we hurtle through the early evening, the sun begins to break through the clouds and enjoying the sensation of being on the road, we continue on heading deeper into

Russia towards the city of Kazan. Caught behind an old red Larda with a mountain of sheep's wool strapped to its roof like an enormous blonde afro-wig, Chris overtakes and we join a convoy of trucks as they transport goods east. Looping around Kazan on a dual carriageway, the sun slowly drops below the horizon behind our heads, filling the car with rich orange light that illuminates our faces. We pullover for the night at a truck stop and watch as Russia slowly fades to black.

Chasing the Trans-Siberian

My sleeping bag is wet on the outside and my breath is clearly visible. I flick on the heater, but quickly turn it off as cold air blows in my face. Si is still sound asleep, so I climb quietly out of the car and look into a new day. Despite a chilly wind, it's bright and fresh outside. I pull up my collars and look across the fields through a morning mist. Sandwiched in the middle of a line of trucks, which tower over the Sierra, I feel protected by their presence. Walking around to the back of the car I notice the truck to our right has a Kazakhstan registration plate, and I find myself trying to imagine what the guy might look like inside. Grabbing the cooking stove and the box of food from the boot, I put a pan of water on the boil and use the car door to shield it from the wind.

Si wakes up and looks over at the pan.

'What you doing?' he mumbles.

'Making breakfast!' I smile. 'I thought this morning I'd whip up something a bit more exotic.'

'It's not noodles again is it?'

'How'd you guess?'

'What flavour?'

'Chicken.'

'For fuck's sake, Chris! How about beef or pork for a change? Why does it always have to be frigging chicken?'

'Because I like chicken.'

The noodles turn out to be delicious, you just add a little ketchup and a slice of ham and you've got yourself one hell of a meal. Si finally comes around to the idea and congratulates me on a fine breakfast. Swilling out the pan, I dry it with some tissue paper and throw all of the equipment back into the boot.

Keen to get moving while it's still early, I kick Si out of the driver's seat and we head merrily into the countryside. The landscape is flat and lush green as we make the 200-mile journey to Perm, an industrial city slap-bang on the Trans-Siberian Railway line. We can see the Ural Mountains on the horizon, which stretch low for 1,250miles from Kazakhstan to the Arctic Kara Sea in the north. Si informs me they contain huge quantities of metals and minerals, and have been vital to Russia for almost 300 years. I recall studying the mountains on a map before we left England, and seeing them now with my very own eyes is strangely surreal. Weaving our way through the thick pine forests, I smile at the sight of hundreds of multi-coloured feather dusters hanging from long wooden racks. What a great product to sell to the passing traffic ... I mean, everybody should have a rainbow coloured feather duster, right? Passing through a number of ancient looking villages that appear to inhabit little more than haggard old women in headscarves, who walk witch-like at the side of the road, we thunder across the Volga Region until late in the afternoon.

Approaching the outskirts of Perm, we get lost down a side road and find ourselves at a dead end. A high brick wall with barbed wire on the top runs parallel with the road. I can just make out the roof of a building behind the wall. It looks like some kind of military base, but I can't be sure.

'This place looks a bit suspicious,' Si mutters, as I swing the car around.

'Yeah, we should be careful. Perm was a restricted area until a few years ago - foreigners weren't allowed to come anywhere near the place.'

Si frowns. 'Why not?'

'Because the Russian government was cloning humans.'

'You what?'

'Yep, it's true.'

'Bollocks!'

'No, I'm telling you the truth, Si. They were cloning the innocent citizens of Perm as an experiment. They were kidnapping them off the streets - men, women and children and cloning them in laboratories outside the city. These poor people were being cloned without their permission. The clones were exactly the same in every possible way ... looks, personality, the sound of their voice. You name it – identical. After the cloning was complete the government returned the individual to the exact location from where they had been kidnapped, and the clone was dumped somewhere deep in the forests of Siberia. It was a very Top Secret operation. No one knew about it until one of the clones managed to find their way back to Perm and spilled the beans. Even today there are thousands and thousands of clones living in the woods.

'Don't be ridiculous,' Si grins.

I crack a smile, and laugh. 'Yeah, I'm only joking. I haven't got a clue what it is.'

'You bastard, you nearly got me there. Cloning ... it's almost believable.'

'Who knows what dark shit is going on. I mean, they could be doing anything behind those walls.'

'Maybe it's a prison?' Si mutters.

'Nah ... I'll bet it's a secret nuclear base or a KGB den?'

'Do you think so?'

I nod. 'Probably.'

'Bloody hell! Maybe we should get moving, then. You know, just in case they think we're spies.'

'That's true. Jesus, listen to us. James Bond, or what!'

Si smiles. 'Cool, isn't it.'

Suddenly, two guards patrolling the perimeter wall walk past carrying large automatic rifles. They look suspiciously in our direction.

'Get moving, Chris! There's no way I'm spending the next six months trying to convince the Russian military that I'm not a spy.'

'I really don't think they'd mistaken you for being James Bond.'

'You never know, buddy boy. I mean, what does a secret agent really look like? I could be trained in martial arts and all sorts for all they know.'

I laugh mockingly. 'Yeah, right…'

We find our way back onto the main road and pick up signs for Perm. The city is 10km away, and as I glance out of the window I'm surprised to see the Trans-Siberian train charging towards us across the lush green fields. This is the first time we've seen the train and it has us both screaming like mad men.

'*IT'S THE TRANS-SIBERIAN!*' Si yells, hitting the steering wheel.

I throw my head out of the window. '*WHOOOOHOOOO!*'

For most normal people seeing the Trans-Siberian is … uh … no big deal. I mean, it's only a train, right? But for us it symbolizes the greatness of our journey, and driving alongside the tracks is absolutely mind blowing. It takes a painstaking 6 days and 6 nights to travel from Moscow to Vladivostok, covering an incredible 6000 miles of track and making it the longest train journey in the world.

The last carriage disappears behind the trees, and as I turn back to the road I suddenly see a GAI officer waving his black and white baton in the air. I slam on the brakes and skid to a halt. He checks through our documents, and I don't know whether it's because we've got business visas stuck in our passports or because the smiley officer got laid last night, but for some reason he speedily welcomes us to Russia and sends us on our way.

Entering the city of Perm, we pass through the centre and admire the leafy green streets. Si informs me that the author Boris Pasternak, who wrote the novel Dr Zhivago lived here and the town called Yuryatin in the story is actually Perm. This means very little to me as I've neither read the book nor seen the film, but the story of writers living here sounds intriguing all the same. With little cash and few reasons to spend a night in Perm, we decide to push on into the evening. We pass another GAI check-point, but much to our relief we drive by without being pulled over.

The sun begins to set behind us in the west as we chase the Trans-Siberian railway line towards Yekaterinburg, a city 41km inside Asia. We travel across the gently undulating Ural Mountains on the only road going east … the only road to Vladivostok. Tearing open a packet of chocolate biscuits, I'm just about to pop one in my mouth when Si suddenly points out blue-flashing lights up ahead. I slow right down, and as we draw closer it becomes clear it's not a GAI checkpoint this time, but instead a head on collision involving a brown Larda and a white saloon. The cars have been crushed beyond recognition and both window screens have been smashed out. Two officers stand beside the body of a bald middle-aged man, who lies stretched out on the tarmac. They look at us as we pass by and their faces say it all. The crumpled bonnet from the Larda has been placed over the man lying on the ground, but you can see his body sticking out underneath – his face is grey and there's a pool of blood above his head. The poor bloke must've gone through the window screen when the cars collided. Inside the white saloon, I think I can see the shape of someone slumped behind the steering wheel, but it's too dark.

Russia has one of the highest road accident rates in the world, and on average there are 520 everyday - 700 people are injured and 95 are killed. 34,000 people died in more than 208,000 road traffic accidents in 2002, that's a massive figure especially when there are only a mere 147 million people living in such a vast country. You only have to see the many roadside graves to understand the magnitude of the problem they have here - you can't drive more than a few miles without seeing one.

I feel a little shaken, particularly as this is the first time I've seen a dead body. Only half an hour ago this brown Larda overtook us at great speed. I remember cursing at the driver and wondering what's the rush? Now he's dead, lying there motionless – the life stolen from his body. He's gone throughout his whole life not knowing when he will die, he's probably thought about it, we all do, but finally that day has arrived. I have witnessed the end of this man's life. It's an image I will never forget.

Keen to put some distance between the accident and ourselves, we eventually stumble across a roadside café. Desperately in need of a cold beer to calm our nerves, we pull off the highway and park up outside. Inside the small wooden building, a stocky guy who looks Turkish stands behind the counter. We study the menu pinned to the wall and point at a couple of dishes in the hope that it will be something edible. Si points at the fridge behind the bar and orders a couple of beers. Grabbing a table, we sit in silence and try not to draw too much attention to ourselves. Four people drinking vodka chat loudly on the table behind us. The older guy looks unlike anyone I have seen before. His face is long and he has an enormous nose. A thick grey moustache hangs from his top lip and his complexion is also dark. It suddenly occurs to me that they could be from Kazakhstan, which is very likely being as we are now directly above it. By the time we receive our food, which is a gigantic spicy sausage and some weird looking beans, I begin to feel quite pissed. Looking at the label on the back of the bottle, I notice that the beer we're drinking has an alcohol volume of 8%. It helps to block out the awful image of the car accident, so we quickly order two more. Paying for our food, I ask the guy if it's OK to sleep in the car outside his café. He seems to understand my sign language and raises his thumb. We bid him goodnight and retire to the car feeling glad to be alive, but equally plagued by the thought of the dangers that lie ahead.

* * *

After an uncomfortable night's sleep, we head cautiously over the last of the Ural Mountains towards Yekaterinburg, the capital of Siberia. Chris seems happy for me to drive, and I wonder if he's still a little shaken after seeing the car accident yesterday. As we approach each bend or brow of a hill, we grit our teeth and expect a drunk Russian to come hurtling towards us on the wrong side of the road. Fortunately, we make it to the outskirts of the city intact, and feel greatly relieved to see signs of civilization as we pass tall concrete buildings eight stories high, displaying huge posters of fashion models advertising jewelry, perfume and designer sunglasses. According to Chris, Yekaterinburg is supposed to be one of the largest and most interesting cities in Western Siberia and, sadly, it was also where the Romanov family got hacked to death by the Bolsheviks in 1918.

Following tramlines into the city centre, we spot a cash machine up ahead. Chris stays with the car while I jump out and wait patiently behind a young couple. The smartly dressed guy glances over his shoulder as he withdraws his card.

I point at the cash machine. 'Is it working?' I ask, hoping

he will understand what I'm saying.

'Yes, you have Visa?' he replies in near perfect English.

I shake my head. 'No, Cirrus.'

The guy peers down at the card. 'Hmm … I think this machine not take Cirrus.'

'Do you know where I can change Traveller's cheques?'

'It is Sunday. The banks are closed. You could try one of the big hotels.'

'OK, thanks, that would be much better for me. Is there one near here?'

The guy converses with the girl stood beside him before glancing down at his wristwatch. 'We can take you there if you like. You have car?'

'Yes, it's the white one over there.'

'OK, please follow me.'

'Spaceeba. Are you sure you have time?' I smile.

The guy nods.

I skip over to the Sierra. 'Good news, Chris! You see that guy and the girl getting into the red car?'

'Uh-huh.'

'Follow them.'

'Why?'

'They're gonna take us to a hotel where we can change Traveller's checks.'

'Great! Where do you find these people?'

'Just lucky I guess.'

Weaving through the quiet streets, we dodge a green tram and watch the Sunday morning couples walking hand-in-hand in the bright sunshine. After passing the impressive Opera and Ballet Theatre and the Sverdlov statue, we're lead down a wide avenue before turning into the car park of the impressive Atrium Palace Hotel, which is part of the World Trade Centre. We park up and follow the guy inside the huge glass building. He storms across the grand entrance hall and makes his way over to the reception desk, where he speaks abruptly to the girl stood behind the counter.

He turns to us and shakes his head gravely. 'The money exchange is closed. It re-opens at one o'clock.'

'That's OK,' I smile. 'We don't mind waiting for a couple of hours.'

Looking defeated the guy sighs. 'I am sorry I could not do more. It is Sunday.'

'No, really, we're very grateful for all your help.'

'Where are you from?' he asks.

'England,' I reply.

'London?'

'Very near.'

'I have been to London two times on business. I work for an oil company here in Yekaterinburg. I like Soho and Camden Market very much.'

'Our older brother used to live in Camden.'

'That is very nice,' he smiles. 'So, you have driven here from England?'

'Yep, all the way,' Chris proudly replies.

'This is amazing! Where do you go now?'

'We're heading for Vladivostok,' I smile.

The guy laughs. 'You drive to Vladivostok? You are comedian, yes?'

I shake my head vigorously. 'No, we really are on our way to Vladivostok. Why doesn't anyone believe us?'

'But there is no road! It is impossible to drive there.'

Chris frowns. 'You what?'

'There is no road. The new highway is not finished yet. This is Russia - it takes a long time to get things done here. They have been talking about the project for over thirty-eight years. You can put your car on the train.'

'Are you sure about that?' I ask.

'Yes. Many people put their vehicles on the train.'

'No, I mean about the road not being finished.'

'Yes, yes, it is true.' The guy looks at us strangely. 'I'm sorry to give you bad news. It seems incredible that you come this far without knowing. Putin is keen to get the

Amur (Chita to Khabarovsk) Highway completed by next year. It is a major highway linking Europe with Asia. I'm sorry to have ended your plans, but I think maybe you live in a fantasy world.'

'Maybe,' I nod. 'It's all a little too much for us to comprehend.'

The guy suddenly looks at his watch and smiles sympathetically. 'I'm afraid I have to go. My girlfriend's mother is cooking today.'

'No problem,' I reply. 'Thanks again for your help.'

'It was very nice meeting you. I wish you good luck.'

We exchange handshakes and watch him leave.

'I fucking knew this was going to happen!' Chris yells.

I catch the receptionist giving us the evils. 'Come on, let's go outside.'

Chris marches across the car park and pounds the roof of the Sierra with his clenched fist.

'*WHAT A FUCKER!*' he shouts.

'Chill out, will ya!'

'*NO, PISS OFF, SI*! We've just driven over five thousand miles. I'm not going to just "chill out!" This journey is officially over!'

'What are you talking about? No it's not. We'll just have to put the car on the train when we get to Chita, just like the guy said.'

'We're not putting the car on a train. It's cheating! And, anyway, how much is that going to frigging cost?'

'Hmm … that's true. Well, maybe we should turn back, then?'

'Si, don't be a prick, what about Lake Baikal?'

I frown. 'Where the fuck's Lake Baikal?'

'It's near Irkutsk. It's one of the biggest lakes in the world! I'm not turning back until I've seen Lake Baikal.'

Chris walks around the car and disappears inside. I rest my forehead against the warm metal roof and take a moment to contemplate our situation. I quickly come to the conclusion that we're well and truly fucked.

'Hey!' Chris suddenly shouts. 'Come and look at this!'

I walk reluctantly to the front of the car and meet Chris at the bonnet. He slides the atlas in front of me.

I look down at the map, and sigh. 'What am I supposed to be looking at exactly?'

'Do you realise we're above the middle of Kazakhstan?'

'Uh-huh, of course I do.'

'We've crossed two time zones in two days!'

Studying the map, I'm amazed by the sheer distance we've covered in the past 48 hours. I follow the route eagerly with my finger.

'I thought the bloody time was wrong,' I smile.

'Forget about what that dude just said, Si. We should keep driving!'

'You've changed your tune.'

'Look, there are still five more time zones to cross before we reach Vladivostok. Let's just see how far we can get. That was always the idea, right? I mean, we never really expected to make it as far as Estonia.'

'That's true.'

'I definitely read somewhere on the internet, that they only have about three hundred and fifty kilometres of road left to finish. Surely there must be a way through. What does that bloke know, anyway? Chita's fucking miles away from here!'

Traversing the Trans-Siberian railway line with a pen, Chris draws a line across Siberia towards the remote cities of Omsk and Novosibirsk. He continues the line across the top of the Altay Mountains, through the never ending forests of Siberia, dips down close to the border with Mongolia, loops around the colossal lake Baikal and comes to a halt at the city of Chita in the Far East.

Chris turns to me with a smile. 'If we make it to Chita I'm gonna buy you a frigging beer.'

'Mate, if we make it to Chita I'm gonna buy us a crate!'

Bandits & Butterflies

With rubles bursting out of our pockets, Si confidently drives the Sierra through the city of Tyumen, a business capital where during World War II Lenin's body was secretly hidden from the invading Germans. A sign to Pokrovskoe springs up from the side of the road and points towards the village and birthplace of Grigory Rasputin – aka 'the priest of sex'. Si isn't keen on straying too far off route, and even though I feel we should visit the village of Pokrovskoe as a mark of respect to a man who had more charm than Leslie Phillips, we continue on to Omsk and the city of Novosibirsk.

Like the Trans-Siberian, we head east and drive and drive and drive - ten hours, eleven hours, twelve hours - we can't get enough of the road, we're addicted. I don't know why? Maybe it's because we're trying to get the thought of Vladivostok out of our minds, or because we want to get to Lake Baikal as quickly as possible before the Sierra decides it's had enough and blows a gasket.

The P402 to Omsk is long and empty and the sky is enormous overhead. Wide-open grass plains stretch out into the distance as far as the eye can see, and we chase telegraph poles that link arms in a line for hundreds of miles. Occasionally, we catch a glimpse of the Trans-Siberian cutting through the landscape, and we feel reassured that if all goes tits up at least we can get the train. In the middle of nowhere, a microlight glides low overhead and I wonder who might be inside. Si guesses it's a rich farmer with a cool mode of transport, but I wonder if it might be some crazy Dutchman attempting a solo round-the-world flight.

Passing through Omsk, we park up for the night at a rest stop 50km outside the city. We sit at a picnic table outside a cafe and are greeted by an interesting looking woman, who informs us she is from Tashkent in Uzbekistan. She's tiny and has a dark brown face and oriental features that are framed by a white Muslim headscarf. She serves us fried chicken and plain rice, and makes us laugh as she stamps her feet with frustration at the mosquitoes nipping around her ankles. She stands by our table in-between serving us beer, and explains in broken English that she has two children living in Tashkent, and has come to Siberia to work for her uncle for six months. Listening to her communicate with us in English, I begin to realise how incredibly ignorant we are about the rest of the world, and the level of intelligence of people who are far less privileged than ourselves. She tells us about the long journey she made from Uzbekistan with her nephew, across the perilous mountain roads of Kazakhstan – a journey she has made out of necessity, not by choice like we have. She deeply misses her children, but hopes to put them through school with the money she'll earn working here. Her eldest daughter is six years old and can already speak a few words in English.

We're up at the crack of dawn and cover 300km before breakfast. What we're doing is no 'Gum Ball Rally', but we're chewing up miles faster than Michael Jackson has facelifts. The weather begins to change from dark and overcast to bright sunshine, with the temperature outside reaching 28°C. Before we started this journey, if someone had asked me what I thought it would be like in Siberia, I would've imagined an empty barren landscape covered in snow. In the winter the temperature drops to minus fifty below, but at this time of year, particularly where we are now, it's as hot as Alicante.

Before long we enter the Khakassia Republic and Novosibirsk, a large city spawned by the Trans-Siberian at the rail crossing of the Ob River in 1893. It's a modern city with orange and white high-rise buildings on the banks of the river. We cross a road bridge over the Ob.

'Hey, Si! Did you know over a million people live in Novosibirsk?'

'Really?'

'Yep, one point three million people live right here in the middle of Siberia.'

'That's insane.'

'We're so ignorant in the west, aren't we? I didn't expect there to be anything out here.'

'Me neither,' Si replies. 'What do all these people do?'

'Well, there's loads of industry. This city was built as an industrial and transport centre between the coal fields a little way to the east of here, and the mineral deposits of the Ural mountains to the west.'

'Right ... so if you think about it. If it weren't for the Trans-Siberian, none of this would exist.'

'Nope.'

Cruising through the centre of the city, we pass a huge dirty colourless car market selling everything to do with ... uh ... cars. There are literally hundreds of makeshift stalls crammed together side-by-side selling headlights, side panels, batteries, hubcaps, engines, wheels, car radios ... you name it someone is selling it. We find the M53 to Kemerovo, and leaving the bustling traffic we find ourselves once again on a long straight road that disappears into the distance. Just as we begin to feel like we're making progress a signpost suddenly zips over our heads, and with genuine surprise we realise we still have a whopping 1778km to go before we make it to Lake Baikal. We console ourselves with the fact that this means we're now more than halfway between the Ural Mountains and Lake Baikal and, considering we've only been driving for roughly two days, we've covered nearly 1,500 miles of tarmac.

We arrive in Kemerovo around 8 o'clock in the evening. It's a lovely little town with numerous outside bars beneath bright yellow canopies. Pretty girls walk arm-in-arm along the pavement, and smart looking guys drive around in their shiny cars. Everything is going swimmingly, when all of a sudden we hear a strange vibrating sound coming from the engine. We ignore it at first, hoping it will disappear, but just like turning up the volume on a stereo, it gets louder until it becomes deafening. People literally stop walking down the street to look at the car. The growling tractor noise howls across the town, and crowds of people standing outside bars watch in amusement as we roar past. Concerned we may have damaged the engine by putting the wrong petrol grade in the tank, we pull over into a rundown tyre garage a few miles outside town.

Si grabs an old piece of hose from the boot. 'Why the fuck did we use seventy-six octane? It's fucked up the engine!'

'It's all they had. I'm sure it shouldn't make any difference.'

'How the fuck do you know? We should've used the petrol from our emergency containers until we got to Novosibirsk.'

Shoving one end of the pipe into the tank, Si gets down on his hands and knees.

I frown. 'Are you sure you know what you're doing?'

Si pauses for a second and looks up from behind his long fringe.

'Yes, I have done this before, you know,' he snaps. 'It

doesn't take a frigging genius to syphon petrol out of a car.'

Looking away, Si takes a deep breath before sealing his mouth around the end of the hose. He sucks vigorously, but turns red and immediately retches before spitting out a mouthful of petrol. I try not to laugh. Clutching his head, the poor bastard drops to his knees and quickly swills his mouth out with water.

'That was disgusting, it's burning my mouth!' He hands me the hose. 'You have a go.'

I shake my head. 'No way!'

'Well, we've got to do something ... the car's shagged.'

Crouching down, I examine the end of the hose. 'Do I have too?'

'Yes!'

Just as I'm about to give it a go, I glance over my shoulder and see a young guy with a shaved head emerging from the tyre garage. With a bare chest beneath his blue overalls and flip-flops on his feet, he makes his way casually over to us. I smile as he peers down at the pipe hanging out of the petrol tank. Si grabs the phrasebook from the car.

'Pamageetee pazhalstra,' the guy mumbles.

I frown. 'What's he say?'

'I don't know,' Si shrugs, flicking through the pages.

The mechanic folds his oily arms and continues to stare at the pipe. Spinning on his heals he strolls into the garage and returns with a big white plastic container. He places it on the ground and begins sucking on the end of the hose. Within seconds, petrol is gushing out the end of the pipe and he quickly shoves it into the container. The guy looks up and nods, we both smile back unsure what to say. The plastic container quickly fills up with the urine-coloured liquid, and he snaps at me in Russian to fetch another container from the garage. As the last few drops of petrol dribble out of the pipe, the guy wipes his hands on his overalls and points to a petrol pump less than thirty yards away.

'Spaceeba,' Si smiles.

The mechanic climbs to his feet and studies our registration plate before disappearing back into the garage.

'Nice bloke,' Si grins, screwing on the petrol cap. 'He could've charged us for that.'

'I guess tourists don't come through these parts all that often. This town isn't a Trans-Siberian stopover.'

Si's eyes light up. 'Hey, we're probably the first foreigners he's met.'

'We could be, but he didn't exactly seem overjoyed to see us.'

'Yeah, but then he doesn't look the type to get over excited.'

We push the car over to one of the petrol pumps and fill up the tank with octane 95, but as we try and drive away the tractor noise continues to roar from under the bonnet.

'Bollocks!' I yell. 'I knew it wasn't the petrol!'

Opening the bonnet, we look down at the rusty engine. Si grabs the tatty old manual that came with the car, and after a few seconds he tosses it to the ground.

'Right, then,' he beams, rubbing his hands together. 'What we have here is a common problem, which effects most cars of this age.'

'You haven't got a clue, have you?'

'No, I haven't got a fucking clue.'

We watch the engine vibrating vigorously from side-to-side.

I click my fingers. 'Wait a minute, I think the noise might be coming from that pipe ... press down the accelerator.'

Si jumps behind the wheel and gently begins to rev the engine.

'It is ... *look!*' I shout. 'The front part of the exhaust has come apart.'

'The front part of the exhaust?' Si replies, switching off the engine.

'Yeah, I think so,' I laugh. 'The bolt that holds it together has popped out.'

'Shit, the engine must've got really hot.'

'Uh-huh. Maybe driving over five hundred miles a day is too much for a sixteen-year old car?'

'That does sound pretty extreme. I can't believe we just threw away a whole tank of petrol.'

I scratch the back of my head. 'So what the fuck do we do now? It's starting to get dark?'

'Try to fix it, I suppose,' Si replies.

'How?'

'I have absolutely no idea.'

'We could bandage it together with some kitchen foil and wire.'

Si frowns. 'Are you sure that'll work?'

'It's worth a try.'

Pushing the two pieces of pipe together, we quickly begin to wrap the foil around the join and just as I'm about to use some wire to hold it all in place, the guy from the tyre garage appears behind us. He glances down at our handy work and begins to laugh. He points at his chest and then at the Sierra. He gestures for us to drive the car into his garage. Feeling embarrassed, but happy to accept some assistance from our new friend, we swing the car around and he directs us into his workshop and onto a ramp. Closing the doors behind him, the guy points to two wooden chairs next to a small table and a rusty stove. We sit down and fight to get comfortable. The mechanic presses a button and we can hear the sound of hydraulics. A ramp slowly lifts the car a few feet above the ground. He jumps down inside the pit and begins tinkering around.

Si turns to me with a puzzled look. 'What's he doing?'

I shrug. 'No idea.'

The mechanic peers over the side of the pit and raises his thumb in the air. We both smile and nod reassuringly. Grabbing a wrench from the side, the guy dives back under the car.

Ten minutes later, he climbs out of the pit with oil on his face and indicates to us that the job is complete.

'Bloody hell, that was quick!' Si beams.

'Don't get too excited,' I whisper. 'He'll probably want us to show him the money.'

We wait patiently for him to present us with a huge bill, but instead he begins to boil the kettle. Picking up a tin of coffee off the floor, he shovels a couple of teaspoons into three stained mugs. He laughs and says something in Russian, but we haven't got a clue what he's talking about, so we just laugh back. We sit in silence for a while and then he whips his wallet out of his pocket. He flips it open and pulls out a picture of a pretty young woman holding a baby in her arms. We smile and study the picture with interest. Taking a sip of coffee, I attempt to try out some Russian words from the phrasebook. He laughs and sparks up a cigarette. Heating up soup on his cooking stove, he pours some into two bowls and for some unknown reason, apart from maybe to break the ice, I suddenly show him a particularly nasty graze on my left elbow. Si quickly joins in and rolls up his jeans to display a large scar on his knee from when he fell off his BMX as a kid, but the guy doesn't seem impressed - he just looks at us strangely. Suddenly he stands up, pulls down his overalls and reveals a deep scar on the back of his thigh. We both look at it and gasp. He then mimes firing a machinegun and uses his hands to imitate an explosion.

'Chechnya,' he nods, pointing to his leg.

He grabs a pen and a piece of paper and writes the date 1994. This guy can't be much older than twenty-six, which means he must have only been about seventeen when he went to war in Chechnya. He tries to act out what happened, and it looks like a piece of shrapnel had embedded itself in his leg when a landmine exploded. Many people were killed. He crosses his chest. You can see in his face that he's not lying; the scar says it all. I feel stupid for showing him my graze, and it makes me think that it doesn't matter how far we drive across Siberia or how many experiences we have, nothing can even come close to what this young guy has seen. Shaking his head he quickly lights another cigarette. Grabbing his diary, he flicks to the back page and starts punching a number into his mobile phone. He stands up and shows us a dirty single bed behind a flimsy divider.

'Dyevachka,' he nods with a smile.

I frown. 'Dyevachka?'

Si already has his face in the phrasebook.

'Dyevachka?' Si mutters. 'Ah, dyevachka means ... uh ... girl.'

'Girl?' I repeat.

The guy grins and points to the bed. 'Dyevachka.'

He dials another number and points to each of us, then once again at the bed.

'He must mean a prostitute,' Si cries. 'He's dialing a frigging hooker!'

'Are you sure?'

'Well, what else is he doing?'

'He's getting a hooker to come here? To the garage?'

Si nods. 'Yeah, I think so.'

'Why? We're here. He can't fuck a hooker while we're here!'

'That seems to be the idea. He probably wants us to pay for it.'

'Really?'

'Yeah, either that or he wants us to join in the fun,' Si smiles.

'What? I'm sorry, but I'm not doing that!'

'Well, let's stop him, then.'

'OK, I will.'

I turn to the guy and shake my head. 'Nyet, spaceeba. Nyet dyevachka.'

The guy's face drops. 'Nyet dyevachka?'

I nod. 'Da. Nyet dyevachka.'

He looks sad. The poor guy, he's probably not getting any action from his wife at the moment.

'Nyet dyevachka?' he repeats sitting down.

'Nyet. We're tired,' I reply, resting my head on my hand.

He puts his mobile phone on the table. We sit in silence for a few minutes. Si tries to liven up the mood by asking him more questions from the phrasebook, but he doesn't seem interested. The guy lights up another cigarette and stares down at his phone. More silence. We eventually make our excuses and crash out in the car.

* * *

I'm woken by the whirring sound of a machine. I peer out of the window and see our new mechanic friend skillfully removing a tyre from its rim. Chris is already up and is sitting at the small table sipping coffee from a mug. Climbing out of the car I throw the tyre guy a friendly wave, but he just ignores me and carries on with his job at hand. Thanks to this dude's kind help, the tractor noise has gone. Without him we would've been up shit creek without a paddle, and all it took to solve the problem was a bolt ... not kitchen foil or wire. He still looks pissed off about last night, and I can only imagine it's because we prevented him from getting laid. No offense to the guy, but I think it was for the best. Feeling as though we've outstayed our welcome, we offer him some money for fixing the car, but he declines. We gather together our belongings and say our goodbyes.

The drive from Kemerovo to Krasnoyarsk is beautiful. The Siberian summer meadows are in full bloom and horses graze peacefully in the fields. Crossing a road bridge over the Yenisey River into the city of Krasnoyarsk, I stick my hand out of the window and ride the air currents.

'Hey, Chris, you can catch a passenger boat from here all the way to the Arctic Kara Sea in the north. Imagine how cool that would be? It's two thousand miles and takes four days going up and six days coming back.'

'Wow,' Chris smiles, 'Ray Mears would be in his element out here ... survival central, or what!'

'Exactly. Mountains, rivers and harsh Arctic conditions in the winter - what more could he possibly need. It's perfect!'

Passing through the city, we enter eastern Siberia and immediately begin to see trucks on the road carrying containers with Japanese writing down the side. The heat inside the car is immense and seeing signs for a rest stop with showers, we decide to clean ourselves up a bit.

Paying to use the shower facilities, we emerge from the brand new shower block feeling like new men. Dumping our soiled clothes in the boot of the car, we grab something to eat in the restaurant and for the first time in days enjoy a mouth-watering meal of hamburger and chips.

'You'll never guess what?' Chris beams, egg yolk running down his chin.

'What?'

'We're above flipping Mongolia!'

'Don't be ridiculous, that's right next to China.'

'I know... *look*!'

Chris slides the map in front of me.

'See,' he grins. 'We're here and the Mongolian border is there, three hundred miles across the Altay Mountains. Now, I reckon we should drive down there and do a bit of trekking. What do you think?'

'Don't be stupid.'

'Why not?'

'Chris, there's no way the Sierra will be able to climb those mountains.'

'Course it will.'

'Use your noodle, fat boy. It's too risky. Let's see how far we can get past Chita first before attempting anything as crazy as that. We've still got a shot at Vladivostok, remember.'

'Do you reckon?'

'Abso-fucking-lutely!'

Wiping our plates clean, we travel deeper and deeper into the Siberian forests, where we drive for a hundred miles along the highway that's a cloud of white butterflies. They flutter in their thousands towards the window screen, some get sucked inside the engine and splat on the front grill, others fly through the windows and pile up on the back parcel shelf. We pull over and look in awe at the white winged creatures that dance in the sky all around us. They gather on the warm tarmac in monstrous heaps like confetti, and scooping up a pile in my hands they tickle my face and get caught in my hair. Thundering through the white swarm, we pass through tiny villages similar to the ones we had seen in European Russia, with the small wooden houses with beautifully carved shutters. Women in brightly coloured headscarves draw water from ancient wells and goats chew on wild flowers growing at the roadside. We wait at a rail crossing and wave at a young kid, who zooms by in an open carriage of a freight train. The wind blows freely in his hair, and he returns our wave as he disappears on his adventure across the top of Asia.

Heading deeper into the wilderness, I'm surprised to see a man standing in the middle of the road. He waves his arms urgently above his head and indicates for us to pull over. I dip the brakes and slow down as we approach him.

'What you stopping for?' Chris snaps.

'We can't just ignore him. I think he's in trouble.'

The guy pops his head through the window and talks

quickly in Russian. He's slightly unshaven, but is smartly dressed in a lime green silky shirt and cream trousers.

'Nyet Rooskey,' Chris replies. 'We don't speak Russian.'

'You speak English!' he grins.

'Yes, we're from England,' I sing, intrigued to meet a fellow English speaker all the way out here in the middle of Siberia.

'You have petrol?' he asks.

'Yes, of course,' I cheerily reply.

Happy to assist a fellow traveller in need, I swing open my door.

'Where are you going?' Chris shouts, as he tries to grab hold of my arm.

I jump out of the car and meet the guy at the back of the Sierra. As I open the boot, I notice a rather dodgy looking kid leaning against a navy blue car on the other side of the road.

'I am from Slovenia,' the guy grins, shaking my hand. 'You know my country?'

'Uh … yeah,' I reply, handing him the petrol can. 'It's near Croatia, isn't it?'

He nods. 'Yes, you know the world very much.'

I smile awkwardly.

The guy suddenly looks a little shifty. He can't quite keep still and keeps glancing up and down the long empty road, almost checking to see if the coast is clear. I suddenly sense something is not quite right. He signals to the kid standing by his car, and he skulks across the road and takes the petrol can. The guy begins to talk urgently at me. He explains how they have run out of petrol and can't afford to buy more. He's a powerful looking bloke with the most unusual emerald green eyes, and for a second I find myself listening to his sob story. My mind races. I suddenly realise where the conversation is heading, and I stop him in mid-sentence and tell him we don't have any money. He pulls a gold ring out of his pocket with a large red rock embedded into it. He tells me it's a ruby.

'Please,' he continues. 'Maybe you buy ring, very cheap, very beautiful. We need to buy petrol.'

He thrusts the ring close to my face, and seeing him glance very quickly up and down the road with those intimidating green eyes, something inside me clicks.

'*No*,' I snap, slamming the boot shut. 'I give you petrol!'

'You buy ring!'

The guy seems to be getting annoyed. He glances up and down the road again before reaching for his back pocket. I freeze. For all I know he may have a knife or a gun. My survival instincts kick in and I sprint around to the driver's door and jump inside the car. I quickly strike the engine as the guy runs around to the passenger window.

'What about your petrol can?' he shouts.

'Keep it!' I shout back, and revving the engine I accelerate away at great speed.

'*YOU FUCKING IDIOT*!' Chris yells. '*WHY DID YOU GET OUT OF THE FUCKING CAR?*'

'Fuck, fuck,' I pant, checking the rearview mirror. 'Are they following us?'

'*SLOW DOWN*!'

I look in the rearview mirror again. 'He was gonna shoot me! That guy was gonna fucking shoot me!'

My hands are shaking and the adrenaline is pumping through my veins.

'Si, what the fuck happened back there?'

'He was going to pull out a gun. I'm sure of it!'

'You're kidding me?'

'No, I'm being deadly serious!'

'You fucking idiot!'

'He started trying to sell me this ring, but I could see in his eyes that he was about to do something.'

Chris hits the dashboard. 'You should never get out of the car in situations like that, it's the first fucking rule, you dumb ass! That's why people travel in convoy around here.'

'Well, how was I supposed to know?'

'You could've got us both killed!'

'Fuck, Chris, I'm sorry. We've been driving for so long, for a moment there I forgot where we are. What the hell is a guy from Slovenia doing out here, anyway?'

Chris shakes his head. 'Jesus Christ! Now we've only got one petrol can.'

'Oh, fuck off! You'd have done the same thing.'

'No I fucking wouldn't have!'

Shaken by the afternoon's events, we both eventually calm down and concentrate on making some distance. Letting Chris take over the driving, we agree to continue on until it gets dark. The never-ending forests and the beautiful meadows of the Siberian countryside slowly begin to disappear. Grey smog hangs heavy in the air, blocking out the sun. We pass through a small industrial town that consists of little more than a grotty housing estate and a rundown processing plant. Rusty pipes loop above the road and kids with grubby faces peer at us as we pass by. On the edge of town, we spy a cafe with a few trucks parked up outside. It's the first place we've seen in hours, and feeling tired and hungry we decide to check it out. Locking up the car, I notice two men and a woman loitering suspiciously outside the gateway to another enormous factory. We ignore them and head quickly through the dark doorway. Walking towards the counter, I'm immediately surprised by how thick the steel bars are that stand between the woman slouched behind the counter and ourselves. They look like they belong to an 18th century jail cell. I hold up the handwritten menu to the bars and point at a couple of different options. Having learnt a few words, I also ask for Borshch (beetroot soup with vegetables and meat), khlyeba (bread) and kartofeeleem (potatoes). Chris peers over my shoulder and orders two beers. The gaunt woman, with a starched cloth tied around her head and bright red lipstick, scowls in our direction. Popping the lids, she thrusts the warm bottles of beer through the bars. We walk across the dimly lit room and sit at a large metal table in the corner. The hard-faced male clientele sit hunched over steaming bowls of soup and glance over at us.

'What a fucking dive,' Chris whispers.

I look around. 'Yeah, they seriously need to slap a bit of paint on the walls. I'm going to the toilet, back in a minute.'

I stand up and walk to the back of the café. There's a door slightly ajar to my left and poking my head inside, I see a dirty toilet with the lid down. Entering the small room, I close the door behind me and grab some tissue paper out of my pocket. Lifting up the lid, I jump back in horror as I see a hypodermic needle lying on top of a pile of black shit. Letting go of the lid, I race out of the toilet and within two seconds I'm sitting back at the table. The woman behind the counter looks over at us.

'There's a used needle in the toilet,' I cry, sneaking peaks around the café.

Chris frowns. 'A needle?'

'Yeah. Someone around here is jacking up. It must be heroin.'

'I didn't know they used that crap out here?'

'Oh yeah, it's probably making its way here from Afghanistan.'

A few minutes later, the woman behind the counter slides a tray beneath the bars with our food on it. I fetch it and return to the table. The food looks disgusting, and half-heartedly pushing the inedible mush around our plates for a while, we quickly head back to the car. It's pitch black outside and locking ourselves inside the safety of the Sierra, we watch as the car park slowly begins to empty. After a while the lights inside the café go out, and we're left alone in the car park feeling incredibly vulnerable. We try to block out our surroundings by getting some shut eye, which is impossible as I've got images of the guy who nearly robbed us haunting my mind. A black shape moving behind the Sierra suddenly attracts my attention. I sit up and glance in the wing mirror, but I'm unable to see anything. I nudge Chris awake. With wide eyes, I roll down my window and peer out into the darkness.

'What is it?' Chris mumbles.

'I just saw something moving outside.'

'You're imagining it.'

'Chris, I definitely saw something moving out there.'

'You're paranoid.'

'I'm not! Fuck knows what it was.'

'It's probably the Grim Reaper coming to get ya,' Chris laughs, as he snuggles inside his sleeping bag.

'Fuck off, its not funny. Those highway robbers could have followed us here.'

'Go to sleep.'

I check all the doors are locked before pulling my sleeping bag tightly around my neck. I feel my heart pounding inside my chest, and just as I'm about to close my eyes I suddenly see the black shape flash by my window.

'*RIGHT, THAT'S IT!*' I scream. '*THERE'S SOMETHING OUT THERE!*'

Chris sits bolt upright and peers out of the window. '*JESUS CHRIST! WHERE?*'

Suddenly, a hand slams against the window. We both scream at the top of our voices. I jump towards Chris, desperate to get away from the glass. A face appears at the window, it's a painfully thin woman with long greasy hair. Her eyes are glazed and bloodshot. Chris tears open his sleeping bag and starts the car as the woman bangs harder against the glass. Flicking on the headlights, Chris reverses at speed away from the crazed woman, who grabs her hair and screams. We wheel spin out onto the road and disappear in a cloud of exhaust fumes.

Pearl of Siberia

Opening my eyes, I look in surprise at a large owl perched in a tree no more than ten metres away from the car. It watches me curiously and I wonder if it's been guarding over us during the night. I quietly take my camera out of Si's bag and raise it slowly to my face. Focusing on the owl through the zoom, I study its huge magnificent yellow eyes. The camera shutter snaps, disturbing the owl and causing it to open its wings and take flight. It swoops low overhead before disappearing into the forest like a creature from a mystical fairytale.

Grabbing some breakfast from inside an old disused train carriage that's been converted into a café, we continue on feeling refreshed and ready for any eventuality that may cross our path. We pass through more remote villages before reaching a busy section of the highway and a GAI checkpoint up ahead. We have begun to hate these bloody checkpoints, not solely because of the risk of being fined for no reason, but it's such a pain having to pull over and explain where we're going all of the time. As we approach the checkpoint, the GAI officer immediately flags us down. Si hands him our passports and points to Lake Baikal on the map. He nods and waves me in the direction of a small brick building, and I head cautiously towards a mean looking officer with a machinegun standing outside the door. Inside it's dark and there's a man in a dark green uniform sitting behind a wooden desk with a white paper funnel in his hand. Four men stand in a line against a concrete wall and I'm told to join them. The policeman waves me over and shoves the paper funnel up to my mouth. He shouts something at me in Russian. I obviously don't understand, so I guess and breathe into it. The policeman whips it away from my face and sniffs hard inside the funnel, which personally I can't help thinking is a really bad idea, particularly as I haven't brushed my teeth for a least 24 hours. He screws up his face and sends me away.

Returning to the car, I'm just about to climb behind the wheel when the GAI officer who pulled us over approaches our vehicle. He mumbles something and points up the highway.

'Nyet Rooskey,' I smile.

Si pokes his head out of the passenger window. 'What's going on?'

'Dunno?'

A cop car suddenly pulls up in front of us.

Si frowns. 'What the hell have you done now?'

'I haven't done anything. I just breathed into a paper funnel. Surely you can't be arrested for having bad breath.'

The young cop indicates for us to follow him. Fearing the worst, I strike the engine and pull out onto the highway.

'He's probably going to buy us some hot dogs,' Si laughs.

'Don't joke around, this could be serious. I mean, where's he taking us?'

We continue to follow the police car into a small concrete town that's not even on the map, and before long we pull up outside a tatty police station.

knew it!' I yell. 'I knew he wasn't taking us for frigging hot dogs!'

'What do you think we've done wrong?' Si frowns.

'How the hell should I know! If they try to get money out

of us, I'm going to write a letter to Vladimir Putin.'

We reluctantly make our way into the police station, but instead of being arrested and thrown in jail we're welcomed with open arms. The top dog sergeant, who looks like he could kill a lion with his nose hair, walks over and shakes our hands. It's like putting your hand in a vice, but we both do well to fight back the tears. There are six other policemen standing behind the sergeant, they all look over at us with fascination. Even the guy locked up in the cell to my right looks through the bars and smiles. I glance around the station and study the main control desk, which could be part of the set from the 1960's sitcom *Z Cars*, with all of its big cheesy dials and switches. A big red telephone begins to ring, and an officer picks up the bone shaped receiver and places it to his ear. He looks hilarious, and I try to hide my amusement. The sergeant slides a book in front of us and hands me a pen. We write down our names and our country of origin while our passports get passed around the room. It seems pretty clear they've never met anyone from England before, so we try to behave as good ambassadors to our country and smile and thank them in Russian at every opportunity.

Escorting us out of the station, all seven policemen crowd around the Sierra. Si speedily grabs the atlas off the back seat and we show them our route on the map. They smile and chatter excitedly. One of the policemen points at the ocean on the map, and I explain to them that we put the car on a boat from England to France. They all seem generally surprised that it's possible to drive from England to the Far East by road, and shaking our hands we feel like pioneers breaking down boundaries and uniting the world. The sergeant asks me to lift up the bonnet. They check out the engine and nod their heads. We haven't washed the car since we left England, and it really does look like it has just driven halfway across the world. It suddenly occurs to me that I haven't seen a Ford

Sierra on the road since St Petersburg, and I get the distinct impression this is the first one they've seen. The excitement of seeing the modern world on their doorstep (even though the Sierra is 16 years old) appears to be a positive sign to them of the future.

We're led back out of town by the same police car. At one point they put on their blue flashing lights and we jump a long queue of traffic. Putting us back on the main road to Irkutsk, we wave out of the window and sound our horn as we tear back onto the road.

* * *

Passing dozens of old gingerbread style log houses, Chris directs me through the quiet streets of Irkutsk, and we're able to imagine what it might have been like here in the 1700's when this town was a bustling trading post. Furs and ivory were sent to Irkutsk from all over Eastern Siberia and were carried to Mongolia, Tibet and China to trade for tea and silk. Around that time it was a starting point for many great expeditions to the far north and east. The famous trader, Grigory Shelekhov, led one expedition across the Bering Strait into Alaska and down to California, which was referred to locally at that time as the 'American district of Irkutsk'.

Taking a celebratory turn around the main square, we pass the statue of Lenin and head out of the city. Chris snaps a photograph of an enormous ugly metal sculpture of a red communist star and a hammer and sickle - an emblem signifying the alliance of workers and peasants, which sits rusting in the centre of a roundabout. Communism had come and gone, leaving these final reminders behind. Seeing these symbols deteriorating at the roadside, I can only assume they haven't removed them out of nostalgia for those days. In fact, I'm sure in the remote villages off the beaten track they still think communism exists. I guess it takes time for people to let go of an ideology that dominated their lives for so long, but eventually they too will disappear along with all of their fears of change and worries about the future. The world will move on.

The sky is thick with smoke as we crawl alongside the Eastern Sayan Mountains towards the legendary Lake Baikal. I had noticed heavy cloud over Irkutsk, but now I can see that it's smoke that hangs in the air over the hills and forests.

'Hey!' Chris beams. 'Did you know Lake Baikal is the size of Belgium and is over a mile deep in places. It also contains nearly one-fifth of the world's unmelted fresh water, which is more than North America's five Great Lakes combined. Also, it's one of the oldest lakes and has been in existence for over twenty-five million years. Almost all other lakes on earth have only been around for twenty thousand years. Pretty interesting stuff, don't you think?'

'Absolutely. So, if there are any monsters on this planet, this is where they'll be.'

'Uh-huh, fuck Loch Ness,' Chris smiles. 'Baikal is a bit like the Galapagos Islands, where animal and plant life has evolved in complete isolation from the rest of the planet. Of over two thousand recorded plant and animal species found at Baikal, seventy to eighty percent can be found nowhere else on earth.'

'That's amazing!'

Chris nods enthusiastically. '*I know*!'

Weaving down the side of the mountain along narrow roads, we excitedly scan the area for any sign of the lake.

'Where the fuck is it?' I cry.

Chris shrugs. 'Dunno. I can't see shit because of all this

smoke. Where's it all coming from?'

'It must be forest fires.'

Reaching the bottom of the steep mountain, we glide alongside a low stone wall and peer into a screen of white smoke.

'Stop the car!' Chris yells. 'I think I just saw something. I think it might be the lake. Yeah, look! There it is!'

We both leap out of the Sierra.

Squinting, I'm unable to see anything.

'Where?' I cry.

Chris points into the white mist. '*There!*'

Suddenly, I catch a glimpse of three ripples through the smoke no more than ten metres away.

'Is that it?' I laugh.

'Yes! This whole area in front of us must be Lake Baikal. It's completely hidden from view by the smoke.'

'But that's ridiculous! How can you hide a lake the size of Belgium?'

'I have absolutely no idea. Bollocks! Imagine what the view would've been like coming down the mountain. That would've been one for my portfolio.'

'Not to worry, fat boy, this road skips around the bottom of the lake for two hundred miles. We're bound to see an area clear of smoke somewhere along the way.'

Jumping back into the Sierra, we continue to make our way slowly alongside the invisible lake. Chris scans the area through an old pair of binoculars, which I can't help thinking is a bit pointless considering we can only see a few metres in front of ourselves. Driving into the evening without seeing another ripple, we stumble across a trucker's cafe at the top of a steep climb and decide to stop here for the night. The smoke at the top of the mountain fills the air, suggesting it must be one hell of a forest fire. Stepping out of the car I look around and observe a family of local Buryats, an indigenous group of Mongol people who live in the Baikal region, selling food at the roadside.

Their faces are incredible with pink rosy cheeks and narrow eyes. The temperature has dropped dramatically and everybody around has coats and hats on. We leave the car and step inside the wooden cabin. It's lovely and warm. I take my coat off and grab an empty table next to a huge Mongolian truck driver.

'Bloody hell, it's Genghis Khan,' Chris smiles.

We watch with fascination as the man slurps soup from a bowl. He has a wispy goaty beard and his straight jet-black hair is tied back in a ponytail. A leather waste coat stretches tightly over his muscular shoulders. He's the first Mongolian I've seen in real life and I realise now how Genghis Khan, the legendary warlord who came from this territory, managed to create history's largest land empire in the 13th century.

Ordering food from a friendly lady working in the kitchen, I return to the table with two bowls of the steaming dumpling soup and a couple of square slices of pizza.

Chris pops a dumpling into his mouth and shakes his head.

'What's up?' I ask. 'Don't you like it?'

'No, it's delicious,' he replies. 'I was just thinking how annoying it is that we haven't seen Lake Baikal yet.'

'I know, these fires must be massive.'

'I was really looking forward to seeing the damn thing.'

'Chris, at the end of the pissing day it's only a lake.'

'Lake Baikal is more than "just a lake"! It's the 'Pearl of Siberia'. The waters are crystal clear. In places it's possible to see down more than forty metres.'

'Well, you'll just have to come back some other time.'

'Yeah, I'll jump in the car one lazy Sunday afternoon and drive the seven thousand miles back here, shall I?'

'You could get the train.'

Chris thinks about this for a second. 'Hey, that's actually not a bad idea. Maybe I could do it in the winter when you can't drive. Apparently, at that time of year the ice on the lake freezes up to a metre thick. They even use it as a temporary road between the remote settlements in the north and south.'

'Wow, that must be awesome.'

'Yeah, but it's incredibly dangerous. They reckon the bottom of the lake is a graveyard of cars and trucks.'

Looking over Chris's shoulder, I see a guy enter the café wearing a bright yellow ski jacket. He's in his late fifties and has a mane of silky grey hair hanging down to his shoulders. He looks over at our table and smiles, almost as if he's seen old friends. He grabs a pizza slice from the counter and makes his way over to our table.

'Dobry vyechyeer,' he grins.

Chris looks up from his bowl of dumplings.

'Hi ... I mean, dobry,' I smile.

'Where you from?' the guy asks in perfect English.

'England,' I reply.

His eyes light up. 'Ah ... The Rolling Stones!'

We both nod vigorously.

'Yeah, great band!' I smile.

'I musician,' the guy announces proudly. 'You play guitar?'

'Yeah, a little...'

Chris sniggers.

'...But not very well.'

'I play all Russia - Moscow, St Petersburg. One time in Warsaw.'

'Wow, are you still in a band now?' I ask.

'Da,' he nods, sitting down at the table. 'I similar to Keith Richards, I play until dead.'

'Nice one,' I grin.

'You in band?' he asks.

'Uh ... nyet, not anymore,' I reply, turning to Chris.

'Why you not in band?'

I shrug. 'I don't know. The band split up and I never did it again.'

He offers me a cigarette. 'If in your blood, you must play!'

Buying the guy a beer, we continue to talk about music and the world. He turns out to be one wise dude, and I'm sure in a past life he would have been a native Indian chief or a spiritual shaman. Completely in-tune with himself this is a man who refuses to grow old in his mind, and I find myself aspiring to be like him. He reaches across the table and tucks something into my jacket pocket.

'Remember the summer of '69',' he smiles, and flicking his silver locks over his shoulders he exits the cafe.

We return to the car with a couple more beers, and reaching inside my pocket I find a perfectly rolled joint. It's a wonderful sight to see and sparking up the cone before bedtime, we get stoned in the car high above Lake Baikal.

Burn Baby Burn

With pasta shell eyes, Si drives on the M55 to Ulan Ude through the burning taiga, the largest forest in the world. Covering five million square kilometers, an area of unbroken forest roughly the size of India, it contains about 25% of the entire planet's wood reserves. On either side of the road, charred trees smolder like burnt matchsticks and flames leap sporadically into the air from patches of green forest. It feels like the world is on fire, and watching a roaring inferno attack an area close to the road, we hear wood crack and watch a tree collapse in flames.

'Hey, Si, keep an eye out for the smokejumpers.'

'Smoke jumpers?'

'Uh-huh. They're the Siberian firefighters, who parachute into the forest from fifty-year old turbo powered Mi-8 helicopters. When there's a fire they're dropped into the forest and spend weeks battling to put them out. They survive by hunting for food and eating raw fish.'

'Now, that's cool!' Si beams.

Not one single car or truck passes by as we make our way through the burning forests, and I begin to feel a little concerned for our safety. Rummaging through the glove box, I dig out the Survival Guide and flick to the section on 'fire'.

'Right, listen to this, Si. It says here, "do not drive through thick smoke."'

Si frowns. 'Bit late for that, isn't it?'

'Yeah, I suppose it is. It also says, "if caught in a fire find a clear area."'

'There aren't any clear areas.'

'Hmm … OK, forget about that one, too. Ah … "turn on the headlights and stay in the car".'

Si quickly flicks the lights on full beam. 'OK, what else?'

'"Close all the windows, turn off the ventilation and stay in your vehicle until the glass begins to melt".'

'*What?*'

'That's what it says! It also mentions there's a danger of the petrol tank exploding.'

Si gulps. 'We're going to die, aren't we?'

'It's highly possible. Although, if the wind does change and the windows melt before the fire passes over the car, there is always the final option of burying ourselves in the earth.'

'Don't be ridiculous.'

'It's true,' I smile, pointing at the page. 'It says, "If there is no natural break or gully in which to shelter and the fire is too deep to run through, you may have to seek the protection of the earth itself."'

'Fuck that!'

All of sudden, a squirrel darts across the road in front of us. Si swerves to avoid it, but we feel a bump as it disappears under one of the back wheels.

I clench my teeth. 'Poor blighter, what's the chances of that? You escape the forest fire by the fluff of your tail, and then you get mowed down by the only car for miles around.'

Si shakes his head. 'Pure tragedy. Life's a bitch, isn't it? I mean, what's the point?'

'In being a squirrel?'

'No, in life.'

'I don't think there is a point,' I reply. 'The fact is, we're on this planet for a nanosecond and then we simply disappear into dust.'

'Very deep, Chris, very deep.'

'Thanks.'

'So, how do you reckon you'll die?'

'Bloody hell, Si, liven up the frigging party!'

'Don't ignore the inevitable, man. It happens to us all eventually.'

'I haven't really thought about it.'

'Chris, you must have thought about it. It crosses everybody's mind at some point.'

'Well, you'd hope of old age, but at the rate things are going I think that's gonna be pretty unlikely. Hopefully I'll suffocate between a huge pair of breasts.'

'Yeah, I guess that would be the ultimate. What about falling off a cliff or having your head cut off?'

I frown. 'You're kidding, right?'

'No. I mean, imagine what would be going through your mind?'

I tap my chin. 'Hmm ... let me think. How about ... *HELP! I'M GONNA DIE!*'

'Fucking hell, wouldn't you like to know how that would feel?' Si laughs. 'You know, to have your head cut off.'

'No, not really.'

'In Medieval times it was entertainment to go and see a public execution. It still is in some countries. Apparently, you can still see and hear for seven seconds after you've been decapitated.'

'How the hell does anyone know that?'

Si shrugs. 'Dunno.'

'I must admit, I've often wondered what it would be like to be eaten alive by a Great White shark.'

'That's the spirit, Chris! You're starting to get into it now.'

'I don't think it would hurt for long. The shock would numb the pain.'

'I hope I get the opportunity to look death in the eyes,' Si smiles. 'Have a moment to say to myself, "so this is how the story ends ... bring it on!"

'Hmm ... nice idea, but I'm not sure that's how it works.'

'Why?'

'Because like I said, in that moment you'll probably be too busy shouting, "*Oh, fuck*! *I don't want to die*!" while your life flashes madly in front of your eyes.'

Escaping death with each mile, we drive through the burning forests for a further 200 miles. Protected by the road we eventually return to civilization ... well, civilization as in a cluster of tin-pot shacks and a roadside café. We decide to take a pit stop. A strange looking guy stood behind the counter welcomes us inside. Dressed in black from head-to-toe, he is ghostly white in colour and has deep blue eyes and long black eyelashes. His nose is huge like a toucan's beak, and smiling politely we grab a table and study the menu. Ordering some food, the young guy seems keen to make conversation and I'm intrigued to learn he is from Armenia. We try to talk about the forest fires, but he just shrugs his shoulders and smiles. The mother, a Jewish looking woman with curly brown hair, immerges from a room at the back of the restaurant. A young boy follows closely behind. I point to England on a map of the world pinned to the wall. They all smile and we exchange handshakes. The young guy looks pleased to see us and enthusiastically points to Armenia, a small country north of Turkey. I vaguely recall the British having some involvement in the Armenia crisis back in the 80's, and suggesting to us that they had not forgotten this we are treated with the greatest respect. The young guy hands me a packet of cigarettes with the brand name 'London' on the box. I gratefully accept the present and dig out a couple of postcards of London from the car. He looks ecstatic and immediately pins them to the wall. Si fishes a couple of English coins out of his pocket and gives them to the kid. It's a shame we can't communicate with them more, as it would be fascinating to hear about their country and find out why they had ended up all the way out here. I wonder if it was because they'd gone in search of a better life, but I can't help feeling their extreme isolation and distance from their homeland suggests something more. The mother cooks us an incredible feast, and we leave the cafe feeling touched by their humble generosity.

Heading back on the road, we quickly reach the city of Ulan Ude, which chokes on the same smoke from the forest fires we'd experienced over 300 miles away. With little reason to stop we push on towards Chita – the frontier of our journey. Winding down the window, the sweet smell of Asia fills the Sierra and I peer out at the barren landscape that dwarfs the car. Si sings lyrics from his band days with, 'The Blood Sucking Flower Fairies', and we play a few stupid games of eye spy. The sky is still smoggy as we cruise through more untouched villages, and to the sound of Si's screams we nearly plough head-on into a horse galloping towards us. Two kids hang on for dear life as they ride the beast bareback through the village. They look so happy and free, and I look in awe at the perfect simplicity of their lives.

We drive pretty much all day. Si places a compass on the boot of the car and we watch the needle settle and point east towards the horizon. For ten days now we've been travelling in the same direction. Each morning the sun rises in front of us in the east; it travels over our heads during the day and sets directly behind us in the west. It feels incredible, like we're heading in the right direction.

Less than ten miles outside Chita, we park up for the night at a rundown roadside café. Like many of the places we've stopped at along our journey, it's a small wooden shack that's badly in need of repair. There's a plastic table on the veranda outside the entrance, so we choose to sit outside and enjoy the remainder of the day. While we try to work out what the hell to eat a guy in a green vest top, with dark stubble and tattoos on his arms, exits the café and walks over to our table. Si orders a couple of beers and some food, and the guy silently nods his head and returns inside.

'Fucking hell,' Si whispers, 'that dude looks like he could go a few rounds with Mike Tyson.'

The guy returns to our table with the beers. They're as warm as bath water, but after a long day on the road it could be a bottle of the dude's piss and I'd probably still drink it. The guy's face is red and his eyes are puffed up. He looks like a heavy drinker and walks with a slight limp. You can tell by his manner that at sometime in his life he was definitely a soldier in the army, and more than likely fought against the Chechens. His attitude is rock hard, and I get the distinct impression that if we stepped out of line he wouldn't hesitate wringing our necks like a couple of chickens. Si flashes him a 'please-don't-kill-us-we're-your-friends' kind of a smile. The guy leaves the table and disappears inside the shack. Suddenly, a beautiful girl carrying a red bucket and a dirty cloth appears in the doorway. She smiles sweetly as she passes by. Si's jaw hits the table, and we both sit dumbfounded for a few seconds before turning to each other.

'Bloody hell, did you see that?' Si stutters, shifting excitedly in his seat. 'Cinda-fucking-rella, or what!'

'Yeah, she must be his daughter.'

'She must be adopted!' Si laughs. 'My God, imagine accidentally getting her up the duff?'

I shiver. 'Ooh, you could say goodbye to your bollocks.'

The guy reappears and throws two plates of burnt mush on the table.

'Spaceeba,' I smile.

As we tuck into our grub, I notice Si keeps looking behind me and smiling. I glance over my shoulder and see the curtain move.

'What are you doing?'

'Fuck, I think I'm in love,' he smiles.

'Not again.'

'Now she's the kind of girl I'd like to marry.'

'The guy's daughter?'

'Uh-huh.'

'Careful, Si, that bloke could snap your skinny body in two.'

'Hey, don't I know it. I'll tell you something, right. That's what's missing from my life right now ... a muse.'

I frown. 'As in a cul-de-sac?'

'No, you idiot, someone who inspires me.'

'Was Emily a muse?'

'The old Emily maybe, but she doesn't exist anymore. I need a new muse.'

'Bloody hell, Si! You need to settle down and get married. You're not cut out for the single life.'

'Yes I am! There's nothing wrong with wanting a muse. Wouldn't you like to have a muse - a reason to breathe?'

'I don't need one. I get enough inspiration from the little booties walking down the street, why have one muse when you can have them all.'

Si nods. 'Good point. The thing is, isn't the love of that one special girl, who spins your world like no other and is perfect in every way, worth a billion other girls?'

I look up at the sky and think about this for a second. 'Uh ... *no*! Imagine how much fun you could have with a billion girls?'

'All right, Ron Jeremy.'

'You're just soft, Si, that's your problem.'

'And you're just a horny mother fucker.'

'It's completely natural.'

'Chris, have you ever actually been in love?'

'Of course I have, you cheeky git.'

'With who?'

'Uh ... well, there was Lucy!'

'Lucy? She was your girlfriend when you were seventeen, wasn't she?'

I glaze over. 'I think she's the only girl I've ever truly been in love with.'

'Hmm ... that depends on how you define the word 'love',' Si smirks, flicking a cigarette into his mouth.

I lean back in my chair and fold my arms. 'Love ... a deep, tender, ineffable feeling of affection and solicitude toward a person, such as that arising from kinship, recognition of attractive qualities, or a sense of underlying oneness.'

'Where did you get that from?'

'The dictionary,' I reply with a grin. 'I memorized it when I was a kid.'

'Why?'

'I don't know? I guess I wanted to know what it meant.'

'And do you now?'

'Yeah, I think so. That feeling of losing your heart for the first time stays with you. I don't think I've really been the same since. She was so beautiful. Those days were great fun, we used to make love in the woods and go horse riding together near Newbury. It was all so innocent. I even bought her a plastic rose from a petrol station.'

Si drops his smile. 'You did what?'

'I bought her a plastic rose.'

'A plastic rose?'

'Uh-huh.'

'Chris, please tell me you're taking the piss.'

'No, I thought it would be romantic! You know ... it would last forever.'

Si places his beer on the table and rubs his eyes. 'Oh my God, only freaks and old people who smell of wee buy plastic roses from a petrol station. What a horrible thought, a plastic rose that lasts forever, not romantic at all, mate.'

'Hey, I was young and clueless.'

'You can say that again. So … she didn't throw it back in your face, then?'

'Nope.'

'Then, why did it end?'

'I don't really know. I think I fucked it up somehow. We did agree to have an open relationship, though.'

Si frowns. 'Really? And what happened?'

'It all went tits up when she started seeing some other guy from her college.'

'But that was the idea, wasn't it … to see other people?'

'I suppose.'

'Well, what about you? Did you start seeing someone else?'

I look down at the table, and sigh. 'I couldn't do it.'

'What do you mean you couldn't do it? Was it because you were still in love with her?'

'Yes. No, I mean, uh … I couldn't do it, all right! I couldn't pull!'

Si bursts out laughing and hits the table. 'You fucking loser!'

The guy suddenly appears at the door with two more bottles of beer. He joins our table.

'Rooskeey peeva,' Si grins. 'Very good.'

The guy shakes his head. 'Nyet, Chech peeva.'

'Chech peeva?'

'Oh, I think he means Chechnya,' I mutter. 'Chechnya Peeva?'

'*NYET CHECHNYA!*' he bellows, slamming his fist down on the table.

'Czech beer!' Si jumps in. 'He means Czech beer!'

'Da. Da. Czech peeva,' the guy nods. He stands up and walks back inside the café.

He returns with a beer for himself and sits back down. His beautiful daughter appears in the doorway like a bright-eyed thorn. She begins to clear away our plates, and I try to restrain myself from looking at her as she disappears back inside.

'Dosh?' Si asks, pointing at the word for 'daughter' in the phrasebook.

'Da,' the guy replies sternly.

We all simultaneously take a swig from our beers.

Breaking the silence, I show the guy our route from England on the map, but he doesn't seem that impressed. Si points at Siberia and shivers. The guy nods his head. He explains to us through hand gestures that during the winter the roads are thick with snow, and he spends much of his time clearing it away from the house. It can reach as deep as the top of the door, and I try to imagine how they survive out here in such extreme conditions, especially when it drops to minus fifty below. Si offers the guy an L&M cigarette, but he declines and pulls a packet of Russian cigarettes out of his pocket. The packet is red and made of cheap cardboard. They look like something my great grandfather might have smoked in the trenches during the battle of the Somme, and encouraging us to try one I study the filterless cigarette between my fingers before accepting a light. Drawing hard, I choke on the harsh tasting smoke that fills my lungs, and quickly wipe away a tear from the corner of my eye. The guy laughs, and reaching over the table he pats me hard on the back. We all sit silently around the table and exhale smoke into the warm evening air.

'Angleeya euro?' the guy suddenly asks, flicking his ash on the table.

'What's he say?' I frown.

Si shrugs. 'I think he's asking if we use euros in England.'

'Nyet,' I reply. 'Pound. Pound Sterling.'

'Euro gutt,' he laughs psychotically. 'Dollar-ruble, nyet.' He makes a face of disapproval.

'Da,' Si grins, whipping a twenty-euro note out of his wallet. 'Euro gutt!'

Placing it on the table in front of the guy, he looks surprised and studies it with intrigue. His beautiful young daughter suddenly appears in the doorway and skips across the grass towards a shed adjacent to the café. Si looks dreamily in her direction. The guy points at Si and then over at his daughter. He nods his head approvingly and says something in Russian. Si blushes and looks shyly down at the table. The guy stubs his cigarette out on the floor and stumbles inside the café, returning seconds later with a book. He hands it to me, and despite the fact it's printed in Russian I instantly recognize it as the Holy Bible. He offers it to us as a present along with an unopened packet of the harsh tasting cigarettes. Overwhelmed by his generosity, Si gets a bit carried away and slides the twenty-euro note across the table towards him.

'For you!' he cries, slurring his words a little.

The guy looks confused and points at the note and then at his chest, as if to say, "you're giving this money to me?"

His daughter suddenly reappears from the shed looking radiant, and I catch myself admiring her slender bare legs as she skips up the steps. I look back to the table and see the guy looking suspiciously in my direction. He quickly stuffs the note into his trouser pocket and speedily clears the table. He looks paranoid as hell, and bidding us goodnight he disappears inside the café and bolts the door shut behind him. The light on the porch suddenly goes out, and we sit dumbfounded for a few seconds clutching our bottles of beer.

'Was it something I said?' Si whispers.

'You just gave the bloke twenty-euros.'

'So?'

'That's shit loads out here. He's lucky to make that in a week.'

'Really?'

'Yeah, he probably thought you wanted to give him money for some quiet time with his daughter.'

Si looks shocked. 'Don't be ridiculous!'

'I'm serious. Did you see how quickly he took the money and ran?'

Feeling slightly uncomfortable sat on the guy's porch in the dark we collect our possessions together and retire quickly to the car.

Guardian Angels

Chita is a city deep in the arse end of nowhere and is by no means a place of beauty or historical importance. It's 6200km from Moscow and is the last major stop before the Trans-Manchurian train line branches off for China 100km east. Feeling a little nervous, Chris drives cautiously through the derelict back streets and glides past a black statue of three soldiers thrusting their rifles aggressively in the air. The usual drunks sit slumped at the roadside, and stare at us intimidatingly as we crawl along the main street.

Keen to stock-up on supplies before we head any further into the unknown, we stumble across a shop with its shutters at half-mast. We manage to purchase an enormous plastic fuel tank and four large bottles of drinking water, each containing six litres. We also grab what food they have, which includes four ginger cakes, a large sack of peanuts, six cans of fish, a packet of dried fruit and a loaf of stale bread.

'Chris, do you think we've got enough food?'

'Yeah, and we've still got some chicken noodles left, remember!'

'Oh, yummy,' I smirk. 'My God, I'm nervous.'

'Why?'

'Well, we're about to enter the great unknown, aren't we? We may never return.'

'That is a possibility. I suppose, this is how Thomas Cook must've felt before heading off on a voyage across the big blue ocean.'

'Chris, it's Captain Cook, you idiot.'

'Yeah, that's what I said.'

'Look, come on, let's be serious for a minute. Where does the road under construction actually start?'

'A few miles outside Chita, I think.'

'You think? Fuck, are we going to die out there?'

Chris shrugs. 'I hope not, because that'd be a real bummer.'

'What if we breakdown? I mean, it's not like we can call the AA.'

'Si, you've got me worried now. I guess we'll just have to see what happens along the way.'

We load up the Sierra and head back through the quiet city streets. Passing a sinister looking 10ft high inflatable gorilla that bobs from side-to-side above the roof of a two-story building, we find a modern petrol station and fill up the car and our new reserve tank with fuel. Chris checks the tyres, water and oil. Everything appears to be in working order, and feeling content that we've done all we can before we attempt driving the incomplete Amur Highway, I pull hastily out of the garage forecourt and straight in front of a cop car. The siren comes on and I curse before swinging the car over at the side of the road. Pushed into the back of the rusty Larda by two policemen of Chinese origin, they stare at me as I hand over my documents. The driver talks quickly into his radio, and turning in his seat he begins to shout at me in Russian. I freeze and show him the phrasebook, but he whacks it out of my hand and continues to scream in my face. I try to remain calm, and sit in silence as he turns away and begins to mutter something to his partner. Desperate to get out of the car, I suffer another verbal attack before he throws my documents back in my face. I quickly gather them together and jump out onto the pavement, feeling incredibly shaken. Watching the police car wheel spin off, I jump into the Sierra and light a cigarette.

'Wankers!'

'What happened?' Chris frowns.

'Fuck knows. Let's just get out of here before they come back.'

We leave Chita and race through the barren countryside. The road suddenly becomes stony and unsurfaced as it stretches out towards the horizon. We drive for twenty miles without seeing a single vehicle. Unsure if we're heading in the right direction, we decide to pull over and wait for any signs of life. Starring out across the dry empty landscape towards Mongolia, there's an eerie silence. There's not one single bird or tree in sight, not a single house or telegraph pole. We're completely alone, vulnerable – there's just the dusty road, the Sierra and us. I begin to feel like we're the last humans on the planet, and if it were not for the dry grass clinging to the rolling hills, we could well be on the surface of Mars.

We wait for what feels like an eternity. Half an hour slowly becomes an hour. I pace around the car and take a leak at the side of the road. Chris becomes impatient and suggests we continue on to the first settlement on the map, but I feel nervous about what might happen if we breakdown out here. Fifty miles in the wilderness is a long way without rescue. We need to be sure that people are using this road. We have to wait for passing traffic. Our morale deteriorates with each passing minute - doubt fills my mind. This route across the top of China has always been impassable, only the construction of the Trans-Siberian train line - an incredible feat of engineering which cost thousands of lives, has managed to connect the cities of Chita and Khabarovsk across the swamps and deep valleys of this hostile terrain.

I fall into the Sierra and drum a tune on the dashboard. The sun is still high in the sky and burning bright. In an attempt to keep us both entertained, I begin to sing lyrics from my old band days with 'The Blood Sucking Flower Fairies'.'

'*I thought you were mine ... the crack in the sink, drowning in the dirt.*

You looked to the sky ... salvation dead, just shit in your eye.

She ... she's got time, she's got the time...

She ... she's got time, to change her own mind.

I want to rub shoulders with the bourgeoisie...

I want to be single I want to be free.

I want to find culture and try to understand,

I guess I want to be in a rock 'n' roll band!'

Chris turns to me with a look of irritation in his eyes.

'*It took time to discover, that you weren't like any other.*

Did you think you could make me suffer?

Well I'll tell you girl I can find another.

Well I'll tell you girl I can find another-er...'

'*SHUT UP!*' Chris yells. '*SHUT UP! SHUT UP!*'

'Chill out, I'm a fucking Rock God!'

'*NO, SI! NO!* You're not a fucking Rock God ... you're an aging hippie! A fucking hippie, who thinks he's a Rock God! Wake up and smell the Horlics, you're living in a fucking dream world!'

'Fuck you, fat boy! I had girls bowing at my feet when I was performing on stage... worshipping my every fucking move ... hanging onto my every verse. I changed girls' lives and made them realise that with my music and my words, not only could I spin them into another dimension, but I could also grab hold of their inner feelings and ... uh ... invite them back to my house for a game of naked Twister.'

Chris smiles. 'Bing-fucking-bong!'

'I was a Rock God, for Christ sake! I had passion and a need for some – hey! What's that?'

'What?'

'Straight ahead, is that a dust cloud on the horizon?'

Chris snatches the binoculars off the dashboard and

leaps out of the car. I run over to him and squint in the bright sunlight.

'What is it?' I cry.

'I don't know!' Chris yells. 'I think it's a car!'

'You'd better not be fucking around.'

'Well, it's definitely not a herd of wildebeest.'

'Please tell me it's a car.'

'It is!' Chris laughs. 'It's a fucking car!'

I leap into the air and begin break dancing in the middle of the road. '*Who's-your-daddy, bitch? Who's-your-daddy?*'

We can see the vehicle clearly now as it thunders towards us.

'Look!' I cry. 'There's another one!'

More cars appear over the horizon - two – four – five. Putting on our headlights for fear of them not seeing us, we sound our horn as they race by. The cars all toot their horns and flash their lights as an enormous dust cloud fills the air.

'They're all Japanese cars,' Chris coughs. 'They must've been shipped to Vladivostok from Japan.'

None of the cars have proper registration plates. Instead they just have a number taped inside the front window screen. Beeping the horn again, we watch as a second convoy speeds past. Some of the drivers wear white gloves, others are stripped to the waist or wearing shades. All of the brand new cars have protective covers over their headlights and masking tape wrapped around their bumpers. As the dust settles we head off in the opposite direction, passing more cars travelling in convoy along the new dirt road. We see brand new Toyota saloons and Mitsubishi estates with tyre blowouts, and watch the drivers change the wheels at great speed like mechanics in the pits at the Grand Prix. Suddenly, from out of nowhere, a huge orange overland truck charges up behind us. We're practically rubbing bumper-to-bumper, so I slow down to let it pass. The massive grill on the front of the truck fills the rear view mirror as it tries desperately to overtake. The driver swerves around our back end, but pulls quickly in as another convoy of cars fly past in the opposite direction. The truck tries again, this time managing to pull up alongside us. I battle to control the Sierra, but I'm forced to slam on the brakes.

'*WHERE'S THE FRIGGING FIRE?*' Chris yells, as the truck zooms by.

I catch a glimpse of the registration plate. They're German. Despite feeling angry by their frantic maneuver, we're excited to see a fellow pioneer on the road – I toot the horn and Chris waves frantically out of the sunroof. The enormous truck ignores us and accelerates away, leaving us choking on a cloud of dust.

'Bastards!' Chris shouts. 'They could've at least beeped their horn!'

'Maybe they weren't pleased to see us,' I reply, regaining control of the car.

'Why the hell not?'

'They probably thought they were the first ones to make it out here.'

'That's ridiculous! Well, fuck them! We've driven all the way from England. That's further, right?'

'Sure is, Crissy boy.'

'So the race is on!'

'Bollocks to that, we're not playing games here. Our only concern is that we make it to Vladivostok in one piece.'

'OK, Si, you're right. We must stay focused.'

'You know it makes sense.'

'I can't believe the size of their truck,' Chris smiles. 'I bet that thing can drive over boulders the size of Pamela Anderson's breasts.'

'Yeah, talk about being kitted out ... they must have some serious equipment with them.'

'But have they got a squeaky foot pump and an SAS Survival Guide?'

'Or a roll of kitchen foil and a rusty coat hanger?'

'Exactly.'

'Actually, Chris, I was thinking about the tyres. If all of these new cars are getting blow outs, what chance do we have?'

'We'll be all right.'

'Are you sure? We've already driven over eight thousand miles on the same four tyres, and we've only got two spares in the boot.'

'Si, don't worry, that's more than enough.'

'Hmm ... maybe we should have brought a tyre repair kit?'

Chris frowns. 'I didn't know you could get them.'

'Well, uh ... you can for bicycles. I guess it's the same for a car, isn't it?'

'I don't know?'

'Neither do I!' I reply. 'The spare tyres are crappy remolds, too, aren't they?'

'Nah, we got them from little Stuart, remember? They'll be the finest tyres money can buy.'

'Really? But I thought he found them at the back of his garage. He took them off an old Ford Cortina.'

'Stop panicking, Si. Remolds or no remolds, we're going to get this bleeding car to Vladivostok even if I have to push it there myself.'

'With no wheels?'

'All right, I'll carry it!'

Tyre marks from the German's truck are clearly visible on the dirt road in front of us, and I begin to feel annoyed by the fact that we're trailing behind in their shadow. The sensation of the open road is scarred by their presence, and I find it hard to relax. At this point in our journey there are very few cars travelling east - the only other people insane enough to attempt driving this unfinished road are the Russians driving the other way in their brand new Japanese cars.

Heading across a wide-open plain, we can hear a low moan in the distance. At first I think it's the sound of the tyres on the road, but it grows louder and we soon realise it's the wind howling across the vast landscape. We slow down and watch as a Mongolian sheepherder crosses the road in front of us with his flock. He carries a crooked staff and skillfully drives the dozens of curly horned creatures safely to the other side. They look unlike any sheep I have seen before, with huge wooly coats that protect them against the harsh Siberian winter. I look in awe at the old man's weatherbeaten face. It looks like it has been carved from wood. He takes little notice of us and continues on his journey. I can't help wondering where the hell he's taking his flock, as there is literally no sign of life in any direction.

Several hours later, we eventually reach a remote frontier town, which Chris pronounces from the road map as being called, "Yephbiwebck". Our guidebook is useless here, and without an English translation for the Russian names on our map we're very much on our own. The town is a grim looking place and consists of tin-roofed shacks and a concrete block of flats around a large industrial factory. Keen to take advantage of what could be our last opportunity to buy fuel, we stop at a junction and gather our bearings. Just as we're about to pull away, some dude in an old brown Larda pulls up beside us. He sticks his white scruffy head of hair out of the window and babbles something in Russian.

'Nyet Rooskeey,' Chris grins.

The guy looks like he's had a few drinks, and falling out of his car he staggers over to us. We stay in the Sierra this time as he peers through the passenger window and looks around inside. I move towards Chris and smile falsely. His breath stinks of booze and cigarettes, and his teeth are brown and rotten. He laughs hysterically.

'Hello!' I cry.

I show him the map and point to the symbol for a petrol station. He leans against the car door and points over his shoulder.

'Banya!' he shouts, pointing to us both.

'What's he say?' Chris chuckles.

'Banya, I think. It's a Russian sauna and steam bath. I think he wants us to join him for a sauna.'

Chris screws up his face. 'Fuck that!'

The guy frowns and begins to laugh. Despite the fact that we probably look as though we need a good scrubbing, we politely decline. He then points at a grotty concrete tower block a few hundred yards away and begins to flick a finger repeatedly against his throat. We get the distinct impression he wants us to go back to his place for a glass of vodka. Not wishing to offend the poor guy, I nod and smile and indicate to him that we're in a hurry. It turns out this is a wise decision, as he starts behaving strangely and proceeds tapping his wrist and simulates jacking-up with heroin. Smiling falsely, Chris slowly rolls the car forward. The guy lets go of the door and stumbles back to his Larda.

Finding the petrol station, which is basically a couple of ancient petrol pumps next to a tin hut, we top up the tank. A brand new Toyota pulls up on the other side of the pump and a tall Russian guy steps out and smiles at us. His mouth is full of sparkling gold teeth, and he looks like the Jaws character from the James Bond movie *Moonraker*. Tucking his smart polo shirt into his jeans, he greets us over the roof of the car. I point at his Toyota and nod approvingly. He taps the roof, and I can tell he's ecstatic to have made it here from Vladivostok in one piece. The car is covered in dust, but with a wash and a few minor repairs I imagine he will be able to fetch a very decent price for it. We try to ask him about the road ahead, but he just grins and shrugs his shoulders. We shake hands and part company.

Leaving the town, we drive for twenty miles before parking up for the night behind a large Volvo digger. There really is no turning back now. If we breakdown out here we're well and truly fucked. All we can do is try and keep an eye out for the Russians, our guardian angels, who will hopefully show us the way to Vladivostok. We devour a tin of fish with some of the bread we bought in Chita, and Chris proceeds to scare the shit out of me with statistics about how far we've travelled and how far we still have to go. We're above China now, and have passed through a staggering eight time zones. We're closer to Tokyo than Moscow and nearer to Seattle than London. Vladivostok is still a great distance away, which leaves me wondering as I snuggle inside my sleeping bag, what the hell lies in between?

The Amur Hellway

The road ahead is blocked. A sign with an arrow pointing to the left diverts us down a narrow dirt track leading into the dark forest. We have absolutely no idea where we're going. We just have to hope the diversion will take us up and around the road works and back onto the main road under construction. Si insists we play it safe, so we wait half-an-hour for a guardian angel to pass by. Seeing the lone car swing around the corner, we feel confident we're heading in the right direction. Potholes are our main problem here, as the exhaust pipe underneath the Sierra takes a pounding every few metres. We cringe with every scrape, but it doesn't seem to make any difference how slow we go or how hard we try to avoid the potholes, the Sierra is just too low to the ground. With no option, other than to turn around and head back to Chita, we're forced to grit our teeth and hope for the best as we push deeper and deeper into the thick forest.

After thirty miles of careful driving, we're brought to a sudden halt by a deep river ... a deep river without a bridge.

'I hope you've brought your arm bands?' Si laughs.

I reverse the car and rev the engine.

He drops his smile. 'You're not seriously going to drive through that, are ya?'

I nod. 'Course I am. What else are we going to do - wait

for the frigging water to evaporate?'

'Well, shouldn't we check to see how deep it is first?'

'It can't be that deep.'

Si frowns. 'How do you know?'

'I don't...'

Slamming my foot on the accelerator pedal, the front wheels spin as the Sierra speeds towards the river.

'*HOLD ON TO YOUR BOLLOCKS, HIPPIE BOY!*'

'*HOLY SHIT!*' Si yells, sinking his fingernails into the dashboard.

With a gigantic splash the car nosedives into the river. The water hits the window screen with a loud thud and sprays dramatically into the air. The buzz is unbelievable as the car burns through the water and flies out onto the other side of the bank.

'*FUCKING HELL!*' Si screams. '*LET'S DO IT AGAIN!*'

The Sierra sparkles bright white. It's never looked so clean. With huge smiles, we high-five and continue to follow the road as it winds through the forest.

After sometime we find ourselves on a relatively flat stretch of road. It carries us through a tiny deserted village and beneath a bridge supporting the Trans-Siberian train line. It's surreal to see signs of civilization out here in the remote wilderness, and following the train tracks for a few miles we stumble across a pretty little house and café at a bend in the road. We're in serious need of some refreshments, so we decide to check it out. Walking through a small yellow gate into the back garden, we find a few wooden tables and chairs dotted around on a patch of freshly cut grass. A Chinese woman looks over at us as she rocks a baby in her arms inside the doorway to the house. We sit down at a table and smile in her direction. She stares vacantly at us and continues to rock her baby gently in her arms. On the other side of the garden, a man wearing a camouflage jacket drives a wooden post into the ground with a sledgehammer.

'Are you sure this is a café?' Si whispers.

'Yeah, I think so.'

'Maybe we should leave? I think we've just walked into someone's back garden.'

The woman calls over to the guy building the fence. He drops his sledgehammer to the ground and marches over to us. He sweats profusely as he dusts himself down. With dark features and thick stubble, he looks more Italian than Russian. We order two bowls of borshch, the refreshing beetroot soup, and some coffee (kof-yeh). He smiles and disappears into the house.

'This is mad!' Si smiles. 'Who'd have thought there'd be people living all the way out here?'

'I know. These little unsurfaced roads must connect places all the way along the route.'

'So what was that potholed track we were just on, then?'

I look down at the map. 'It must be one of these grey dotted lines, seasonal roads and paths. Some of these places must be completely cut off in the winter. What an insane place to live.'

After our little feed, the man walks over and points to our map. He seems to take interest in where we are from. Si points to England and the man points to Azerbaijan.

'Caspian Sea,' I beam.

The man nods vigorously. 'Da, Caspian!'

He points past the house and over at the train tracks.

'Chita?' he grins.

Si frowns. 'Chita?'

The guy points to us both. 'Chita?'

'No, no,' Si replies. 'Vladivostok.'

He looks surprised.

I try to ask the guy which direction Vladivostok is in, just to be sure we're heading in the right direction, and he encourages us to follow him across the garden. He swings open the garden gate and waves us over. We follow him across the dirt road and through knee length grass onto the railway tracks. Two train lines run parallel to each other, one going east to Moscow and the other going west to Vladivostok. With caution we stand on the wooden sleepers. The guy points up the line towards the eastern horizon.

'Vladivostok,' he smiles.

The train tracks stretch out into the distance, and I look with excitement in the direction of a city we've been driving continually towards now for over five weeks. The man slaps Si on the back and smiles before returning to the café. I take one last look around and savour this incredible opportunity to stand with my feet on the legendary Trans-Siberian railway line. Returning to the café, we pay the bill and shake the guy by the hand. We head over to the car, and just as I'm about to jump inside I suddenly hear the roaring sound of an approaching train.

'It's the Trans-Siberian!' Si grins.

We sprint as fast as we can back through the long grass and stand at the side of the tracks. The guy from the café runs to the garden gate and points in its direction.

'*VLADIVOSTOK*!' he cries.

A huge dark green train approaches. My heart pounds inside my chest as the train grows bigger and bigger until it thunders past us at great speed, whipping Si's hair across his face. We jump in the air and dance around like excited kids at a fun fair, as each carriage zooms by one by one. A western guy with long hair peers out of the window. We think he might be a tourist, so we wave madly at him.

'*HELLOOOO*!' Si screams. '*WE'RE FROM ENGLAND*!'

The guy does a double take as he zips past. Out of breath, we watch the last carriage disappear into the distance.

As we continue on through the forest the road suddenly becomes incredibly narrow and steep, and we're forced to use the whole road in order to maneuver the Sierra over craters that are literally the size of the car. This tends to be a disruption for the guardian angels driving down the hill in the opposite direction, as they have to wait for us to pass by. It occurs to me that we must be the first people ever to cause a traffic jam in deepest Siberia. From the state of the road, it's clear this track has been heavily used for quite some time. The potholes are worn away more steeply on the far side, making it nearly impossible for us to pull the car out of the pothole without scraping the exhaust pipe along the ground. This becomes a major problem, and we can't drive for more than a few meters without getting stuck. Forced to drive into one particularly deep crater, Si revs the engine and accelerates up the steep side of the pothole. There's a loud crunch. Jumping out, we run around to the back and examine the damage. The exhaust pipe hangs in two pieces beneath the car, the join in the middle has been completely torn apart.

'*BOLLOCKS*!' Si yells. '*NOW WHAT DO WE DO*?'

'Chill the fuck out, will ya! We'll just have to fix it!'

'Easier said than done, you idiot. It's broken in the middle!'

'We can plug it back together. At least everything's still attached to the car.'

Si grabs the ariel and jabs the piece of metal into the boot lock. It springs open and he quickly gathers together the equipment. I lay a mat on the dry earth and slide underneath the car. Within a jiffy I've connected the two pipes together, sealed them with exhaust paste and wrapped kitchen foil and wire around them for extra strength.

It takes us four hours to reach the summit of this treacherous climb – covering a total distance of about six miles. I quickly gulp down a litre of water and fall out of the car. Si turns off the engine and leans back. He looks physically and mentally drained. On the bushes all around us there are colourful pieces of ribbon, socks and strips of plastic tied to the branches. They dangle like Christmas decorations, and examining them closer we notice one or two have messages scribbled on them in Russian.

'This must be the halfway point,' I beam. 'Everyone who has reached the top has tied something to the tree.'

'Hey, I've read about this!' Si cries. 'They're called wishing trees. It's a bit similar to prayer flags of Tibetan Buddhism, the religion of most Buryats.'

'Buryats?'

'Yeah, you know, the Mongol people we saw around Lake Baikal. The ancestors of that warlord dude, Genghis Khan.'

'Wishing trees ... cool! We should make a wish.'

Si smiles. 'What shall we wish for?'

'That a car full of sexy girls pulls up.'

'Nah ... something realistic.'

'OK, how about we wish for world peace?'

'Chris, I said something realistic, you prick.'

'A four day working week?'

'Not bad.'

'Free chocolate and tampons?'

'Tampons?'

'I'm thinking of the ladies here...'

'Fair enough.'

'Ah-ha, hold the frigging phones!' I cry. 'How about we wish for a safe journey to Vladivostok?'

'Perfect!' Si grins.

Grabbing a carrier bag from the boot, I cut one of the handles off with my blunt penknife and flatten it out on the bonnet.

'All righty, what shall we write?' Si mumbles, chewing on the end of a permanent marker.

'How about "Yippeeeeeee! We're in Siberia ... yippeeeeeee!"'

Si shakes his head. 'Uh ... no.'

'OK, how about "UK to Vladivostok – The Raven Brothers, June 2003?"'

'Like it!'

Scribbling down the message, Si loops the plastic around a branch and ties it firmly to the tree.

We stand back and admire it as though it were a piece of artwork.

I turn away and look down the other side of the hill. 'Right, then, brother - now all we have to do is get down!'

* * *

Reaching a remote village at the bottom of the mountain, a couple of guardian angels stand by their vehicles and prepare for the climb. You can tell by the worried expression on their faces that this section of the road is notorious, and having barely survived it ourselves we throw them a wave and wish them luck. We drive past a derelict building and see three dirty little faces appear over the rubble. The hostile looking savages, who can't be older than five or six, are stripped to the waist and scramble rat-like towards the car. I wave at them out of the window, but they respond by hurling bricks and concrete at us. One jagged piece of slate scuffs across the bonnet of the car and Chris sounds the horn and accelerates away.

The village is perfectly simple, and it's clear it has been completely locked away from the outside world until now. It feels like we've travelled back in time a hundred years, and I wonder what they make of all these futuristic vehicles suddenly descending on their world and ruining their tranquility. An old man staggers out of his garden gate and flags us down. He grips onto the side of the car and rants and rages at us. Chris tries to ask him which direction we need to go for Vladivostok, but looking confused he blinks at us - quite understandably really as Vladivostok is still a few thousand miles away. He won't let go of the door and continues to shout at us as we try to explain to him that we don't speak Russian. Chris points to England on the map, and this is all too much for a man who has probably spent his entire life in the remote wilderness. He looks about eighty-years-old, and it suddenly occurs to me that he was a young boy of about ten when the Gulags (labour camps) were put into operation. As part of Stalin's grand plan to turn the USSR into an industrial power in 1929, he forced collectivisation of agriculture with the aim of getting peasants to fulfill production quotas, which would feed the growing cities and provide food exports to pay for imported heavy machinery. Farmers who resisted were either killed or deported to labour camps in there millions and it occurs to me that this guy must have lived through that entire period. Looking into his pale grey eyes, I wonder what stories he has to tell about that time. He seems pretty upset by this sudden invasion to his world, and I can only assume his life must be pretty OK for him to stay out here after the collapse of communism. He finally loses his grip on the door and throws up his hands in despair. I feel guilty as we pull away. I guess he has spent his whole life out here building a new life in a community that had been up-routed and forced to work for the good of the nation. In his mind perhaps, especially in his old age, he felt at least he should be given the right to enjoy peace and quiet in a place his family had been forced to call home. We leave the town and head back through the countryside towards the new highway, and studying the map I console myself with the thought that before long the Amur Highway will be complete and this village will be returned to the wilderness once more.

We eventually find our way back onto the highway. We cruise at 20mph along a stony, but relatively good section of the road until it gets dark. Pulling up close to the impenetrable forest, we pass out exhausted from nearly sixteen hours on the road.

Chris crawls under the Sierra and patches up the torn kitchen foil wrapped around the exhaust. He does a pretty good job, and putting some air in the tyres with the squeaky foot pump, we feel confident to head back on the road. We drive through the morning until we reach a stretch of the highway that is in full construction. Enormous diggers shovel tons of earth as they clear a path for the road. Volvo dumper trucks tower over the Sierra as they transport rocks and stones along never ending stretches of the highway. We feel nervous as we crawl beneath their huge wheels and weave along tracks that tail off into deep canyons. We battle against the road works from dawn until dusk, at an average speed of roughly five miles an hour. Sections of the road force us to drive up steep hills at a frightening angle of 45 degrees, and we approach each turn cautiously for fear of colliding with a digger or one of the many guardian angels travelling in the opposite direction. Reversing and shunting, we carefully manoeuvre the car along the edge of sheer drops and around huge boulders. At one point we nearly tip sideways down a twenty foot drop. It takes incredible concentration, and pounding the underneath of the car against sharp rocks and smashing the bumper into the ground, we curse out of anger and laugh out of insanity with every knock and scrape. Desperately trying to stay sane, we head slowly towards the never-ending horizon.

We pass through the small town of "HeBep" around noon the next day. The place feels like a city after more than three days on the Amur Hellway, and we grin with excitement at making it this far without any major setbacks. That said, the car looks like shit. The front bumper hangs close to the ground and is held in place by little more than some electrical tape and a fist full of rubber bands. The bodywork is caked in mud and blue exhaust fumes leak from under the car. To make matters worse there appears to be something wrong with the starter motor, because when we turn off the ignition the car rattles and shakes for about thirty seconds before the engine stalls. We fill up with petrol, grab more supplies from a small shop and try to find our way out of the town. We quickly become lost and find ourselves heading up a road, which Chris thinks might be the M56 to Yakutsk and Magadan. In 1932, Stalin sent thousands of prisoners to Magadan to build docks and piers, so they could transport gold found in the Kolyma region. It became a major marshalling point for the prisoners who were sent there to work in the mines. Being sent to Magadan was a death sentence. Of over the estimated 20 million people who were either shot, starved, beaten, tortured or worked to death in Stalin's Gulag camps, an estimated one fifth died in camps around the Kolyma region. The road to Magadan is even called the Road of Bones because of the thousands of prisoners who died building it.

'We're on the M56, for fuck's sake,' Chris yells. 'We're going the wrong way!'

'Are you sure?'

'Course I'm sure!'

Suddenly, we see an orange vehicle heading towards us.

'Oh my God!' I cry. 'It's the Germans!'

'No way,' Chris laughs. 'Let's flag them down.'

We flash our lights and stick our arms out of the windows. They pull over close to the grass verge on the opposite side of the road. Chris switches off the ignition, but the engine continues to rattle beneath the bonnet and the car shakes vigorously from side-to-side before cutting out. We meet the driver at the front of his massive truck.

The German dude stares at the Sierra, and frowns. 'You drive from England in this?'

Chris nods. 'Yeah. Hard to believe, isn't it?'

'It's kaput, ya?'

'Nah ... it's just temporarily fucked,' I reply.

'If we ignore it, hopefully it'll go away?' Chris grins.

The German dude looks confused. He's a fairly young guy in his early thirties with rectangular metal-framed glasses, and a ridiculous bright green scarf tied around his neck. He looks like a nerdy accountant or a rich city boy, who has sold up and spent all of his money on this amazing adventure. His girlfriend stays in the truck and glares at us sulkily through the huge window screen.

'So, we meet at last!' Chris smiles.

'Ya, hallo,' the guy replies. 'We are on the wrong road. This road goes to Magadan.'

'I told you,' Chris beams proudly.

'Yeah, yeah, whatever.'

'Where are you going?' the German guy asks.

'Vladivostok,' I reply.

He sighs. 'Ya, we go there, too.'

'Really?' I beam, trying to look surprised. '*That's great!*'

'You've got an amazing truck,' Chris interrupts, resting his hand on the bodywork.

The German guy freezes and watches him grope the side panel with his grubby fingers.

'Do you want to swap?' Chris jokingly smiles. 'How about we swap vehicles, we'll take this and you can have our Sierra?'

The guy shakes his head vigorously. 'Nein. This is not possible. I do not want to.'

'I'm only joking,' Chris laughs, patting him firmly on the back.

The German guy looks extremely uncomfortable.

'Sorry about my brother, he's slightly retarded.'

'It is fine,' the guy replies, trying desperately to crack a smile.

'So you've driven from Germany?' I ask.

'Ya, from Munich.'

'Ooh ... the Oktoberfest,' Chris beams. 'I've never been, but I'd love to go!'

'Ya, it is very good.' The German guy looks over at the Sierra and shakes his head. 'Your car will not make it, I think.'

'Yeah it will,' I reply.

'You sleep in this car?' he asks.

'Uh-huh, it's really uncomfortable. I'll bet it's nice inside your truck, isn't it?'

'Ya, we have a bed and a shower. You have GPS?'

'No, but we've got a map!' Chris laughs.

The German guy doesn't look impressed.

'I think we are the first Europeans to drive this road,' he suddenly smiles.

'Do you think so?' I reply.

He nods. 'Ya. A Russian man in Irkutsk told us it was not possible last year. We are the first westerners to drive on this road to Vladivostok.'

'*Really*?'

We both grin with excitement. The German guy slowly begins to back away.

'We are the first,' he continues. '*The first*!'

'Who would've thought it,' Chris smiles.

The guy edges his way around the truck.

'How long have you been on the road?' I ask.

He swings open the driver's door. 'We have been on the road for two months. We are going to ship our truck to Australia from Vladivostok.'

'Wow,' Chris smiles. 'What a mad adventure.'

'Ya,' the guy nods, climbing inside the truck. 'We are the first ones to drive this road.'

I consider asking the guy if they'd like to join us for a cup of tea, but he seems in a hurry to leave and suddenly strikes the engine. Smiling falsely, he bids us farewell and accelerates away at great speed without so much as a toot. We stand in the middle of the road for a few seconds, a little confused by their hasty departure.

'What the fuck!' Chris yells. 'What's he doing?'

'Quick, get in the car!' I shout.
'Why?'
I slide across the bonnet. 'It looks like the race is on!'

The Final Frontier

'*FASTER!*' Si yells, as I whack the Sierra into third gear.

The windows are down, the sunroof is open and Si's crazy hair dances in the wind. We skid back onto the main road under construction and literally fly through the air, hitting pothole after pothole like they're little more than small obstacles in our path. The suspension takes a pounding, but determined to catch up with the Germans we happily risk destroying the car. Less than an hour ago we were driving on this road at 5mph, now it's more like 50mph.

'*COME ON, FASTER!*' Si screams, as rocks disintegrate under the tyres.

'*I'M GOING AS FAST AS I CAN!*' I shout back.

The risk of the suspension collapsing is high, but this almost seems irrelevant to us at this moment in time.

Si turns to me with a smile. 'I can see their truck up ahead. We're gaining on them, Vladivostok will be ours!'

All of a sudden, the front left tyre explodes. The Sierra swerves sharply to the left, then to the right before sliding across the highway and crashing sideways into a huge pile of gravel.

'Fuck!' I stutter, gripping the steering wheel tightly. 'Are you OK?'

Si rubs his head. 'Yeah, I'm fine.'

I force a smile. 'Now we've blown it.'

Looking extremely pale and feeling slightly shaken, we push the car back onto the road. The tyre has been completely shredded.

Si leans against the car and massages his temple. 'Idiots!' he spits.

'Looks like they've won,' I mutter, staring down at the tyre.

'Fuck the Germans!' Si cries. 'What the fuck we going to do now?'

'I don't know, do I?'

Si walks away from the car and sparks up a cigarette.

'Hey, let's not panic, bro. At least we've got two spares.'

Si looks over his shoulder and shakes his head. 'Hardly. The front right needs changing, too. It's buckled to buggery.'

'Yeah, but it still works ... it still rolls.'

I dig out the jack and one of the spare tyres from the boot. Si loosens the nuts and tries to remove the wheel, but it won't budge an inch.

'I can't get it off,' he grunts. 'The damn thing is welded tight.'

'Let me have a go.'

I grab hold of the wheel and pull with all of my might. A sharp pain shoots down my left arm, so I let go and fall backwards onto the gravel.

'We're really fucked now!' Si cries.

We both stand back and try to think for a second. Suddenly, a huge Volvo dump truck carrying mud and rocks skids to a halt beside us. A muscular guy with a bare chest leaps out of the driver's cab and strolls over. He looks down at the shredded tyre.

Si reaches through the driver's window and grabs the phrasebook. He flicks to a page. 'Shina prakolata,' he beams.

I frown. 'What does that mean?'

'It means, "I have a puncture".'

The guy nods and spins the wheel. He then tries to pull it off without any luck. Rising to his feet, he walks back to his truck and returns with a crowbar. He's built like a brick shit house, and after a few attempts he manages to wrench the tyre loose.

'Spaceeba!' I cry.

The guy seems pleased to have been of some assistance. We try to communicate through the phrasebook, and from what we gather he's just finished work for a few days. Thrusting his hips backwards and forwards, he dry humps the car and kindly informs us that he's now off to bang his girlfriend from behind all weekend. We throw him a high five. The guy jumps back into his truck and grins widely before tearing off down the road.

Successfully changing the wheel, we both agree that if we're going to make it to Vladivostok in one piece, we need to retire from the race and travel at our own – incredibly slow pace. Heading off, we begin to pass fly-overs that are under construction and cross over fast flowing rivers and wide canyons. Workmen wearing yellow hard hats sweat in the heat as they move huge concrete pillars with cranes and shift millions of tons of earth. This is the first time we've seen fly-overs on the Amur Hellway and it's a very surreal sight. We follow a dirt track that skims alongside these huge concrete pillars, which sprout out of the ground like bizarre monuments. The highway that will run over the top hasn't even been built yet, and it's amazing to witness this incredible feat of engineering with our very own eyes. In a couple of years this dirt road we're driving on will disappear as it's reclaimed by the forest and returned to the wilderness once more.

* * *

The sun on my face stirs me from my sleep. It's early morning and we're parked on an elevated muddy bank overlooking the vast forest. Chris drives for an hour before we pass a large camp where the hundreds of men working on this stretch of the road must sleep. Huge trucks and diggers line up outside a long row of portacabins, and it suddenly occurs to me that we haven't seen a guardian angel for ages. We begin to wonder if we're going the right way. I find myself distracted for a moment by chronic stomach cramps. Feeling the need to release some pressure from inside my bowls, I squeeze out a fart. My eyes widen in sheer panic as I empty the entire contents of my stomach into my pants.

'*STOP THE CAR!*' I shriek.

'Why?'

'*JUST STOP THE FUCKING CAR!*'

Chris slams on the brakes. Leaping out of the Sierra, I quickly disappear into the bushes and whip off my jeans. How degrading I think to myself, as I squat in the long grass and fling my soiled boxer shorts over my shoulder. Returning to the car, I grab some clean underpants from my rucksack and put on the pair of trousers I'd been saving for Vladivostok.

Chris screws up his face and points at my shit stained jeans. 'What are you gonna do with them? You're not putting them in the car.'

'Oh, yes I am.'

'Fuck you, Si! This is my bedroom too, you know.'

'They're my favourite jeans. I'm not throwing them away!'

'Well, put them in the boot.'

Chris looks disgusted and sprays half a can of deodorant over his shoulder.

'How embarrassing,' I grin. 'I've just pooed my pants in the middle of Siberia.'

Chris cracks a smile. 'Yeah, how humiliating. You're a twenty-seven year old man, and you've just pooed your pants like a child.'

Trying to put this awful event out of my mind, I get

Chris to spray water from the car window washers so I can wash my hands. The water rebounds off the glass and jumps in my eyes. At this moment in time we both look like dirty street urchins and, apart from splashing our faces once in a while, we have neither changed our clothes nor had a proper strip-wash in days. Chris's hair looks grey from the dust that covers the dashboard and the entire interior of the car. I lick my finger and rub an area on the back of my wrist, a white patch appears under the dirt. Dusting down our rucksacks we attempt to clean things up a bit, but we just end up creating an enormous dust cloud.

'Hey, Si,' Chris coughs, 'we're running low on petrol. When's the next village?'

I glance down at the map. 'Uh ... about thirty miles away, but its one hell of a diversion.'

'It doesn't matter, there might not be anywhere else for ages.'

Putting some air into the buckled wheel, we continue to drive along the dirt road and stop when we reach a long track tailing off into the forest.

I throw Chris a look of concern. 'Are you sure this is the right road?'

'It must be.'

'You're not too sure, are you?'

'Course I'm sure. It must lead somewhere.'

Even though the idea of leaving the main highway seems completely insane, we decide to risk it anyway. Gritting our teeth, we make our way cautiously through the forest. We drive in a straight line for about twenty minutes. The thought of breaking down out here makes me feel physically sick, as the chances of anyone passing by are incredibly slim. At least if we get stuck on the Amur Hellway there's a small chance someone will come to our aid within a few hours, but if it happens here we'll have to walk back to the main highway and persuade someone to come to our rescue. Much to our relief, we eventually see a few wooden houses in the distance on the far side of a river. Chris draws up in front of a rickety wooden bridge.

'No fucking way, Chris! We're not driving across that!'

'Shut up, Si! Of course we are.'

I tap Chris's head with my finger. 'Have you lost your frigging mind?'

'What's the big deal?'

'Look at it, you crazy fool! There's no way that bridge is strong enough to support the weight of a car.'

'Yes it is. If it can support a horse and cart, surely it can support a car.'

'But it looks like something out of an Indiana Jones film.'

'I know, isn't it cool!'

'No … it's fucking dangerous! Let's find somewhere else to get fuel.'

Chris laughs. 'Where? There isn't anywhere else. If we turn back now we're in serious danger of running out of petrol.'

'What about the reserves in the boot?'

'We've already used one tank.'

'OK, so let's use the other one, then?'

'Si, that's for emergencies.'

'*THIS IS AN EMERGENCY*!'

'Hey, fuck you! We've got to have some reserves. We need to get more!'

'Oh my God, I think I'm losing my mind.'

Jumping out of the car, I step onto the rotten bridge and peer over the edge.

'This is suicide, Chris! How can we be sure it won't collapse?'

'There's a petrol station in the village on the other side. It's marked on the map. Cars must cross this bridge all of the time.'

I frown. 'What cars? There aren't any cars. Oh, how I

dream to be on a tarmac highway right now ... oh, how I dream to be on the M25.'

'Shut up and get in.'

way, I'll walk in front.'

Chris inches slowly forward, while I help him line up the front wheels with the wooden planks. There's a wide gap running down the middle of the bridge and I can see the rushing water below. As the front tyres mount the wooden slats, they creek under the weight of the car.

'Slowly!' I shout.

With wide eyes, Chris lets out the clutch again and crawls steadily across the bridge. There's a hole about a foot wide in one of the slats, but Chris skillfully maneuvers the car around it. I can feel my heart pounding inside my chest. This is ridiculous, what are we doing? The bridge sways a little and continues to creek, but thankfully we make it safely across to the other side.

Feeling relieved, we pass the deserted wooden shacks and see a rusty sign depicting a petrol pump. A huge pile of coal has been dumped in front of a house, obstructing the view outside their window. There doesn't appear to be anyone around, and I wonder if the inhabitants are all at work in the quarries or mines that surround this area. We pass under a large railway bridge and see a small dirty coal-mining town in the distance. Another sign diverts us away from the town, so we follow the road until we reach a big yard in the shadow of the railway line. Chris pulls up beside an antique petrol pump, and we look in awe at an old rusty steam engine deteriorating in the long grass. While Chris sorts out the petrol, I stretch my legs and decide to check out this incredible relic of Russia's past. It's in serious need of restoration, but with a slap of paint it would look great in a museum. Suddenly, I see something in the corner of my eye. I turn and look in terror as an enormous black dog sprints towards me across the yard. Frozen to the spot, I'm virtually paralyzed from the eyes down and find I'm unable to cry for help. The rabid beast leaps for my throat, but luckily the chain around its neck goes taught and it's pulled violently back. This only torments the monster more, causing it to growl savagely and foam at the mouth. It really is the biggest dog I have ever seen. It's twice the size of an Alsatian and looks more like a bear. Its piercing bark penetrates my eardrums and its sharp three-inch long teeth drip saliva. I return quickly to the Sierra. The young lad filling up the car in a blue boiler suit laughs at me as I approach. He has bright orange hair and a splatter of freckles across the bridge of his nose. He looks like a cheeky kid who used to live three doors down from our house, which is pretty amazing considering we're less than fifty miles away from the Chinese border and slap-bang in the middle of the Siberian wilderness.

We wave goodbye to the carrot-topped kid and return cautiously back across the bridge to the safety of the highway. We reach a section of the road that is relatively flat, and after a few miles we blink in amazement at the sight of a signpost in the distance. This is the first signpost we've seen on the Amur Hellway, so we cheer loudly and dance around it in wild celebration. It's an amazing sight to see, particularly as it informs us that we are now only 600 miles from Khabarovsk in the Far East of Siberia, and a city that is within pissing distance of the legendary Vladivostok.

The Executioner

We drive into the night. I massage my forehead and rub my eyes as I struggle to focus on the road ahead. Car headlights dazzle as they flash by, and blinking I look over at Chris who sits glazed in the passenger seat. It feels deeply surreal to be back on a tarmac highway after being in the remote wilderness for so long and, seeing the orange glow of a city in the distance, a combination of relief and anxiousness washes over me at the sight of civilization. I had grown used to the imposing wilderness despite my fears of becoming stranded, and for a second I had almost forgotten about the chaos of the world outside. Our focus had been to survive the notorious 'road under construction', and making it to the other side it feels strange to be suddenly zapped back to reality, into a world without the problems of crossing rivers and negotiating hazardous terrain.

A white figure suddenly flashes across my field of vision.

'Wow, did you see that?' I cry feeling strangely intoxicated.

Chris jumps in his seat and looks around the car. 'You what?'

'I just saw something cross the road. A white figure.'

'A white figure?'

'Yeah.'

'A ghost?'

'I don't know, didn't you see it?'

'No, I was half asleep.'

'Shit, I don't feel too good.'

Pulling over into an empty lay by I stumble out of the car and spin around in circles, clutching my forehead.

'Are you OK?' Chris shouts.

'Head rush, I feel fucked!'

'Yeah, me too.'

I lie down on the cool tarmac and look up at the stars. The beautiful night sky is spinning above my head. I feel like I've just stepped off a ride at the fair or downed eight double vodkas in one go. Chris sits cross-legged on the ground next to me and covers his eyes.

'Maybe it's the exhaust fumes?'

I sit up and burp, feeling nauseous. 'Do you think so?'

'Yeah, now we've picked up speed it could be carbon monoxide leaking into the car from the broken exhaust.'

Climbing unsteadily to my feet, I feel as high as a kite. The ground swells like the ocean beneath me. I stumble over to the car and begin to tear large chunks out of an incredibly dry loaf of bread. I sit back down and take a swig of water - it hits my stomach with a bang and I immediately projectile vomit onto the tarmac.

'Fucking hell!' Chris cries, leaping out of the way. 'We've poisoned ourselves ... the end is frigging nigh!'

'My God, I feel bad ... so bad.'

Chris slaps me hard around the face, which does little more than numb my cheek.

'*OUCH! WHAT DID YOU DO THAT FOR?*'

'Si, stay calm! You've got carbon monoxide poisoning.'

'*I AM CALM!*' I cry, tearing another huge chunk out of the bread.

Chris slaps me around the face again, this time numbing the other cheek.

'*YOU BASTARD!*'

'*I SAID STAY CALM!*'

I fall back down onto the tarmac and blink as I try to regain my vision.

'Don't fall asleep, Si. Keep your eyes open!'

I rub my cheek and continue to devour the loaf of bread. It really does feel like I'm drunk. Afraid to sleep incase we don't wake up, I look out into the night and moan feverishly.

* * *

A scrapping sound beneath the car wakes me with a start. It takes me a few minutes to find the strength to investigate the noise, and stepping outside my head begins to pound at the temple like someone has just smacked me over the head with a crowbar. I climb into the bright sunlight and see Si's bare feet sticking out from under the car. I squat down on my hands and knees and take a peek underneath.

'Si, are you OK?'

'Morning!' he cries.

'What you doing?'

'I'm fixing the exhaust.'

'Are you sure you should be doing that?'

'Why not?'

'Well, how are you feeling? I mean, can you remember what happened last night?'

Si smiles. 'Of course! I feel better now.'

'We were lucky. If you hadn't pulled over when you did, I dread to think what might have happened.'

'Tell me about it. I was practically in a vegetative state during the night. I was dribbling down my chin and everything.'

'I know, I've never seen you like that before. You really scared me. Are you sure you feel all right now?'

'Yeah, I think so. I'm still a bit confused. I think the carbon monoxide has killed a few brain cells, but who needs brain cells anyway, right?'

I nod. 'Yeah … they just get in the way of making a decision.'

Si wriggles from beneath the car and jumps to his feet. 'That should do the trick!' he smiles, dusting down his jeans. 'I hope so anyway, because I've used up all the kitchen foil and exhaust paste.'

'Yeah, it'll be fine. The quicker we get to Vladivostok the better. We can't drive the car in this state for much longer.'

Si tosses the empty kitchen foil box onto the back seat. 'Come on, let's drive to a café and sort things out.'

To avoid poisoning ourselves any further, Si insists we drive with all four windows down and the sunroof open. Rubbish flies around inside the car as the temperature outside begins to soar. Putting my arm out of the window I surf the hot air currents with my hand. We drive steadily for a few hours through the lush green countryside, and seeing a rest stop up ahead we pull off the road and park outside a garage. Fetching the burst tyre from the boot, I roll it across the hot tarmac and show it to a young guy inside the workshop. He takes one look at it and shakes his head. I show him money and suggest we want to buy a new one, but he just barks something at me in Russian, giving me the distinct impression that he's not interested in doing business with us. Feeling defeated, we decide to grab something to eat from inside a scruffy trucker's cafe. We enter the joint and take a seat at a table near the window. It's incredibly hot inside, and a plague of flies buzz angrily behind the grotty wire mesh placed at the window. Si peers down at the coffee stained menu. A sweaty woman wearing a dirty apron, who looks like she's just given birth behind the counter, walks over and waits for our order. A fat guy sits at a table behind. He looks like a Mafia Godfather, with big yellow tinted shades hiding his eyes and a stomach that swells beneath his white vest.

Devouring a plate of mashed potato and fried eggs, he looks over at us and says something to the waitress in a gravely voice. She turns to the guy and shakes her head in disgust. He roars with laughter. I try to avoid eye contact with him, but I find it difficult not too. Si looks deeply uncomfortable and wipes sweat from his forehead. We quickly lose our appetites and decide to make our escape while we've still got kneecaps.

We continue on towards the town of Birobidzhan, where we find a more respectable looking restaurant. I head inside to check things out, but I'm surprised to see a kid's party in full swing. I quickly exit the place and return to the car.

'What's up?' Si cries, fanning himself with the torn road map.

'There's some kind of party going on inside.'

Si frowns. 'Are you sure it's a party?'

'Course I am. There's music, balloons and everyone is dancing. The girls are wearing pretty little frocks with ribbons in their hair, and all the boys are wearing smart shirts and those little caps on their heads like Jewish people wear.'

'Kippots.'

'Bless you.'

'No, that's what they're called, Kippots.'

'Oh, I see!'

'This is a Jewish area.'

'Really?'

Si nods. 'Yeah. Birobidzhan is the capital of the Jewish Autonomous region, they came here from European Russia in the twenties.'

'Bloody hell, I didn't know that.'

'You're slacking, fat boy. Hey, maybe it's a bar Mitzvah?'

'At eleven o'clock in the morning?'

'Why not? They probably prefer to party earlier around these parts.'

Deciding to eat up the remainder of our supplies, we continue on the road towards Khabarovsk. The temperature seems to be rising the further east we drive, and by the time we reach the impressive city of Khabarovsk we're sweating like pigs. Cruising through the colourful streets, the place has a surprisingly European feel considering it's so close to China and I notice there's hardly a Larda in sight, only Japanese cars and 4x4's. Gorgeous women stroll along the main street, and we're taunted by the promise of a night out. Staying strong we manage to tear ourselves away, unprepared to risk anything happening to the car or ourselves when we're so close to the finish line.

Racing into the early afternoon, we quickly find ourselves on the M60 heading south for Vladivostok. Si begins to suffer in the heat and stumbling across a small lake, we see a group of kids plunging into the water from the bank. We decide to pull over for an emergency 'clean up' operation, and within seconds Si is stripped down to his pants and swimming in the refreshing shallows. Following his lead, I jump off the side and dunk my head under the water. It feels great, and just as I begin to contemplate staying right here for the remainder of the day, I'm disturbed by the sight of some green slime sticking to my chest hair. I pick it off and fling it away, but as soon as I do more of the horrible stuff attaches itself to my skin. This is all a bit too much for me, so I swim to the bank and stagger out of the water like a green slimy swamp monster. Si doesn't seem to mind the green slime and continues to splash around in the water. Fetching a razor from the car, I attempt to shave my thick stubble in the cracked wing mirror. I grab some soap and work up a creamy lather on my face. The blunt, slightly rusty razor scrapes across my stubble as salty beads of sweat run into my eyes. If this doesn't make the job difficult enough, I'm suddenly attacked by a swarm of giant flies. They land on my face, pricking the skin with their spiky legs and buzz maliciously around my ears and nostrils. Spinning around, I swipe the air with irritation and throwing away the razor, I resort to towel whipping the bastards. I hear Si's screams from the water and through blurry eyes, I see his white chicken legs sprinting across the grass towards me with a cloud of the insects buzzing above his mullet. We both hop around the car like Laurel and Hardy, desperately trying to pull on our shorts while frantically waving our arms above our heads. Diving into the Sierra we slam the doors shut, but the vicious flies dart through the open windows and sunroof and continue to launch their attack. Cursing and swatting the air, I reverse the car out onto the highway. The majority of the flies abandon ship, but those stupid enough to stay suffer a terrible fate at the hands of Si 'the executioner' and join the dead butterflies on the back parcel shelf.

PART 3

Lords of the East

The Chinese border is less than 15 miles away. Excitedly
following our route on the map as we head south down
the tail end of Russia, Chris informs me that the forests
we're driving through now are called the Ussuriland,
which are completely different to the taiga. It's monsoon
forest filled with an exotic array of animal species including wolves, the Asian black bear and the Siberian tiger.

'No way!' I cry. 'So lurking somewhere in those trees,
there could be a tiger watching us and waiting to pounce?'

Chris nods. 'Yep, the Siberian tiger ... the largest cat of
them all! Some have been measured at three point five
metres in length.'

'That's huge!'

'I know. If one of those gets ya, you're dog food.'

'Don't you mean cat food?' I smile.

'Ha-ha! Si, you kill me do you know that? Unfortunately,
the sad truth is, the chances of being eaten by one around
here are practically zero.'

'Why?'

'Because there are fuck all left! A few years back, this
guy spent six weeks trying to track a tiger in Siberia, but
all he found was paws prints in the snow.'

'He should've gone to the zoo, it would have saved him
a lot of trouble.'

'That's not the point, you idiot. The idea was to see a tiger in the wild. They estimate there are only around three hundred left. Poachers hunt them for their bones, genitals and bile. They can fetch a fortune for them on the black market in Korea.'

'Fucking humans! I dread to think how many other species are on their way out.'

'Si, you don't want to know. This area we're in is also home to the Asian leopard, which roams the land between China and North Korea. There are only an estimated thirty of those left in the wild.'

I shake my head. 'Absolutely criminal.'

The drive through the Ussuriland is perfect, with good surfaced roads winding through the beautiful countryside. We stop for lunch at a roadside café and enjoy a bowl of meaty stew and a cup of green tea. I've got no idea what the name of the village is called we're passing trhough; we've almost given up trying to pronounce the names in Russian. All I know is, Vladivostok is at the very bottom of a red road that ends at the Sea of Japan. This is the last stretch.

From across the dimly lit canteen, I watch a Chinese woman gnaw savagely on a chicken leg. I'm shocked and a little disgusted by her urgency, it's like she hasn't eaten for weeks. The guy and girl sitting with her seem totally oblivious to her outrageous table manners. I've never seen anyone eat like this before, well, maybe apart from Chris when he's devouring a helpless kebab on the way home from the pub. Suddenly, the woman begins to choke on a chicken bone, which isn't surprising at all. Gasping desperately for air, she clutches her throat and turns a deep shade of purple. The young guy runs around the table and slaps her firmly on the back. She's thrown forward and her plate crashes to the floor. We both look on in shock. The kid continues to whack the woman on the back, and she raises her hand almost signaling for him to stop. You can see the desperation in her bulging eyes, as she gasps for air more and more urgently with each second that ticks away. Grabbing her arm, the guy drags her to her feet and proceeds to attempt the Heinrick Maneuver.

'We should help!' Chris yells.

'It's OK, he's doing the Heinrick Maneuver!'

The Chinese guy thrusts hard from behind, pushing into her diaphragm. Everyone in the café stops eating and watches the show. Even the employees standing behind the counter stop work and take front row seats. Just as she looks like she's about to croak her last breath, the guy thrusts again and the chicken bone shoots out of her mouth and lands on the floor by Chris's feet. The woman wheezes and collapses onto her chair. With the show over everyone continues to tuck into their meals and the women behind the counter get back to work.

Chris turns to me with a smile. 'Ooh, now that was close!'

'Too right,' I reply. 'Three cheers to Mr. Heinrick.'

We drive for 300 miles along the M60. We must be literally on top of Vladivostok by now. Cruising through the countryside on the last leg of our journey, there's only the promise of Vladivostok ahead, a city at the end of the world and a place that meant very little to us two months ago, and everything now. With each turn in the road we draw closer. It feels like a magnet is pulling us towards it, and as the sun shines we devour mile-after-mile propelled by a momentum that's six weeks strong. The traffic suddenly begins to build up and billboards advertising Japanese cars for sale start to appear - every man and his dog seem to be cashing in on the action.

We pass through a GAI checkpoint without any problems, and I feel butterflies in my stomach as we approach a steep hill. The Sierra climbs the gradient with surprising ease and, unless I'm completely mistaken, I could swear is running better now than it was before we left England. Breaking sharply at the top of the hill, Chris indicates and pulls hastily into a lay by.

'What are you doing?' I shout.

'We're here!' he smiles.

'You what?'

'*Look*!'

Chris points across the road at a crowd of people stood in front of a small monument. 3D letters cast in iron, which sit above a waist height concrete alter project the word "*VLADIVOSTOK*" at us in Russian. It's a sight as magical as seeing the Hollywood sign, and it renders us both speechless. Chris grabs his camera and takes a picture of my twisted, psychotic face next to the Sierra with the sign in the background. We have made it to Vladivostok in our clapped out £300 Ford Sierra – *overland*! For six weeks we have been heading in the same direction with one destination in mind, and seeing these letters on top of this hill is by far the most surreal moment of my existence so far. We have come to the end of the road ... quite literally! A complete sense of euphoria washes over me. It's all happened so suddenly. One minute we were deep in the wilderness and the next thing we know we've arrived ... *bang* ... it's almost like I'm not ready for it all to come to an end yet. I guess it will take some time for it to sink in.

A bride appears in a huge white meringue of a wedding dress and stands with the groom in front of the Vladivostok sign. A photographer snaps away at the smiling faces, and a brass band begins to play music under the trees. It almost feels like this whole event has been organized for our arrival - to welcome us to the Far East, and as a mark of respect for completing our epic journey. Sadly, it isn't for us at all, but we still enjoy the atmosphere and pretend all the same. We dance and sing and, although everyone around us probably thinks we're little more than two freaks cashing in on the free music, it gives us a buzz to think that they have no idea what we've just been through. I feel overwhelmed with emotion. A young guy in a badly fitted suit looks over and smiles. I'm unable to contain my excitement. I march over and shake him vigorously by the hand.

'Vladivostok!' I beam. 'Vladivostok!'

The guy frowns. 'Da, da, Vladivostok.'

I turn to Chris. 'My God, we made it, fat boy!'

'I know!' he yells. 'Come on, let's get out of here.'

Striking the engine Chris accelerates over the brow of the hill, and with huge grins we watch as the city of Vladivostok falls dramatically into view.

* * *

Si sings 'The Final Countdown' by Foreigner at the top of his voice, as we descend the enormous hill above the city of Vladivostok. It feels like we're coming into land. The road splits into a two-lane carriageway and we're sucked into a line of traffic, which takes us under a large concrete fly-over and spits us out in the direction of the ocean. We quickly find ourselves in the city centre, weaving around trams and suicidal shoppers. Nudging around the main square, a large monument dedicated to the Fighters for Soviet Power in the Far East, looms above the traffic. We continue on past the train station, and follow a steep coastal road around the Amursky Gulf until we finally arrive at a car park over looking the Sea of Japan.

'This is incredible!' Si beams.

'I know, I can't believe we're here!'

Si leaps out of the car and perches himself on the bonnet. 'So, what the fuck do we do now?' he laughs.

I join him on the bonnet, and shrug. 'Fucks knows.'

We sit in silence for a moment and look out across the ocean.

'We could get a ferry to Japan,' Si suggests.

'Yeah, that's one option. We could eat sushi in Tokyo, climb Mt Fuji, drink sake with pretty geisha girls and buy a really cool Samurai sword and cut off people's heads. Ah, hold on a minute, there's a problem.'

Si lights a cigarette. 'What's that, then?'

'Japan's expensive.'

'You don't say.'

'I'm serious, Si. A bag of sugar in Tokyo is about fifty quid.'

Si takes a long drag on his cigarette. 'Oh well, not to worry. To be honest with you, Chris, I'm feeling a little tired. Maybe we should just finish this last cigarette and think about heading home, what do you say?'

I laugh. 'Yeah, if we leave now we should be home in time for tea in about six weeks.'

'That's true. OK, let's get going.'

I turn to Si, and frown. 'You're taking the piss, right?'

He sighs. 'Of course I am, you prick.'

Si glances around and spots a grey concrete hotel on the hill behind.

'The Hotel Vladivostok!' he nods. 'That's where we'll stay tonight. We can decide what we're gonna do in the morning.'

'Sounds like a plan!'

We jump back in the car and make our way to the gates of the hotel. The guy at the barrier hands me a ticket and we find an empty space by the main doors.

'So where's the welcome party, then?' I smile. 'Where's the checkered flag? Where are all the pretty girls with banners with "I love Chris" on them? The Champagne should be flowing, God damn it.'

We make our way over to the hotel entrance and enter a bustling foyer. The smartly dressed woman standing behind the reception desk checks us in without any fuss and we head on up to the eighth floor. The room is $60, which is a little pricey considering our slim line budget, but happy to push out the boat in celebration of our arrival, we agree to forget about money for one night. The hotel room is clean and very spacious, and dumping our bags on the floor we're both asleep within seconds.

I'm disturbed by a telephone ringing in my ear. I lift my head off the pillow and try to focus on my unfamiliar sur-roundings. Saliva dribbles from the corner of my mouth and my vision is blurred. The loud ringing starts to annoy me. I reach over and fumble for the receiver. Unable to find it, I begin to get agitated and accidentally knock over the bedside lamp. It crashes to the floor and wakes Si. He too jerks his head off the pillow, and with pasta shell eyes he peers over in my direction. The phone continues to ring as I search desperately for the receiver.

'Answer the bloody phone!' Si grumbles.

Rolling onto my back, I swing my legs off the bed and pick up the phone.

'Hello?' I croak.

'Dobraye ootra, Mr Raven.'

'Who is this?'

'This is reception.'

I smile at the cute voice on the other end of the line. 'Oh, hello, dobraye ootra.'

'Sorry to disturb you, but it is nearly check out. Will you be staying another night?'

'Oh ... uh, yes, please,' I quickly reply. 'We're definitely staying tonight.'

'Spaceeba, Mr Raven, sorry to have disturbed you.'

I put the receiver down and fall back onto the bed.

'Who was that?' Si slurs, rubbing his eyes.

'It was some cute honey on reception. She wanted to know if we're staying another night. It must be nearly twelve o'clock.'

Si sits up and blinks at the glowing curtains. 'Twelve noon?'

'Uh-huh.'

'But that would mean we've been asleep for nearly fifteen hours.'

I nod. 'Yep, we must've needed it. I mean, we haven't slept in a proper bed since that church dorm in Vologda.'

'Yeah, that's true. Bloody hell, I feel shagged! My whole body aches.'

'Mine, too. That road certainly gave us a good thrashing.'

'*Hey*!' Si suddenly shouts. 'What are we still doing here? We've arrived in Vladi-cockin-vostok. Lets check out this town!'

It's a Kind of Magic

We wander through the bustling streets of the city and find ourselves down by the waterfront. Weaving between crowds of people gathered around brightly painted kiosks and beer tents, we head in the direction of a lively restaurant nestled beneath a green canopy. Treating ourselves to a steak, we watch a group of drunken youth's sing out of tune around a portable karaoke machine.

'This is great,' Chris laughs. 'What a bizarre city!'

'Yeah, three cheers to Vladivostok. Three cheers to Lord of the Dance.'

Chris frowns. 'Lord of the Dance?'

'Yeah, Vladivostok means Lord of the Dance.'

'Don't you mean Lord of the East?'

'Yeah, that's it!'

'Si, you're an idiot, do you know that?'

'Hey, cockhead, no one's perfect.'

'True. Anyway, you can see how Vladivostok has been compared to San Francisco, can't you?'

'Can you?'

'Yeah, it's similar, isn't it,' Chris replies. 'With all of its steep hills, tramlines and ocean views.'

'How do you know? You've never been to San Francisco.'

'Yeah, but I've seen *Herbie Rides Again*.'

'Fair enough.'

With bellies bursting, we take another stroll around the city and take in more sights before returning to the hotel around seven for a drink. Entering the lobby, we follow signs to a bar and quickly find ourselves in the doorway of a tiny room in the basement. A middle-aged woman and a very attractive girl in her twenties with curly brown hair, greet us as we enter the room. Much to our relief the younger girl speaks English, she shows us to the only table close to the bar. Chris orders a whiskey and I settle for a vodka on the rocks. We sip the drinks and quickly fall into conversation with the magnificent girl called Anika. She's six feet tall and has the longest legs I have ever seen. She sits beside me and lights a cigarette. Her short black dress clings to the tops of her thighs, and I distract myself by peering down into my vodka glass.

'In Vladivostok we think English people are cold,' she smiles.

'Cold?' I reply.

'Da.'

'Are James Bond and Robbie Williams, cold?'

She nods vigorously. 'Da, I don't like them. I like Brad Pitt and T.A.T.U.'

I turn to Chris. 'Who the hell are T.A.T.U?'

'They're those hot bisexual honeys from Russia. They performed at this year's Eurovision song contest, remember?'

I turn back to the girl and smile. 'Yeah, T.A.T.U are amazing.'

Chris tells the story about how we have driven to Vladivostok from the UK. Anika laughs and quickly changes the subject, but Chris perseveres and continues to share details of our adventure. Suddenly, an enormous guy in a purple tracksuit enters the room and walks over to the bar. He overhears our conversation and confidently joins our table. We quickly discover that Roman is an ex-Olympic Russian heavyweight boxing champion, who lived in Beverly Hills for ten years and once lived in a mansion next door to MC Hammer. Much to our surprise he seems genuinely fascinated by our story of driving from the UK to Vladivostok.

'I welcome you to Vladivostok,' he smiles, raising his glass.

We both raise our drinks.

'Nastrovia,' Chris replies.

Anika seems star struck by Roman's presence, and immediately fixes us all new drinks. Roman is the strongest guy I have ever seen. His hands are the size of Chris's head and his neck is as thick as a tree trunk. He whips out his wallet and shows us a picture of his wife, who is in the Russian Olympic karate team, and a faded photo of himself in his prime stood next to his coach. With spiky blonde hair and a ridiculously square jaw, he has exactly the same features as Dolph Lundgren, who played the Russian boxer in the 1985 classic, *Rocky IV*. He impresses us with his story of how he had to quit boxing after he was shot in the stomach. He lifts up his T-shirt and shows us the scar. We gasp in amazement as he explains to us how he was a bodyguard later in his career, and took a bullet for some rich businessman he was protecting. He hasn't been able to box professionally since, but he is now an Olympic coach. The guy's enthusiasm and energy amazes me. He seems as soft as a pussycat, and I can only imagine that it's the knowledge of his strength and abilities, which allow him to be himself. He doesn't need to put up a front, or prove that he is stronger or more capable – it's just an unspoken fact, an inner confidence that naturally demands respect. Chris looks miniature sat next to this giant and challenging him to an arm wrestle, the guy swiftly offers Chris his index finger. Taking up the challenge, Chris wraps the palm of his hand around the guy's enormous digit and takes the strain. Roman beats him with incredible ease and I sit back and look in awe at this guy's outrageous strength.

Skipping off to the toilet, I pass six Japanese guys exiting the hotel sauna. Dressed in little swimming trunks, they chatter loudly with their bottles of Ashai beer and disappear into a side room. Swaying at the urinal, I catch myself humming 'Hammer Time' and amused when I remember why, I up-tempo and dance Hammer-style over to the sink. As I exit the toilet, I hear singing coming from inside the room, which the Japanese guys disappeared into. Peeking through a gap in the door, I smile when I see them all sat around a table in their trunks listening to one of the dudes singing a sentimental love song into a microphone. Suddenly, Anika enters the corridor and walks towards me with a tray full of Ashai beer. I quickly leap back and lean against the wall.

'Oh, hi,' I grin.

'You like karaoke, Simon?'

'No ... I mean, *yes*! It's great.'

'You would like to use machine?'

I blush. 'Uh ... maybe later.'

'OK,' Anika smiles, gracefully swinging the tray into the karaoke room.

I drop my smile and make a dash for the bar. Re-joining the others at the table, Chris introduces me to a new recruit called Seung, a bizarre looking chap in his late twenties from Seoul in South Korea. Seung wears big thick glasses and has a sharp bowl cut, and is quick to inform me that he is paralyzed down the left side of his face. He tells me that his affliction is stress related and that he is unable to smile - one morning he woke up and couldn't use any of the muscles down one side of his face. It has really affected his life and he has lost a lot of confidence, especially with the girls.

'Girls like a guy with a smile,' he sighs, '...and I can't smile.'

Close to spitting out my vodka, I contain myself and listen with intrigue as Seung informs me that society in

South Korea is incredibly competitive, and that many people suffer from stress related illness. He seems fascinated by our travels, and shows great admiration for tossing aside our careers and heading off on an adventure. It is something he admits he could never imagine doing in South Korea, where the measure of success is directly related to material wealth and the achievements in your career. His family would be ashamed of him if he were to turn his back on the family business and disappear on a whim.

'Hey, Si!' Chris interrupts. 'Roman knows someone who might be interested in buying the Sierra.'

'Really?'

Roman nods. 'Yes. My friend, Artur, is croupier in the hotel casino. He has many connections. He may buy car from you.'

Seeing Anika return to the bar, she throws me a testicle-tingling gaze and starts chatting to the older woman crushing ice behind the counter.

'We go!' Roman commands, downing his vodka.

'Where?' I frown disappointed by the idea of a sudden departure.

'To meet Artur,' Chris grins.

'Oh, right. Actually, I might chill out here with Seung for a bit. You go.'

Chris looks a bit surprised by my unenthusiastic response.

Roman looks over at Anika and then throws me a wink. 'I wish you luck,' he smiles.

* * *

What the hell am I doing? I'm in a lift with an ex-Olympic boxer, who definitely has connections with the Russian Mafia and an index finger that could break my spine.

266

Roman is apparently taking me up to his penthouse suite to introduce me to his mate, Artur. The elevator seems to be taking ages - it's the slowest lift in the bloody world. He looks down at me and smiles. I crank my neck and smile back. Come on lift, how long does it take to go up thirteen floors? I know Roman must weigh roughly the same as a blue whale, but this is ridiculous. The silence is killing me. I have to say something.

'So, uh ... did it hurt when you got shot?' I mumble.

For fuck's sake! What kind of a question is that? Roman furrows his brow, while I clench my buttocks together and cringe with embarrassment. Luckily, the elevator doors open before he has time to answer. We exit the lift and walk towards a door at the far end of the corridor. Roman swings it open and welcomes me inside. The place is incredible. It's huge with an impressive view of the ocean. Roman takes me through to the lounge, where a smartly dressed guy and a pretty girl in hot pants sit slouched on a white leather sofa. I immediately notice two lines of cocaine on the glass coffee table in front of them. Roman introduces me to Artur and Katya. Artur works in the hotel casino and, I think, Katya is ... uh ... a lady of the night. Here in Russia sleeping with a prostitute appears to be as normal as brushing your teeth, although, I could be wrong, she could be Artur's girlfriend. Artur wipes his nose and sniffs before shaking my hand.

'Dobry,' he smiles.

'Dobry,' I reply shyly, nodding at Katya.

Artur leans forward, and using a rolled up note he snorts one of the lines of cocaine up his left nostril. He throws his head back and hands Katya the note. She then leans forward and clears the other line in a swift motion. There's something quite disturbing about watching a pretty girl snort cocaine, but I try not to look surprised and quickly glance down at her breasts. They both sniff hard and simultaneously grab their drinks off the coffee table.

'Please,' Roman smiles, 'take a seat.'

I do as I'm told. Artur immediately opens up a small bag and begins lining up more cocaine with a credit card.

'You would like?' he asks.

'Uh … sure,' I reply.

Katya looks over at me, and sniffs. She stares deep into my eyes.

'Chris, you want vodka?' Roman shouts from across the lounge.

'Yes, that would be great, spaceeba.'

Roman pours the drink and places it in front of me.

'Drink and be merry,' he laughs.

Rolling up a ten dollar note, I shuffle to the edge of my seat. I haven't been white line dancing for about a year, not since I went to a fancy dress party dressed as Zoro. The cocaine is as smooth as silk and hits me with a bang. Artur quickly makes me another line. I don't hesitate to accept and before you can say "Oh, the okey-cokey", I've hoovered it all up my nostril and I'm sniffing like a mad man.

Roman sits down beside Artur and talks to him in Russian. Artur listens carefully and nods his head. They both lean back and sip their drinks.

'Chris, I tell Artur about your car.'

I wipe my nose, and nod. 'Yeah, it's a Ford Sierra.'

'Maybe I interested,' Artur smiles.

'Really?'

'Da, how much you sell?'

Feeling a little off-chops, I glance quickly around the room. 'Uh … I don't know. It's pretty fucked up.'

'It is old car?'

'It's about sixteen years old.'

'Ah, it is very old car. It has big engine?'

'About that big,' I smile, holding my hands roughly three feet apart.

Artur laughs. 'You are very funny.'

He feeds me more cocaine and knocking back my vodka, I find myself jabbering away like I'm with old friends. Roman makes a call and, suddenly two beautiful girls arrive at the door. Roman immediately disappears into the bedroom with one of the girls.

Katya switches on MTV and blasts up the volume.

* * *

Seung half yawns and heads off to bed. He's as sober as a judge and seems to be slightly depressed. From what I gather he doesn't have one single ounce of enthusiasm or excitement left in his over worked body. I know he's here on business for a few days at some trade show, but why should that stop him from getting his credit card out and having some fun at the company's expense? Surely he deserves it, he's only 27 years old. I know he has a face disability, which would certainly lower your enthusiasm to 'get up and go', but to sit here all night and moan constantly while sipping a pathetic glass of orange juice, is truly incredible.

I watch as the bar slowly begins to empty. The Japanese guys stop singing karaoke and make their way to the casino, and the older woman working behind the bar kisses her colleague goodnight and heads off home. As I'd hoped, Anika seems keen for me to stick around. More than happy to keep her company, I feel deeply aroused as she dims the lights and pours us both a drink.

'Simon, do you believe in magic?'

'Magic?' I reply.

'Da, magic,' she smiles, sitting down beside me.

'Uh … I'm not sure.'

'Why not sure? I believe in magic.'

'Really?'

She nods and takes a sip of her drink.

'What kind of magic do you believe in?'

'Good magic,' she smiles. 'I read a lot of … how do you call it … fantasy.'

'Stories about witches and wizards, that kind of thing?'

'Da.'

'Wow, that's pretty cool. I haven't read anything like that for years.'

'Close your eyes.'

'Why?' I laugh nervously.

'I want to show you magic.'

Reluctantly I do as she asks, and feeling her soft fingertips against my temple, I smile at the sensation of the intimacy and silence. After sometime, I relax and begin to feel a warm energy flowing into my body through her fingers. It trickles past my ears and down either side of my neck, and spreads quickly across my shoulders and down my spine.

'Can you feel it?' she whispers, breaking the silence.

'Yeah, I think I can.'

'It is magic, Simon.'

The warm sensation fills my entire body, reaching the ends of my fingers and the tips of my toes. I shift in my seat and clear my throat as I feel my trousers becoming tighter around the crotch. Anika drops her hands and sits back as the warm energy continues to circulate around my body.

'How do you feel?' she whispers softly.

'That was amazing.'

'You see,' she smiles, looking pleased, 'I told you there is magic.'

Composing myself, I take a sip of my drink.

'What is your symbol?' she asks.

'Symbol?'

'Da. You say in English astrologic?'

'Oh, my astrological star sign.'

'Da, da, what is it?'

'Scorpio.'

'Ah, this explains a lot. And what is your Chinese animal?'

'Uh … year of the Tiger, I think.'

She throws her head back, and gasps.

'What's the matter?'

'Nothing. It is very powerful combination. We are compatible!'

'*Really*?'

'Yes, in head and heart.'

'Excellent,' I grin.

'What makes you happy in life, Simon?'

'Happy?'

'Yes. Just answer the question,' she snaps, grinding her teeth together.

I shrug. 'Dunno. I hate it when people are sad.'

'Yes! I see this in you, Simon. You cannot be happy unless the people around you are happy. You search for this?'

'Yeah, maybe I do. I've been searching a lot just recently.'

'I hope you find what you look for.'

'Hmm, I was thinking maybe it's better I don't. I'm enjoying just looking for it right now.'

'Ah, I see! It is the journey you love. This is very wise.'

Anika's eyes flicker in the dim light. I can feel her warm breath on my neck.

'Simon, you like to go somewhere?'

'Go where?' I hesitantly reply.

'Somewhere private.'

She begins to draw her nails across my back. We kiss.

'I like you, Simon,' she whispers, pushing her tongue into my mouth.

'I like you, too.'

'You have money?'

I'm surprised by her question. 'Money?'

'Da.'

I nod shyly. 'Yes, I have money.'

Taking my hand, Anika rises to her feet and leads me out into the corridor.

* * *

With half a gram of the finest cocaine in my bloodstream and a room full of beautiful girls to keep me inspired, I hoover up another line and pat Artur on the back.

'I like you, Artur. You're a good man,' I smile.

'Da, I am, Spaceeba,' Artur arrogantly replies. 'So, Chris, now you in Vladivostok what you do?'

'Well, I only have a small amount of money left, so I need to return home pretty soon.'

'Where is home?'

'Daventry.'

Artur frowns. 'Dovintery?'

'No, Daventry. It's in England.'

'Ah ... da, da, England. David Beckham!' he smiles.

'Yes! You like David Beckham?'

'Da, he has cool hair.'

Artur looks embarrassed by what he has just said and darts paranoid glances around the room. 'So why you not drive home to Dovintery?' he asks with wide eyes.

'No way, it's too far! I don't think my body would be able to withstand the pain. We thought about getting the boat to Japan and flying home from there, but our money situation is a problem.'

'Get train to Moscow,' Artur suggests.

'I was thinking about that.'

Artur clicks his fingers and beams a smile. 'You go to China!'

'Hey ... now there's an idea! Ah, but we don't have visas.'

'There is Consulate in Khabarovsk. You are very close ... you should go! China is cheap and nice girls for you in China.'

'I like what you're saying! You should come with us?'

272

Artur drops his smile. 'Impossible,' he replies, shaking his head. 'I have work and no money.'

I nod sympathetically. 'Maybe next time.'

He shrugs his shoulders and lights a cigarette.

'Hey, Artur!' I suddenly cry. 'You still want the car?'

'Da, I still interested. But how much for car?'

'For you … *nothing*!'

'Nothing?'

'You're a good man, so I give it to you for free.'

Artur looks confused. 'You give me car for free?'

'Yes, I want you to have the Sierra. No money!'

'You joke with me, Chris.'

'No, I'm serious. I want you to have the car.'

Artur still looks confused. 'But…'

'No buts … the car is yours!'

'Spaceeba, Chris!' he beams, shaking my hand vigorously.

I jab around inside my pockets for the keys, but I remember I've left them in the room … my mind races.

'I want to give you the keys!' I cry.

'The keys?' Artur frowns.

'Da. *The keys*! I want to give you the keys to the car!'

Artur nods vigorously.

We sit in silence and smile at each other, confused and waiting for the next move. Leaping to my feet, I suddenly march across the penthouse suite like a soldier on parade. Artur charges after me and meets me at the door.

'Where you go?' Artur shouts.

'To room 806 … to get the keys for the car!'

'Room 806?'

'Da.'

His pupils are huge and his face looks slightly twisted.

'But, what about girls?' he whispers, pointing over his shoulder.

I see Katya dancing in front of the TV with the girl in thigh length boots. She blows me a kiss.

'You want boom-boom?' he winks.

A sneaky grin appears across my sweaty face. 'I'll be right back!'

Charging out of the room, I make my way speedily down the corridor. Did he just say what I thought he said? I pick up pace and decide to take the stairs. Jumping two to three steps at a time, I arrive quickly at the eighth floor. Finding the room, I fumble with the key in the lock and leap inside. I zip around the beds like Speedy Gonzalez and snatch the car keys from the bedside table. I dive into the bathroom and check my appearance. Fuck, I'm sweating. I reach for the towel and wipe my face. I pace around the bathroom and look in the mirror again.

'Calm down, Chris, you're looking cool,' I mutter under my breath. 'You're just a little off-chops, that's all.'

Stripping off my clothes, I impulsively decide to take a shower. I turn the temperature to cold and dance around under the powerful jet of water. Feeling refreshed, I throw on a bathrobe and begin brushing my teeth. Struggling to concentrate, I suddenly remember what I'm supposed to be doing.

'The keys! I must give Artur the keys!'

Just as I'm about to throw my clothes back on, I hear a knock at the door. I'm immediately paranoid. Creeping up to the door I peer through the spy hole. To my great surprise, I see Katya stood outside the room with the girl in the thigh length boots. I blink and rub my eyes. Dabbing my face on the corner of the bathrobe, I take a deep breath and swing open the door.

'Hello,' I beam.

The girls giggle and push their way past me. I stumble to one side and watch them jump playfully on my bed. My God they're sexy, but what the hell are they doing here?

'I'm supposed to be going back to see Artur,' I smile, fidgeting uncomfortably. 'To give him the keys for the car.'

The girls giggle.

'Artur sent us,' Katya smiles, licking her red lips.

'He sent you to my room?'

They both look at me and nod.

Katya is absolutely beautiful. She has blonde bobbed hair and big blue watery eyes. The other girl is also incredible, with long jet-black hair tied back in a ponytail and a piercing above her right eyebrow. You just want to wrap her up in cotton wool and pop her in your pocket. I still feel really coked up, so I race into the bathroom and slap my face. It's all too good to be true - I'm alone in a room with two girls who seem to be, well ... up for it! I grab the towel and dab my face. Skidding out of the bathroom, I catwalk up to the girls. Katya grabs my hand and pulls me onto the bed. She begins kissing me on the lips while the other girl begins to unzip her hot pants. I lie back in amazement and watch the girls undress each other. I keep expecting to wake up and find myself sitting in the car on an empty road in the middle of Siberia, but I don't. This really is happening. Within seconds, the girls are naked and kissing each other. I stand over them, my legs turn to jelly and without any warning Katya unties my robe and starts working away on my bad boy. The other girl kneels forward and begins to join in. It's impossible for me to describe how I feel at this moment in time, nothing in my entire life has even come close to being as pleasurable as this. Katya looks up at me and holds up a condom. I smile and quickly remove my robe. Both girls throw me back onto the bed and quite literally eat me alive.

Foot People

It's eleven o'clock in the morning and I'm dancing around in the shower like a freak on heat, massaging shampoo excitedly into my scalp and humming an annoying tune that I can't seem to get out of my head. I feel great, I feel so very, very great! OK, so I've got a banging headache and my body aches after nearly two months of sleeping upright, but the pain is almost irrelevant right now, because earlier this morning I had sex with two beautiful girls ... at the same time! Whipping the shower curtain to one side, I leap onto the bathroom floor and grab the bottle of shampoo off the sink. Using it as a microphone, I spin around and punch the air. I've never felt like this before ... I feel so alive!

Last night I had entertained the girls for a couple of hours, or should I say they'd entertained me, and when the naughty little chick-a-dees finally left my room, they bumped into Si in the corridor. His face was priceless. "I can't believe it!" he yelled. "Two girls! You lucky bastard!" Si's night had been pretty eventful too, though. The beautiful girl who worked in the bar downstairs, had certainly performed some magic on him all right – and magic that had very little to do with white gloves, top hats and fluffy bunny rabbits. Well, at least as far as I know.

Drying myself with a warm towel, I contemplate whether or not we should feel guilty about paying for sex.

In hindsight, I hadn't actually paid for it as the girls had visited me as a favour to Artur in return for giving him the car. Si, on the other hand, had paid a girl for sex in hard cash … no excuses. I don't think he felt particularly proud of himself, because when he got back to the room in the early hours of the morning he mentioned it straight away. I think he felt it was wrong in some way, even though she had told him she only did it very occasionally, and had only done so because she found him attractive. I'd tried to console the poor lad by informing him that in Russia they viewed prostitution quite differently to how we do in England, but it didn't appear to help much.

Skidding out of the bathroom, I find Si lying on his bed spread eagle in his pants. Grabbing a towel off the back of the chair, I proceed to towel whip him a few times.

'Fuck off!' he cries, leaping off the bed. He stands shivering and confused in the corner of the room.

'Morning, stud!' I laugh, messing up his hair.

'Leave me alone! What time is it?'

'Just after eleven.'

'In the morning?'

'Yes, in the morning, numb-nuts. Come on, we've got to get moving. We have to check out at twelve.'

'Why, where are we going?'

'China!'

Si frowns. '*China*?'

'Yep.'

'Since when?'

'Since last night, don't you remember what we talked about?'

'No!'

'Shit, maybe I forgot to tell you.'

'Tell me what?'

'What Artur suggested we should do. We're going to China, hippie boy! There's a Chinese Consulate in Khabarovsk, we can get the train.'

'Wait a minute,' Si mutters. 'China? As in kung fu, chopsticks and sweet and sour pork balls?'

'Yes!'

'Are you sure we've got enough cash?'

I shake my head. 'Not really, but China's cheap as chicken shit, and we've got to get home somehow. We may as well fly home from Beijing or Hong Kong instead of backtracking to Moscow. Hey, we might even be able to make it overland to Bangkok!'

'Bangkok? Chris, you're talking out of your arse.'

'I'm not, use your noodle! Flights from Bangkok to London are cheap. The money we save flying from there might give us enough to travel for a few more weeks overland.'

A smile appears across Si's face.

'You're right, excellent idea!' he cries, boxing the air. He freezes in mid-punch. 'Hey, but what are we gonna do about the car?'

'Oh, you don't have to worry about that. It's sorted!'

'What do you mean?'

I scratch the back of my head. 'Well, I probably should have consulted you first, but in all of the excitement I kind of forgot.'

'Chris! Forgot what?'

'Well ... last night, I sort of gave the car to Artur.'

'*What*? What do you mean, "gave"?'

'He's a nice bloke, and I kind of felt guilty that he doesn't earn much money, so ... I gave it to him.'

'For free?'

'Uh ... yeah.'

'*You idiot*!'

'Come on, Si, what else are we gonna do with it? It's not like we were gonna drive it back to England, and we haven't got the money to hang around here for too long. This works out easier all round.'

Si walks over to the window. 'I suppose you're right. Although, I thought the idea was to sell it to him - not give it away.'

'Yeah, well...'

Si looks over his shoulder and eyes me suspiciously. 'Hang on a minute ... cocaine ... threesome?'

'Ah, well, yes ... I guess in a way that's what I got in exchange for the car.'

'You sold *our* car for a gram of cocaine and a threesome?'

'Hmm ... I suppose I did.'

Si thinks about this for a second. '...*Awesome*!'

With clothes spilling out of our rucksacks, we stumble into the reception area and look around for Artur. He's nowhere to be seen.

'Where is he?' Si moans.

'If he's got any sense he'll still be in bed. Tell you what, why don't you go and check us out of the hotel, while I wait here for Artur.'

Si nods and heads over to the reception desk.

Suddenly, Artur slides up beside me with his eyes half-closed and his bright blue shirt buttoned up the wrong way.

'Sorry I late,' he pants darting his eyes around the foyer.

'No problem,' I smile, 'we've only just got here.'

I pat him lightly on the shoulder. 'Thanks for sending down the girls last night,' I wink.

'Girls? Oh, no problem. You had good time, Chris?'

'Absolutely! What can I say, it was a nice surprise.'

Artur grins. 'You give me car for free, I give you girls for free. I am man of respect.'

I nod vigorously. 'You are indeed!'

'If you happy, I happy,' he beams.

'I have the keys for you now, Artur. Do you want to see the car?'

'Da. Can you drive car to hill behind hotel? I come in five minutes. I don't want boss to see.'

'Yeah, the hill just outside?'

'Da.'

'No problem,' I smile.

On that note, Artur sprints off and disappears around the corner. Si returns with a piece of paper in his hand.

'That Artur dude was right,' Si grins. 'There's a Chinese Consulate in Khabarovsk. It's an eight-hour train journey from here.'

'Eight hours! Is it that far?'

'Yeah, we passed through it two days ago, you numb-nuts. Have you forgotten already?'

'Of course not.'

'It's about five hundred miles, it should be fun,' Si smiles. 'Let someone else do the driving for a change. Where's Artur gone?'

I shrug. 'Dunno. He wants us to meet him on the hill behind the hotel.'

'Why?'

'He doesn't want his boss to find out about the car. Don't know why? Fuck it, let's go!'

We drive the car up the hill and park over looking the Sea of Japan. It's weird to be back in the Sierra again, and it really puzzles me how the hell we managed to live for so long in a car in this condition. When we were on the road it felt normal, we were in the same state as the Sierra - all filthy and clapped out, and I realise now how close we were to failing in our mission. The interior is completely covered in dust and the floor is littered with food wrappers and empty water bottles. It smells disgusting, and the thought of having to sleep in here makes me feel physically sick. How we did it I'll never know. Adrenaline, determination and complete insanity can be the only answer. I walk around to the boot and scribble 'UK to Vladivostok' in the dirt. Even though the exhaust is wrecked and all four tyres are flat, Artur is one lucky guy. For a start, there aren't any Ford Sierra's in Vladivostok, so he'll be driving around in one of the coolest cars in the city. Well, maybe not the coolest car in the city, but certainly one of the most original. In years to come I'd love to return to Vladivostok and see if it's still cruising around the streets. I'm sure it will be. Looking through the paper work, it suddenly occurs to us that we had signed a customs declaration form when entering the country. Si begins to worry that leaving the car here in Russia might actually be illegal. We persuade ourselves that there's little we can do, and that we'll just have to trust Artur to sort things out.

Artur meets us on the hill. His eyes light up when he sees the Sierra, which is incredible considering it looks like its about to collapse in a heap. He loves the car and circles around it, peering through the windows. I quickly take a picture of Artur holding up the car keys.

'Russia and England, friends!' he cries. 'Russia and England, friends!'

He looks so happy. We show him the customs declaration form, and he puts our minds at rest by informing us that his girlfriend's father is a cop, and that anything can be arranged in Russia if you know the right people. We feel a little reluctant to give him the V5, but he insists that it's necessary in order to register the car as a Russian vehicle.

Shaking his hand vigorously, it's time for us to depart and say farewell to our trusty time machine. Artur leaps into the car without even flinching at the smell, and strikes the engine. It roars like a sports car, well, sort of, and we fight back the tears as we watch our beloved Sierra disappear out of sight.

'I can't believe it's gone,' Si sniffles, swinging his bag over his shoulder.

'Yep, it looks like we're on our own again. Back to being just simple foot people.'

We both smile and glance out across the ocean.

Walking over to flight of steep steps that cling to the side of the hill, we're just about to make the journey down to the train station when Si suddenly sees something making its way up the winding road.

'*NO WAY!*' he cries. '*IT'S THE GERMANS! WE FUCKING BEAT THEM!*'

Their unmistakable huge bright orange truck skids into the hotel car park. With massive smiles on our faces, we watch the excited couple leap out of their truck and swing each other around in celebration of their arrival.

I turn to Si and raise an eyebrow. 'Shall we go down and say hi?'

'Nah ... let them enjoy their moment. They've come a long way, they deserve it.'

'Where's the fun in that? I think it'd be rude if we didn't. Come on, let's go down there and surprise them.'

Si smirks. 'Yeah, but how much cooler is it that we know we got here first. It's almost too perfect.'

'Uh ... fuck that!'

Cupping my hands around my mouth, I shout at the top of my voice. '*GUTEN TAG, AMIGOS! HELLOOOOO...!*'

The Germans stop hugging each other and look up in our direction.

We both stand proud and wave.

'*WE BEAT YOU!*'

They glare at us in stunned silence. We wave one last time before disappearing down the hill in childish fits of laugher.

* * *

Looking like a right couple of backpackers, I follow Chris through the busy city streets. Feeling extremely vulnerable without the safety of the Sierra, we join the chaos inside the train station and look up at the departure board. Khabarovsk is nowhere to be seen, so we race down the main stairs and join a long queue at the ticket desk. As we slowly inch forward with our rucksacks between our thighs, a guy dressed in a mustard coloured military uniform pushes through to the front of the queue. The people behind mutter under their breath. We eventually make it to the window, and I peer through the glass and smile at the woman sat behind the desk.

'Khabarovsk?' I smile.

'Adeen?' she sternly replies raising a finger.

'Uh … nyet, dva,' I reply, raising two fingers.

She nods her head and proceeds to print out two tickets. She circles the price on one of the tickets with a green pen and slides them beneath the window. We rummage around in our pockets and collect the cash together. She throws the change at us, and wrestling with our bags we haul ourselves to one side.

'Shit, we didn't ask her when the train leaves?' Chris yells.

'It must say on the ticket.'

Chris begins to scan his ticket. 'Ah, it leaves at seven forty-five.'

'What time is it now?'

'Nearly five.'

'Perfect! Let's grab something to eat in the restaurant.'

Sliding our heavy bags over to a small crowded cafeteria, we ignore the stares and order a selection of dry boring rolls, which appear to have absolutely no filling. We wash them down with a couple of beers and clock watch until it's time to go.

Feeling a little tipsy, we head for the platform and find the correct carriage. The Khabarovsk-Vladivostok express train is surprisingly quiet, which is great because we have the whole cabin to ourselves. We sit on the bottom bunks and stare out of the window as the train pulls out of the station. The journey to Khabarovsk is relaxing, but I feel detached from what's happening outside. The landscape and the villages flash by at great speed, and I smile in satisfaction that we know what it's really like out there in the depths of the Far East. We call it a night after a bite to eat in the buffet car, and collapsing onto my bunk I fall quickly asleep to the awesome sound of the clattering carriages.

The door to our compartment slams open and a deep voice shouts "Khabarovsk".

'Chris!' I cry, reaching over and shaking his dead weight. 'Wake up, we're here!'

He groans and turns over.

'Come on, we have to get off!'

Chris sits up and looks around the carriage. Still fully dressed, we quickly gather together our belongings and shuffle off the train. We stand for a few moments on the platform, feeling incredibly dazed. Hoards of people make their way quickly towards the exit, knocking us to one side as they rush by. It's just after 6 o'clock in the morning, and even though I slept like a baby last night my eyes refuse to open.

'What do we do now?' Chris asks, his face greasy and his eyes swollen.

'I haven't got a clue.'

I sit down on my rucksack and fish my contact lens case out of my pocket. Balancing the white plastic case on my knee, I manage to rinse out each lens with solution before forcing them into my eyes. Chris fishes a bottle of water out of his bag and pours half of it down his throat.

'Ah, water tastes so good when you're thirsty,' he gasps.

'OK!' I cry, leaping to my feet. 'We need to get ourselves a Chinese visa. Time is against us.'

Wrestling with our bags, we make our way out of the train station and into the street. Studying a handy street map of Khabarovsk in the guidebook, we decide to grab a taxi to the Hotel Intourist, which is close to the Chinese Consulate. After a twenty minute ride through the back streets, the taxi driver pulls up outside the main entrance to the hotel, and in true 'you're-tourists-so-I'm-going-to-con-the-shit-out-of-you' style, the hard looking dude vastly over charges us. We reluctantly hand over $15, and feeling cheated we step inside the hotel and make a beeline for the tourist desk. We wait patiently for the girl behind the counter to finish talking on the phone. She lowers the receiver and looks blankly in our direction.

'Dobry den,' I smile. 'Do you speak English?'

'A little,' she sulkily replies. 'How can I help you?'

'We'd like to go to China, please.'

'China?'

'Yes.'

'You must go by boat,' she sighs.

'By boat?'

'Da.'

'Can we arrange this here?'

'I must ask, please wait.'

The girl makes a call and before she's replaced the receiver, a smartly dressed middle-aged woman with bleached blonde hair appears from an office across the foyer and walks over..

'Good morning,' she smiles. 'Please forgive me, my English is not good.'

'That's OK,' I reply. 'My Russian is probably a lot worse.'

'How can I help you?'

'We'd like to go to China. Can we arrange a ticket for the boat here?'

'When would you like to go?' she asks.

'We were hoping to leave ... well, as soon as possible,' I smile.

'Did you know the border has been closed for six-months?'

'No, we had no idea!'

'It re-opened two days ago.'

'Really? That's a bit of luck,' I smile. 'Why has it been

closed?'

'You know SARS?'

'*SARS*?' Chris replies.

'Yes, there was an outbreak in China. We are very angry. Not many Japanese tourists come now. Very much problems for just a stupid flu.'

'That's terrible,' I mutter.

'Where are you from?' she asks, sounding keen to change the subject.

'Daventry,' Chris grins.

She frowns.

'England,' I smile.

She looks suddenly excited. 'You are the first English people I have met. I thought you were Italian. What are you doing here in Khabarovsk?'

'We've been travelling across Russia,' Chris replies. 'We drove here by car.'

'Wow, this is big adventure!' she beams. 'You put your car on the train at Chita?'

'No way, we drove on the new Amur Highway,' Chris announces proudly. 'Well, that's if you can call it a highway.'

'You must be very brave.'

Chris drops his gaze and turns red. 'Nah, not really.'

'Please allow me to welcome you to Khabarovsk.'

'Thanks very much,' I grin.

'OK, so you go to the Chinese border town of Fuyuan tomorrow on day trip?'

'No, we would like to depart Russia from here,' I reply.

She frowns. 'You do not return?'

'No, we want to travel into China.'

She looks serious for a minute. 'This is not normal. I will have to make a few telephone calls. Please wait here for a moment.'

The woman quickly disappears into her office.

Pacing around the reception area, we wait for over half-an-hour for the woman to return. We begin to wonder if it might not be possible to go to China after all, and on top of this we begin to worry about the threat of SARS.

She immerges from her office and marches over to us with a piece of paper in her hand.

'I can arrange everything for you,' she nods, 'including the boat to Fuyuan and a bus transfer to Harbin, but it will cost sixty dollars each.'

Chris looks uncomfortable. 'Why does it cost so much?' he asks.

'I will be honest with you, we must bribe the officials to let you cross the border.'

'Wow, sounds exciting,' I smile.

'Yes, my contact in China seems to think it will be OK, but there is a risk they might not let you in. As far as I know, no tourist has crossed this border into China since 1996. It was a Ukrainian man who came here. He never returned, so I assume he managed to enter China on the other side without problem.'

I throw Chris a look of concern.

'Most people who cross this border are Russians buying products from the market in Fuyuan, to sell here in Khabarovsk.'

'Right, so nothing is guaranteed,' Chris smiles.

'You will be part of tour group, so I think it will be OK.'

I turn to Chris. 'What do you think?'

He shrugs. 'I dunno, maybe it's worth the risk. What about visas?'

'You can get a tourist visa from the Chinese Consulate today,' she replies.

Excited by the challenge, a devilish grin spreads across my face. 'OK, we'll do it!'

She nods. 'Are you staying here in the hotel?'

I look down at our dirty bags lying in a heap on the floor. 'Yeah, I guess so. We haven't sorted anything out yet.'

'I will have your tickets ready by this afternoon, so please arrange your visas and I'll give you all the information you need when you return from the Consulate.'

Checking in at reception, we grit our teeth and pay $100 for a double room. Entering the large suite, we dump our bags and look out of the window over the Amur River.

Chris tilts his head and looks up river. 'China here we come!'

'Yeah, do you think this SARS malarkey is a problem?'

'Best not think about it.'

'Maybe we should think about it?'

'Why?'

'Well, it's pretty serious, isn't it?'

'Don't worry about it, Si. I'm sure it's all media hype.'

'I bloody hope so! What is SARS, anyway?'

'SARS stands for Severe Acute Respiratory Syndrome. It's basically a killer virus that's not dissimilar to the virus that causes the common cold, except, we don't have any immunity to it.'

'Sounds nasty, what are the chances of getting it?'

Chris shrugs. 'Pretty slim I would imagine. I mean, as far as we know only a handful of cases have been reported, and there are over 1.3 billion people in China. I'm sure we'll be fine.'

'Don't count your dirty chickens, fat boy! The Chinese Government is notorious for covering things up and hiding the facts. I'll bet there have been thousands of cases that we haven't even heard about. What are the symptoms?'

'High fever and headaches.'

I press my hand against my forehead. 'I feel a tad feverish right now.'

'Nah ... don't worry, Si. That'll be the vast quantities of alcohol you consumed in Vladivostok, and a perfectly normal reaction to getting your end away for hours in a hotel sauna.'

I try to hide my smile. 'Pleasure in the face of danger, isn't it ironic?'

'What is?' Chris replies.

'That we can be stood here looking death right in the eyes, and yet simultaneously feel so fantastically alive.'

Chris glazes over. I can tell his thoughts are back in the hotel room in Vladivostok with the two girls. 'Yeah...' he smiles, 'I know what you mean. It's true. I really have never felt more alive.'

Exiting the hotel, we follow a path that leads around the back of the building and down some steps. We cross a pleasant tree lined park that runs alongside the river, and pass the impressive Lenin Stadium with its large statues of a boxer and an ice skater outside the gates. The next building along is the Chinese Consulate. A group of people queue up outside, so we grab a ticket and wait patiently in the sunshine. It takes about three hours and a further $60 to get a one month visa glued inside our passports. Returning to the hotel via the banks of the river, we admire the blue piece of paper with Chinese characters printed on it, like it's some kind of certificate of achievement for making it this far. Dropping by the hotel tourist office, we're presented with our tickets for the boat. The woman informs us that the hydrofoil departs tomorrow morning at 7am. All the necessary arrangements have been made, and we're to be met on the boat by a Chinese tour operator called Yut. Feeling completely exhausted, and utterly relieved to have sorted everything out, we thank the lady again and crash out in the hotel room.

I lie paralyzed on my bed and stare up at the ceiling. The night sweats take hold of my body and I'm tormented by a feverish sleep. Images from our journey flash through my mind and I struggle to remember where we are. I replay the scene of the horrific car accident we saw on the road, and I see the ghostly figure of the dead driver lying stretched out on the tarmac. I pass through the remote Siberian villages that are locked in time. I see children playing with rusty metal hoops - a pretty girl dressed in a pink party frock with ribbons tied in her hair sings as she rocks backwards and forwards on a swing hung from the branches of a tree. Chimneys bellow smoke into the air as we pass through concrete city suburbs. Flames reach out towards me from the forest fires and I can feel the immense heat on my face. My mind races and we're driving along a dusty potholed track, we pass hunched over figures who turn for a brief second as we pass by - their faces like masks, carved from dark wood.

A Touch of SARS

Startled by the bleeping sound of my alarm clock, I sit up and wipe my sticky face on a towel. I climb out of bed and grunt at Si, who sits on the edge of his bed with his head in his hands. We quickly get dressed and head down to reception with our heavy bags. The lady from the tourist office greets us outside the elevator.

'Good morning!' she sings from behind a pair of enormous sunglasses. 'Your transport to the boat terminal is waiting outside. Please follow me.'

'What about breakfast?' I whisper to Si.

'Later!' he snaps.

We clamber inside the back of a taxi, and look sleepily out of the window as we head through the quiet city streets. Within no time at all we arrive at the boat port. Si quickly grabs some water and a sack of plain crisps from a small kiosk. The lady from the hotel escorts us to the small hydrofoil terminal, and we join a long queue at passport control. The woman shakes our hands, and with genuine sincerity she wishes us a safe journey.

'Yut will meet you on the other side,' she shouts over the noise of the crowd. 'Good luck!'

Like two confused toddlers on their first day at school, we slowly wave and watch her leave.

'Hey, wait a minute!' Si cries. 'I thought Yut was meeting us on the boat?'

'Don't worry, it's all cool.'

Reaching the front of the queue, we approach the glass screen and hand over our passports to the stern looking Russian official behind the desk. A spotlight glares in my face, and I'm made to stand behind a yellow line with my hands by my sides. I suddenly remember the Sierra, and begin to worry they'll quiz us about its whereabouts. Thankfully, the guy doesn't say anything, he just hands back our passports and waves us right. We head towards the exit where we're greeted at the gangplank by two female customs officials dressed in military uniform. With short skirts and black leather boots, both women are blonde and extremely attractive. They look like the stars of a low budget pornographic movie, or a couple of strip-o-grams in costume. I struggle to hold my composure. The dirtier looking of the two wears blood red lipstick and glares at me coldly. They check our exit stamps and dismiss us without so much as a smile. We find our way onto the boat, and sit at a table with two friendly women and a young lad of about fifteen years old. The kid looks sulkily out of the window, and it seems clear that even out here in the depths of the Far East, teenagers suffer from the same hormonal roller coaster ride as the rest of the world. I can hear his thoughts. "I hate you! I didn't ask to be born! Why can't you all just leave me alone?" The woman sat next to him opens a plastic tub filled with sandwiches and places them in the centre of the table. She offers us both one and feeling it would be impolite to decline, we both gratefully accept. Si tears open the sack of crisps in a gesture of good will, and we all munch happily in silence as the boat pulls away from the pier.

The hydrofoil rockets down the Amur River for three hours. I catch forty winks and study the map of China in my pocket atlas. We haven't a clue where we're going. We don't even have a guidebook for China, and apart from being able to say "hello" and "thank you" in Chinese, taught by Kong who owns the local Chinese takeaway near our house, it suddenly occurs to me that this could potentially be a bit of a problem.

All of a sudden the engines cut out. I glance out of the window and see a small pier jutting out from the river-bank. Si opens his eyes, as the other passengers begin to gather their possessions together in anticipation of their arrival. As the boat comes to a halt, I look over the crowd of heads and watch as one of the crew opens the exit doors. Two Chinese customs officials in dark green uniforms immediately climb aboard, and I'm surprised to see they are both wearing white surgical masks. The female customs official carries some kind of scan gun in her hand. She works her way from one end of the boat to the other, methodically firing a red beam of light against the forehead of each of the passengers.

I turn to Si. 'What the hell is she doing?'

'Don't look into the light!' Si laughs. 'She's erasing everybody's memory.'

I watch with fascination as she fires the gun at a chubby lady a few seats away. The Russian woman looks stunned as the laser bounces off her wrinkled forehead.

'I think she's taking everybody's temperature,' I mutter. 'Yeah, that must be it … they're checking to see if anyone has SARS.'

'Don't be so naive, Chris. SARS is just a mythical disease that was invented by a secret inter-planetary organization to scare people from going to China. Communism kept people away until recent times, but as the country has opened up to the rest of the world they had to invent something else. People love a good epidemic, so they invented the SARS outbreak. The Chinese aren't really human at all, you see. They're Mohogs from the planet Zorg. They lost their planet zeons ago and have been living here ever since. That's why they built the Great Wall of China. It's basically a signpost for passing spaceships. We wouldn't want UFO's just landing anywhere, would we? It might freak out the little people, although, a few have made the odd mistake over the years.'

'Wow, I had no idea!' I smirk.

Feeling suddenly hot and sweaty, I begin to worry my temperature might be somehow artificially higher than it should be, and I'll be quarantined inside an oxygen bubble for years in some remote hospital in northern China. The official approaches me and raises the gun to my forehead. I brace myself as she pulls the trigger and hearing a healthy bleeping sound, I breathe a sigh of relief as she continues on down the line. Making our way slowly off the boat, we step down from the gangplank and plant our feet firmly on Chinese soil. A huge Chinese flag flaps vigorously in the breeze above our heads, and a boyish looking Chinese woman with short black hair approaches us. It's Yut. She personally escorts us through customs, and we're greatly surprised by the welcoming reception we receive from the Chinese officials. They quickly stamp our passports, and we're made to feel like VIP's as we're led to an awaiting mini bus outside. Tossing our rucksacks on the roof, we peer excitedly out of the window as we're transported through the back streets of town. The bus drops everyone off at a busy market and we're asked to remain on board while they unload. It's absolute mayhem outside. Everywhere we look there are boxes stacked high containing; TV's, stereos, satellite dishes and portable karaoke machines. Hoards of people sit around in the street eating noodles and chatting loudly.

Within seconds, we find ourselves hurtling down the main street of Fuyuan. The town looks fairly modern, with newly constructed concrete buildings either side of a tarmac road. Large red Chinese characters printed on silky banners hang across the front of the buildings along the main street, and splashes of gold paint decorate the roofs in a weak attempt at providing some colour. We pull up outside one of these large concrete buildings, which I presume is the bus station, and follow Yut inside. She pays in cash for two tickets to Harbin, China's northern-most city, and hands them over to Si. Mutely showing our appreciation, we follow her to a beaten-up sleeper coach outside. The luggage handlers immediately tear our rucksacks off our shoulders and add them to the pile of junk on the pavement that's waiting to be loaded onto the coach. A brown sack next to my rucksack moves by itself and I hear growling and yapping coming from inside. Much to my astonishment I realise it's a bag of puppies, most probably on-route to the nearest Harbin restaurant. Bowing her head, Yut says something to us in Chinese. We thank her and watch as she scurries off back to the mini bus. We stand there for a second scratching our balls at the roadside, and feel suddenly vulnerable again as we're left to fend for ourselves in this completely alien world. Everybody around the bus stares at us, and two teenage girls sitting on a wall close by giggle and point at our big feet. It's impossible to blend in here. At least in Russia if we kept our mouth's shut they could have mistaken us for being Russian, but here it's pretty obvious we're not locals.

People eventually start to board the bus, so we follow their lead. It's very cramped inside and the putrid smell of sweaty feet hits me hard as we squeeze down the narrow aisle between the beds. It's immediately obvious the bus has been designed with Chinese proportions in mind, but fortunately we're both pretty skinny and we reach our bunks without too much trouble. My bed is on the top bunk, and the guy sitting on the bottom bed stares up at me as I haul myself over his head. The bunks are less than one and a half meters long, and it's impossible for me to stretch out my legs. I console myself with the thought that it's only a fifteen-hour journey. The driver of the bus stands outside my window and talks to a guy on a scooter. He seems quite oblivious to the fact that his bus is ready to depart and everyone on board is ready to go. I think about jumping off and having a quick cigarette, but I can't be arsed to fight my way back down the aisle. Finally, the driver finishes his conversation and rocks this dirty bus out of town. I grin at Si with excitement as we head into the barren countryside of northern China. A surreal end to a surreal journey I think to myself, as the driver switches on the onboard entertainment system and blasts weird sounding Chinese music from the stereo. Si's head is literally three inches away from the speaker embedded in the roof, and I try not to laugh as we're flung from side-to-side on the bumpy road to Harbin.

Observing the alien world outside, the extent of our journey becomes a very clear reality. Have we really driven all this way? It seems too bizarre to comprehend now. Passing through small towns, we watch dogs scavenge for food and study the hard faces of the people who live in a corner of the world I barely knew existed. Featherless chickens scratch and peck at the dry earth, while toothless hags thrust inedible offerings through the bus windows. Hardened by our journey across Siberia, we lie back and embrace the surreal and the unknown. In a world where anything can and will happen - fear for us has finally left the building, and when and where our journey will come to an end, it seems clear now is a question we have always faced.

Back to Bateman

'All right now, guys, settle down!' Bateman, the nightshift supervisor yells. 'It's another busy night tonight, we've got ninety-five thousand to pick, so I want you all to pull your fingers out of your backsides and get stacking those boxes. Any questions?'

The time is 6:58pm. It's getting dark outside and I'm sitting in a canteen with Chris surrounded by a hundred exhausted fellow freezer workers. We're all dressed like we're about to ski down Mont Blanc, and are literally minutes away from throwing ourselves into a 12 hour nightshift in the harsh conditions of the -30°C freezer.

'OK,' Bateman barks. 'What are you still doing here? Come on! *Move*! There's work to be done!'

A loud groan fills the canteen.

Bateman claps his hands together, and laughs. 'Don't look so miserable! A bit of hard work will soon cheer you up.'

'He's such a prick,' Chris mumbles, as we make our way out of the canteen.

The two weeks we spent in China had been incredible. It's a country bursting with culture, and it's impossible to leave the place without a smile on your face or a nice piece of dog meat in your belly. From the industrial city of Harbin, we caught a train to Beijing, the Mecca of the People's Republic of China, and from there we continued directly south to Zhengzhou to see the Shaolin temple and the 10,000 students who train Kung Fu. Onwards to Xian to see the Terracotta Warriors, then Chengdu to see the Pandas, Linjang, Dali and across to Kunming, where we travelled south and crossed the border into the South East Asian country of Laos. Travelling by bus to Louangphrabang and onwards to the capital of Vientiane, we finally crossed the border into Thailand 'the land of smiles', and that is exactly what greeted us. We caught a train to Bangkok, one of the craziest cities in the world with its fast-paced sticky street life, amazing temples, great bars and disturbing ping-pong shows, and headed south to the paradise island of Koh Phangan. We spent our last few weeks swimming in the beautiful blue ocean, eating fresh fish, swinging in hammocks, drinking buckets of Thai whiskey and becoming very friendly with a group of incredibly attractive girls from the north of England. We had certainly ended our trip in style. We waved goodbye to paradise and headed back to Bangkok, where we purchased a one-way ticket to Heathrow via Kuwait City for £195. The Iraq War had been in full swing for a while now. Baghdad was heavily bombed only six months ago, so it was crazy to fly over the desert and see enormous oil fields out of the window of the plane, and US soldiers in military uniform milling around the airport terminal.

Much to our relief, we made it back to old Blighty "God save our Queen" without being blown out of the sky by a rocket launcher. Catching a National Express coach to our hometown of Daventry, we walked the last mile to our mum's house where our journey had first begun. With dirty rucksacks over our shoulders we felt like men returning home from war … well, not quite, but it felt pretty good all the same. I wanted to shout out to everyone walking down the street "we've just driven to Vladivostok in a £300 Ford Sierra", but of course I didn't. I bottled it up and promised myself to wait until we'd developed the hundreds of photographs we'd taken on our journey, so we could bore the living shit out of everyone with a three-hour slide show when we got home. Our family was stood in the kitchen when we arrived at the house. It was a lovely surprise.

Standing by a busy chute rammed with heavy boxes of frozen oven chips, I physically and mentally prepare myself for the long cold night ahead. Glancing around I notice nothing has changed, it's all exactly the same. The Kurdish guys seem really pleased to see us again, and Lefty is always full of energy and ready to crack a joke, which is incredible considering he's been working pretty much twelve hours a night, seven days a week for five months now to pay off some debts. In a harsh environment like this you need characters like Lefty to keep up your morale, otherwise you'd end up slitting your wrists before it was time to clock-out.

Chris suddenly appears from across the freezer and slaps me around the back of the head.

'Have you heard the gossip?' he laughs. 'Savage has been banged up again for GBH!'

I ignore him and continue to stack boxes into a cage.

'Hey, and Lefty just told me Shooter's got his girlfriend up the duff.'

'Chris, if Bateman catches us talking we're fucked!'

'Fuck, Bateman. It's not prison!'

Suddenly, a voice cries out from across the factory. '*RAVENS*!'

We turn to see Bateman storming towards us.

'*RAVENS! WHAT THE FUCK DO YOU THINK YOU'RE DOING?*'

'Déjà-fucking-vu!' Chris laughs.

Bateman slides up beside us and folds his fat arms. 'Are you guys deaf, or something? It's a busy night tonight. Why aren't you working?'

'We are,' I reply.

'Do I look stupid?' he cries. 'I know your game, one more strike and you're out!'

I watch Lefty tiptoe up behind Bateman and whip his Everton bobble hat off his head. We both look in surprise, as a huge mass of curly black hair flops down either side of his ugly face.

'Leave them alone, Bateman!' Lefty cheekily cries disappearing behind chute 48.

Bateman looks embarrassed and turns red. The whole hard man image immediately disappears. He quickly attempts to tidy up his mass of curly locks, but gives up and smiles awkwardly before chasing after Lefty between the chutes.

'What a loser,' Chris smirks.

We're interrupted by a voice calling over from the next chute. 'Excuse me, please. You help?'

We turn and see a young lad with a dark complexion cradling a box of frozen vegetables in his arms.

'You tell me if vegetables go in cage four or six, please?'

'Cage six is for frozen bread and cage four is for meat,' Chris shouts back. 'Vegetables go in cage three.'

'Thank you,' the guy smiles.

'Hey, where are you from?' Chris asks.

'I am from São Paulo in Brazil'

Chris turns to me, and grins *'Brazil...'*

THE END

The Linger *Loco*!

SIMON RAVEN   CHRIS RAVEN

From Tango in Buenos Aires to Samba on the beaches of Brazil, join the Raven brothers on a new adventure in South America as they cross the Atacama Desert, scale the Peruvian Andes and fight their way through the hot Amazon jungle. Traveling by bus along the Trans-Oceanic Highway from the Pacific to the Atlantic coast, our trusty heroes chase their muse from one end of the continent to the other with only one idea in mind – to go in search of the real carnival!

'The Linger *Loco*!' is the third book in The Linger Series.

Order your copy of 'The Linger *Loco*!' online at:

www.samosirbooks.com

OUT NOW!

Living the Linger

SIMON RAVEN   CHRIS RAVEN

The sudden break-up with girlfriend, Emily Willow, finds Simon Raven, ex-amateur rock God and bored internet producer, on a Boeing 747 bound for Seattle. Led by his twin brother, Chris, who's more than happy to exchange a career in fashion photography for the open road, they embark on a personal mission to survive outside the system.

Leaving London life far behind, the brothers are taken on a roller coaster ride of paranoia and self-doubt as they bumble through bear infested wilderness, encounter modern-day ogres in the form of bullwhip wielding maniacs and explore the evils of Las Vegas. Testing their friendship to the limit, they eventually find inspiration on a journey that exposes the stark truth about work and relationships and which asks the question – what do you really want to do with your life?

'*Living the Linger*' is the first book in The *Linger Series*.

Order your copy of '*Living the Linger*' online at:

www.samosirbooks.com

Email the authors:
simon.raven@samosirbooks.com
chris.raven@samosirbooks.com